Graham Seal is an award-winning biographer, songwriter and poet. He is the bestselling author of many books, including *Great Australian Stories*, *Great Bush Stories*, *Great Convict Stories*, *Great Australian Mysteries* and *Australia's Most Infamous Criminals*. He is Emeritus Professor of Folklore at Curtin University.

Also by Graham Seal

Praise for other books by Graham Seal

Australia's Most Infamous Criminals

'From robbery to fraud, this collection of tales from Australia's cold cases is brought together by a master storyteller.' —*New Idea*

Great Australian Places

'Seal reveals much about Australia—and Australians—on a storytelling tour from iconic destinations to tiny settlements, remote landmarks and little-known corners.' —*The Senior*

Great Australian Mysteries

'Seal brings to life the enigmas and puzzles behind unsolved crimes, lost treasures and strange phenomena . . . a fascinating read.' —*Canberra Weekly*

Australia's Funniest Yarns

'Full of songs, stories, poems, rules and quizzes. It is a lovely book for those who want to catch a glimpse of the old characters who used their stories and language to make the Australia of the past much more colourful than it is today.' —*Glam Adelaide*

Great Bush Stories

'Takes us back to a time when "the bush" was central to popular notions of Australian identity, with the likes of Henry Lawson and "Banjo" Paterson serving to both celebrate and mythologise it.' —*Writing WA*

Great Convict Stories

'With a cast of colourful characters from around the country—the real Artful Dodger, intrepid bushrangers ... *Great Convict Stories* offers a fascinating insight into life in Australia's first decades.'
—*Sunraysia Daily*

Great Australian Journeys

'Readers familiar with Graham Seal's work will know he finds and writes ripper, fair-dinkum, true blue Aussie yarns. His books are great reads and do a lot for ensuring cultural stories are not lost.'
—*The Weekly Times*

The Savage Shore

'A gripping account of danger at sea, dramatic shipwrecks, courageous castaways, murder, much missing gold and terrible loss of life.' —*Queensland Times*

Larrikins, Bush Tales and Other Great Australian Stories

'Another collection of yarns, tall tales, bush legends and colourful characters ... from one of our master storytellers.' —*Queensland Times*

Great Anzac Stories

'. . . allows you to feel as if you are there in the trenches with them.'
—*Weekly Times*

Great Australian Stories

'A treasure trove of material from our nation's historical past.'
—*Courier Mail*

AUSTRALIA'S GREATEST STORIES

True Tales, Legends and Larrikins

GRAHAM SEAL

ALLEN&UNWIN
SYDNEY·MELBOURNE·AUCKLAND·LONDON

Allen & Unwin
Cammeraygal Country
83 Alexander Street
Crows Nest NSW 2065
Australia
Phone: (61 2) 8425 0100
Email: info@allenandunwin.com
Web: www.allenandunwin.com

Allen & Unwin acknowledges the Traditional Owners of the Country on which we live and work. We pay our respects to all Aboriginal and Torres Strait Islander Elders, past and present.

 A catalogue record for this book is available from the National Library of Australia

ISBN 978 1 76147 113 1

Set in 11.5/17.2 pt Stempel Schneidler Std by Bookhouse, Sydney
Printed and bound in Australia by the Opus Group

10 9 8 7 6 5 4 3 2 1

The paper in this book is FSC® certified. FSC® promotes environmentally responsible, socially beneficial and economically viable management of the world's forests.

CONTENTS

NOTE

In traditional Aboriginal communities it is customary not to mention the name of, or reproduce images of, the recently deceased. Care and discretion should therefore be exercised in using this book within Arnhem Land, Central Australia and the Kimberley.

TIMELINE

Around a billion to 540 or more million years ago the landmass of Gondwana forms.

Around 335 million years ago the supercontinent Pangaea forms from the collision of Laurentia (North America), Baltica (northeastern Europe) and Siberia.

Around 2.6 million years ago the paleocontinent of Sahul (including Australia and New Guinea) forms

Around 2.5 million years ago to possibly around 25,000 years ago, or even less, megafauna lived in Australia.

Perhaps 75,000 years ago, humans first inhabit Australia.

Between 7000 and 12,000 years ago sea levels rise, cutting off Tasmania and New Guinea from the mainland.

1606 Willem Janz(oon) and his Dutch East India Company sailors are the first recorded Europeans in Australia.

Mid-18th century, possibly earlier, Macassan trepang fishers make annual voyages to northern Australia.

1770 Lieutenant ('Captain') James Cook RN sails along the east coast of Australia and claims it for the British Crown. He gives it the name 'New South Wales'.

1788 The First Fleet arrives and establishes a military–penal colony at Sydney Cove and environs. Over 160,000 men, women and children will be transported to the continent before the last convict ship arrives in 1868.

1790 Beginning of First Nations resistance to colonisation, actions that will continue throughout Australia until the 1930s.

1813 The Blue Mountains are crossed by Gregory Blaxland, William Lawson and William Charles Wentworth, assisted by a Dharug guide whose name wasn't recorded. A route to the fertile western plains is established.

1838 First official public Australia Day observation, though it is not observed uniformly across the country until 1994.

1840 Penal transportation to New South Wales is prohibited but continues to Van Diemen's Land until 1853. Penal transportation to Western Australia (men only) begins in 1850.

1851 Edward Hargraves finds gold near Bathurst, New South Wales. The precious mineral has been found before, but his discovery ignites major gold rushes in the east of the country.

1854 The Eureka Stockade battle on the goldfields of Ballarat in Victoria leads to political reform in Victoria and becomes a celebrated event for Australian democracy and identity.

1854 The first steam railway, in Melbourne, begins a new era of goods and passenger transportation.

1856 The eight-hour working day is achieved for some workers in New South Wales and Victoria but not realised nationally until the 1920s, and then not in all industries, with some having to wait until 1948.

1858 The first game played by Europeans of what becomes Australian Rules Football takes place in Melbourne, between Melbourne Grammar and Scotch College.

1868 The last convict transport ship lands, in Western Australia.

1872 The Overland Telegraph from Adelaide to Darwin (then called Palmerston) is completed, connecting Australia with the world.

1872 The Victorian *Education Act* establishes free, secular and compulsory education, taken up in all states by 1908.

1880 Bushranger Ned Kelly is hanged in Melbourne, but his controversial legend continues.

1885 Broken Hill Proprietary Company (BHP) is formed. As this book goes to print, after several restructures, BHP is the largest Australian mining company and the third-largest in the world.

1885 The first gold rush in Western Australia is in the Kimberley region, followed by several others leading up to the large rushes of the 1890s in and around Kalgoorlie and Coolgardie.

1891 Industrial conflict and economic depression begin, ending in a viable trade union movement and the formation of the Australian Labor Party (ALP).

1894 South Australian women—but not First Nations women—win the vote and the right to stand for parliament. (New Zealand was the first country in the world to enfranchise women, in 1893.)

1895 'Waltzing Matilda' is composed near Winton, Queensland, by A.B. 'Banjo' Paterson and Christina Macpherson.

1901 The Commonwealth of Australia is formed on 1 January 1901. It was narrowly approved after referendums across the colonies between 1898 and 1900.

1901 The *Immigration Restriction Act* is passed, establishing a 'white Australia policy'. Although this Act was replaced in 1958, some elements remained until the 1970s.

1902 Women gain the right to vote and to stand for parliament in federal elections. The following year, Vida Goldstein, Nellie

Martel, Mary Moore-Bentley and Selina Siggins are the first women to stand for election to the national parliament.

1907 The Bondi Surf Bathers' Life Saving Club is the first of many surf lifesaving clubs to be established, forming a national surf lifesaving movement.

1914–1918 World War I. In 1915 the Australian and New Zealand Army Corps (ANZAC) lands at Gallipoli, Turkey, as part of a combined Allied invasion force. The Anzac tradition begins.

1916 The national scientific research body, later to become the Commonwealth Scientific and Industrial Research Organisation (CSIRO), is formed.

1917 The Trans-Australian Railway is completed, linking the east and west coasts of Australia by rail for the first time.

1921 Edith Cowan becomes the first woman elected to an Australian parliament, in Western Australia.

1921 The first radio licence is issued, for 2CM, Sydney.

1922 The first scheduled Qantas flights take place.

1924 The human voice is first transmitted by radio from England to Australia.

1929 The Great Depression begins. For many, it lasts until the start of World War II.

1938 First Australia Day observance of Day of Mourning.

1939–1945 World War II. In 1941 Prime Minister John Curtin looks to the United States of America for support rather than to the United Kingdom.

1942 Japanese planes bomb Darwin. The fall of Singapore.

1942 *The Statute of Westminster Adoption Act 1942* confirms the independence of Australia's government, following the *Statute of Westminster* act passed in Britain in 1931. Australia remains subject to the Crown.

1945 The Commonwealth post-war assisted immigration program begins and runs in various forms until 1982.

1948 The first Holden automobile comes off the assembly line at the General Motors–Holden plant at Fishermans Bend, Victoria.

1956 Television is first broadcast to the public by HSV7, Melbourne. Colour television broadcasts begin in 1975.

1965 The Freedom Ride highlights deep discrimination against First Nations people.

1966 Decimal currency is introduced, replacing pounds, shillings and pence. Metric measurements followed from 1970.

1967 Referendum 'yes' vote ensures Aboriginal and Torres Strait Islander peoples are counted in the national population and that the Commonwealth can make laws for them.

1969 Equal pay for some women in some industries is instituted, though inequalities persist to the present.

1971 Senator Neville Bonner is elected to the Australian Senate, becoming the first known First Nations member of any Australian parliament.

1976 The first 'boat people' arrive in Darwin after the end of the Vietnam War.

1978 A gay activist protest in Sydney is broken up by police but subsequently evolves into the annual Gay and Lesbian Mardi Gras. It goes on to become one of the world's largest such events.

1983 The Australian dollar is moved onto the floating exchange rate and valued within international currency markets.

1984 Medicare begins, providing government-funded medical care for all Australians.

1984 'Advance Australia Fair' becomes the national anthem, replacing 'God Save the Queen', which becomes known as the 'Royal Anthem'.

1986 The *Australia Act* makes Australian law independent of the United Kingdom and is proclaimed by Queen Elizabeth II at a ceremony in Canberra.

1987 Australia's first mobile phone call is made.

1989 Australia is connected to the global internet, later to the World Wide Web (www).

1992 CSIRO scientists file a wireless local area network (WLAN) patent, the basis of wi-fi.

1992 Concluding a case brought by Eddie Koiki Mabo and other Traditional Owners, the High Court recognises the land rights of the Meriam people, overturning the doctrine of *terra nullius* (empty land) previously used to justify colonisation and opening the way for the *Native Title Act* of 1993.

1999 Failure of the Australian republic referendum.

2001 The *Tampa* refugee crisis begins, leading to an era of immigration control and detention of asylum seekers. In Western Australia, Carole Anne Martin is the first First Nations woman elected to any Australian parliament.

2002 The first Bali bombing; this is followed by another in 2005.

2004 The Darwin to Alice Springs railway link is finally completed after construction began in 1878.

2008 Prime Minister Kevin Rudd's Apology to the Stolen Generation.

2013 The National Disability Insurance Scheme (NDIS) is legislated and in full operation by 2020.

2017 After many years of advocacy, and after the passing of the Same-Sex Marriage Bill 2016 and the subsequent National Marriage Law Postal Survey, same-sex marriage becomes legal.

2020–23 The COVID pandemic.

2021 A trilateral security partnership between Australia, the United States and the United Kingdom, known as AUKUS, is established.

2023 The referendum on the 'Uluru Voice from the Heart' fails.

2023 The High Court rules that indefinite immigration detention is illegal.

Introduction

A JOURNEY THROUGH TIME

This book takes a journey through time. A very long time. It begins with the coming of humans to the land we now call Australia and ends as planet Earth's spacecraft sail towards an unknown future. Along the way you will meet a few interesting people and read about some of the things Australians have done and continue to do. Many of those things have been momentous, with lasting consequences. Others involve ordinary folk going about their everyday lives, yet often doing extraordinary things. A few are characteristically quirky. They are the small stories behind the big story of Australia and its people.

When people first came to the massive southern continent now given the name 'Sahul' they found animals and plants mostly unknown elsewhere. They had to see the country and learn how to make it work for them by understanding and using its unique geography and environment for survival, travel and trade. In doing that, they evolved one of the world's oldest and most impressive bodies of mythology and belief. They saw stories in the stars and turned geological events, such as the rising of the sea and volcanic eruptions, into legends that survive today.

Europeans began to arrive in the early seventeenth century and they also had to learn to see and understand the country as well as the people who had been living on it for millennia. First contacts were a mixed bag of hospitality, hostility and mutual misunderstandings that only increased as convicts and settlers began to spread across the continent from 1788. The newcomers always had the advantages of technology, especially weapons, and of resources flowing into the country from Europe and elsewhere in the world as more and more immigrants arrived and trade developed accordingly.

One legacy of colonisation was the growth of an assortment of legends that often reflected a lasting discomfort about the land. Lost peoples, monsters and deadly magic feature in First Nations traditions, or at least in the settler interpretation of those traditions. These have been joined by newer legends of lonely pioneer graves, hauntings and contemporary yarns of dangerous journeys across borders and boundaries. Many of these stories are more folklore than history, but they are an important part of the way we try to make sense of an often fractured past.

The extreme nature of Australia's geography and climate led to many heroic deeds in the pioneering past and into the present. Floods, isolation and extreme weather are an inescapable aspect of this environment. Australia's unusual experience of war has involved most conflicts, other than those of the frontier, being fought elsewhere. Heroism, whether real or invented for propaganda purposes, inevitably features in these events, usually involving the valour and sacrifice of soldiers. The courage of wartime nurses and post-war advocates for the families of dead heroes is not so often hailed. Quiet persistence can also be heroic, as in the once hidden story of Edith Emery and the unusual sporting techniques of the 'Gumboot Tortoise'. Usually, though, people had to make a lot of noise to be heard and recognised, particularly if they were 'the fair sex' seeking a fair go in political representation.

It's often difficult to tell the difference between heroism and wilful defiance, or even eccentricity. Just a few of Australia's many notable rebels and ratbags appear here. You've probably never heard of William Carr-Boyd or Paddy the Poet, but they deserve their place in the roll of colourful and memorable people that also includes the contradictory Robert Lyon (if that was his name), rioting gold diggers, a Queensland bushranger and the man who inspired the famous film character 'Crocodile Dundee'. Some of these people came to sad ends, some seem to have achieved a redemption of sorts, while others passed into the extensive legendry of the land.

There are no periods of Australian history since 1788 in which one or more groups of people have not experienced hardship and struggle, from the frontier resistance of First Nations people to the COVID pandemic of the early 2020s that brought trouble to everyone. Suffering, protest, crime and community fear are a vivid thread through the past and into the present. Bushranger and controversial icon Ned Kelly makes a dramatic and satanic appearance in an eye-opening account of the Glenrowan shootout. A few of Australia's many riots—one in war and one in the Great Depression—highlight the tensions and conflicts of their respective moments, as does the story of the Peace Ship.

Balancing the tough times, Australia has a rich tradition of celebration. We don't think much about the calendar that underpins all our daily lives, determining when we holiday, when we worship—if we do—when we commemorate or when we party. The official annual timekeeper of the country is the Christian Gregorian calendar inherited from Britain and takes little or no account of the many other methods of marking time operating here. If we look at all of those calendars, some observed by a great many believers, we quickly see that there are few days or periods of any year when one or another religious or cultural group is not marking a moment of significance. Some of these events are also the focus of extensive retail and marketing efforts, with the yearly cycle of calendar events increasingly commercialised and, in some cases, the focus of community tensions and conflict.

Another tradition, innovation, has always been seen as a particularly Australian characteristic. It is a form of creativity that can be seen in First Nations adaptations of European technologies and languages, as well as practical inventions such as the stump-jump plough and wi-fi, and artistic expressions of all kinds, even advertisements. Writers, musicians, artists, soldiers and tellers of very tall tales have contributed to the varied stream of the national imagination, often engaging with the distinctiveness of colloquial speech and the social and political experiences of particular times and places.

We all belong to one or multiple communities. They can take many forms, from families to nations, with any number of possible variations of religion, ethnicity and personal preference in between. Urban and rural Australia includes a vast number and variety of groups who identify with each other and the places they live, work, relax and even where they shop. Before the invention of the internet and the World Wide Web, radio programs and the postal service were important forms of interaction that joined distant groups of people spread thinly across a vast continent into communities of the air, not unlike today's interactions on social media.

Can the diverse experiences of people on such a large continent and from so many places, over such a large period of time ever produce a sense of shared purpose and identity? Who we are—and, perhaps more importantly, who we are not—is an increasingly contested issue. Controversies include whether and how to recognise Australia Day, the Anzac tradition, certain other public holidays, commemorative representations of the colonial past, sovereignty in an increasingly polarised world and gender identities. And these are only some of the debates about what it means and doesn't mean to say we are 'Australian'. The question of national identity is not new. People have been arguing about it for a long time—with some occasionally odd results. What is new are the number and variety of contested issues and the vehemence with which they are often pursued. Is this a sign that the idea of Australia is fragmenting, or is it simply the modern version of old debates? Perhaps there never was just one Australian identity, but many? If so, how can that diversity be combined into a reasonably harmonious unity? Should it be?

These tales of ratbags, rebels, heroes and villains, unsettling legends, clever creations, celebrations and communities are part of a rich storyscape of the land, its people, its history and its folklore, none of which can be separated from the other, good and bad. The past of every nation is tainted with discrimination and oppression; Australia is no different. While there is a lot to celebrate, there are also acts of violence and injustice to acknowledge and accept, important steps on a long journey from prehistory to whatever the future might hold. How the future will unfold cannot be known, but it is sure to include many of the themes of this book—and who knows what others?

A few notes:

Money values and measurements

Where necessary, historical monetary values are given as closely as possible to their contemporary value.

Distances, weights and other measurements are converted to their decimal equivalents.

Language

There are plenty of quotations from historical documents and other sources in this book. These sometimes contain terms and convey attitudes no longer considered acceptable. Where they have been included, they are intended to give readers a sense of how people of the past thought, spoke, wrote and acted.

Spelling

Spelling of First Nations names and places varies considerably. Generally, I have used what seems to be the most commonly accepted version at the moment, indicating where necessary some alternative spellings. There may well be others.

Names in colonial newspapers and other documents are frequently spelled in a bewildering variety of forms, leaving the author to settle on the most common version, if there is one.

A group of Pitcairn Islanders photographed on Norfolk Island in 1861. The descendants of the Bounty mutineers were moved to Norfolk Island from their increasingly unviable life on Pitcairn. They joined a long line of Norfolk Island settlers, including Polynesians, convicts and Norfolkers.

1

SEEING THE COUNTRY

The Superhighways of Sahul

She was a slight, short woman, a young adult. He was around fifty years old, built lightly and around 1.7 metres tall. They were both buried 42,000 years ago. Mungo Lady's remains were recovered in 1968 and those of Mungo Man in 1974. Until these discoveries, humans were thought to have occupied Australia for only around 10,000 or 12,000 years. More recent evidence suggests that the ancestors of First Nations people arrived here much earlier.

Mungo Lady and Mungo Man were buried only around five hundred metres apart yet they did not know each other. Later excavations revealed many more sets of human remains and a community of humans living for generations in the usually well-watered area, hunting, harvesting, procreating, dying and being ritually buried—she by cremation, crushing and interment; he face upwards, hands folded on his lap and his body sprinkled with red ochre. Ancient though these people were, their forebears may have lived in Australia for 30,000 years or more.

Scientists are rewriting what we thought we knew about early human history and a prehistoric supercontinent called 'Sahul' has an outsize role in the story. Existing in the Pleistocene Epoch, from around 2.6 million to around 12,000 years ago, it consisted of mainland Australia, attached to Tasmania, and to many of the islands we know as New Guinea and to what is now called Timor. From perhaps as long as 75,000 years ago, large groups of technologically sophisticated humans crossed from the northern reaches of the supercontinent to begin the peopling of Australia. More followed at later times, probably by sea, and within around 10,000 years of first arrival the ancestors of the First Nations peoples had reached the southern tip of Sahul.

The routes these first comers travelled on their epic journeys—continental 'superhighways'—began in Timor and New Guinea then passed, broadly, along the west and east coasts and through the centre, looping through the Nullarbor and eventually reaching Tasmania. There were secondary connecting routes but the superhighways were created by waves of people moving towards and through 'highly visible terrain', basically the mountain ranges of the continent. These tracks became trade routes and songlines and often correlate with later stock routes and even modern highways.

We have long held the idea that Australia and the people living here before colonisation were unknown and isolated from the rest of the world. For many centuries, stories of an unknown continent at the southern end of the globe circulated through the northern hemisphere. Often called 'the unknown south land', or *terra australis incognita*, this continent was shrouded in mystery and myth. Any people who might live there would necessarily walk upside down, it was said, and there would be strange beasts and flowers growing there—wherever it might be.

Beginning in the seventeenth century, European navigators began to slowly peel back the mysteries of the land as they came into contact with it and, sometimes, with its original inhabitants. Gradually, coastlines were charted, the odd river or island was hastily explored and by the time James Cook came to make his celebrated voyage along the east coast in 1770, Europeans had some idea of the size and shape of what we now call Australia. But at that time there was almost complete ignorance of the inland and it was not clear whether Tasmania was attached to the rest of the continent. Answers to those questions would come in time, but the dominant story was that the great south land was completely unknown—other than to its original occupants—until 'discovered' and colonised by Europeans. It followed that there had been no outside contact for millennia. But in recent years, other possibilities have arisen.

The north-west of Arnhem Land has a wealth of rock paintings depicting sea creatures, European sailing ships and other scenes. Among these paintings are two intriguing images that archaeologists believe to be war craft from the Maluku Islands. It has long been known that trepang fishers from the area usually known as Macassar regularly visited and sojourned in Arnhem Land from around 1700. But these were, as far as we know, peaceful visits by fishing boats. The paintings on the rock shelters of Awunbarna (Mount Borradaile) show craft with pennants and other indications that they were designed and fitted out for war rather than trade. To date, no one has found any indications of conflict between First Nations people and whoever might have sailed the warships, but the paintings are evidence of pre-European interactions with people from islands to the north of Australia.

In Queensland's Channel Country, the Mithaka have been quarrying stone for seed grinding for several thousand years. Their quarries are spread across an area of more than 30,000 square kilometres, in which there are dwellings and elaborate stone arrangements thought to be of ceremonial significance. The stones are also part of an ancient industrial production and trade system dubbed 'Australia's Silk Road' that runs from the Gulf of Carpentaria to the Flinders Ranges in South Australia. Archaeologist Michael Westaway observed that the route 'connected large numbers of Aboriginal groups throughout that arid interior area on the eastern margins of the Simpson Desert' and that 'You get people interacting all across the continent, exchanging ideas, trading objects and items and ceremonies and songs'.

It is possible that this transcontinental Silk Road also connected with trade routes beyond Australia. There is strong evidence of interchange between Torres Strait Islanders and what is now Papua New Guinea for more than 2000 years. The discovery of a platypus carved into a sixteenth-century church pew in Portugal and the documented presence of cockatoos in medieval Sicily suggests that there were links between Australia, south Asia and, ultimately, southern Europe, for centuries before Europeans began to arrive at the unknown south land.

First Nations people also travelled beyond Australia to islands in the north, even forming family attachments there. These places were linked to other parts of the world through trading networks we are only beginning to uncover, and it would have been possible to send Australian wildlife, as well as other items, along these routes. Ongoing research will reveal more information about the pre-modern world and its extensive connections, so the image of an unknown south land might need to be even more radically reshaped. First Australians were not completely isolated from the rest of the world, though they, and almost everything else about Australia, would remain a mystery to the European colonists who came much later. In the many millennia before that there was enough time for even geological and cosmic events to become part of Australia's story.

Nurundere Makes the Sea Flow

Tales of a great flood appear so often in the world's traditions that many have concluded there must have been some such event or events in antiquity. Noah and his Ark may be the most familiar version of the story but there are an immense number of variations on the theme. Until recently the trend has been to dismiss oral traditions of historical or prehistoric events as fantasies or myths. But research linking scientific evidence with Indigenous stories has brought about intriguing new interpretations.

One topic that can now be linked to provable prehistoric events is the drowning of land by rising seawaters. In 2020, archaeologists working in north-western Australia discovered First Nations settlements beneath the sea near the Burrup Peninsula at Cape Bruguieres. The drowning of these sites is thought to have occurred between 7000 to 8500 years ago, when the last ice age ended, a major event recorded in oral traditions.

In the 1840s, the Narrinyeri (Ngarrindjeri and other spellings) people of Lake Alexandrina and the Lower Murray region of what is now South Australia recounted a tradition of their great ancestor, Nurundere (also Martummere) to Heinrich August Eduard Meyer. Eduard, as he was known, and his wife, Friederike, were German Lutheran missionaries who established a close relationship with the people they hoped to convert to Christianity. Whatever we might now think of such acts of colonial indoctrination and the motivations behind them, many missionaries collected cultural information that would otherwise have been lost and now is often the basis for revivals of First Nations language, tradition and identity. This version of the story, part of a longer sequence, tells how Nurundere came to create a passage between Kangaroo Island and the mainland by causing the sea to 'flow' and so punishing his two fleeing wives.

> He was a tall and powerful man, and lived in the east with two wives, and had several children. Upon one occasion his two wives ran away from him, and he went in search of them. Wherever he arrived he spread terror amongst the people, who were dwarfs compared with him. Continuing his pursuit, he arrived at Freeman's Nob. Disappointed at not finding his wives, he threw two small nets, called witti, into the sea, and immediately two small rocky islands arose, which ever since have been called Wittungenggul. He went on to Ramong, where, by stamping with his feet, he created Kungkengguwar (Rosetta Head). From [t]hence he threw spears in different directions, and wherever they fell small

rocky islands arose. At length he found his two wives at Toppong. After beating them they again endeavoured to escape. Now tired of pursuing them, he ordered the sea to flow and drown them. They were transformed into rock, and are still to be seen at low water. Discontented and unhappy, he removed with his children to a great distance towards the West, where he still lives, a very old man, scarcely able to move.

Another twenty or more First Nations stories of rising sea levels are also thought to be around 10,000 years old.

Other First Nations oral traditions are also turning out to be traceable to verifiable events rather than myths. Some of these relate to a 4700-year-old meteor impact south of where Alice Springs now stands. Luritja Elders explain their belief that this area, now known as the Henbury Meteorites Conservation Reserve, is evil. Their lore tells of a fire devil running down from the sun to set the earth alight. Anyone who goes there breaks sacred law and will be consumed by the fire. Related research suggests that other traditions might also carry memories of the megafauna that were extinct by 40,000 years ago.

In 2020, a team of geologists suggested that the south-eastern Victorian Gunditjmara story explaining the origins of the volcano they call Budj Bim might relate to an eruption that occurred around 37,000 years ago. They say that 'If aspects of oral traditions pertaining to Budj Bim or its surrounding lava landforms reflect volcanic activity, this could be interpreted as evidence for these being some of the oldest oral traditions in existence'.

The extensive archaeological and palaeontological research currently underway in all parts of the world is revealing new evidence of human occupation, journeying and interacting. In recent years some of these discoveries and interpretations of them have rewritten the history of humankind around the world. It might even be that some of the world's oldest stories were told beneath Australian skies.

Star Stories

The original inhabitants of the continent had thousands of years to observe and understand the night skies above them. The patterns, movements and colours of stars and constellations provided information about the change of the seasons, vital for food gathering, hunting and medicine. The stars were also an atlas by which people were able to find their way around the country. Much of this essential knowledge was held and transmitted through traditional stories.

As in many world cultures, the Milky Way was important. The Kamilaroi and Euahlayi people and their neighbours, the Murrawarri and Ngemba, in north-west and north central New South Wales, knew it as the Warramul, or river. It was the place where everything began before being tipped over, scattering people, animals, plants, landscapes and all that we know onto the Earth. The creation beings who are found in Warramul include the Emu, the Kangaroo and the Crocodile, and all these figures can be traced in the night sky at different times of the year. In March, the Emu is a female figure running through the sky in pursuit of males to begin the mating season. The eggs of the emu on the ground will be laid around this time, signalling that they are available for hatching.

The Emu in the sky becomes male in June and July. It is then seen to be sitting on the nest and hatching the eggs, like the earthly emu. It is likely that there is a connection with the main Kamilaroi culture hero, Baiame, and the initiation of adolescent males, as male Elders are responsible for their passage into manhood through a ceremony linked to the Milky Way. Although these ceremonies or bora usually take place in summer, preparations may be made in August and September. At that time, the Emu in the sky again changes to a representation of the physical layout of the bora, a large circle generally aligned south to south-west of a smaller one.

Around November, Kamilaroi country is usually blessed with plenty of rain. Then, the sky Emu loses its feathers and only the outline of its body can be seen as the constellations change position. The Emu is now sitting in a waterhole, which those observing hoped would mean similarly full waterholes on Earth. The disappearance of the Emu from the night sky in late summer reflects the drying up of water sources that is usual at this time of the year.

The Emu on the Milky Way is found in one version or another in the traditions of many First Nations groups where it has various meanings. The Kamilaroi story is an especially rich one that shows the intricate connections between the seasonal patterns and movements observed in the night sky as it appears in that part of the continent, the management of resources and the spiritual aspects of Kamilaroi tradition.

Another story may also link Australia's first inhabitants directly with everyone's African ancestors. The star patterns known, respectively, as Orion and the Pleiades are the subjects of myth-making in many cultures. In Australian First Nations traditions, Orion, who is known as Wati Nyiru, is often portrayed as a male hunter, or hunters, who pursue seven sisters, represented by the stars in the Pleiades group. Versions of this story are widely told and are the basis of the famous Seven Sisters songline that stretches across the country. But only six stars are usually visible in that group. The missing sister may be accounted for in storytelling by saying that she is hiding or missing for some reason. Now, researchers in the field of cultural astronomy, as well as astronomers using the Gaia space telescope, have shown that the night sky of 100,000 years ago would have contained a visible seventh star in the Pleiades group, strongly suggesting that the Australian Seven Sisters songline, the Greek story of the seven daughters of Atlas and similar tales in African, Native American and Asian traditions had their origins in the way things were in the night sky one hundred millennia ago. This story may go back to the earliest efforts of humanity to interpret the mysteries of the stars, an endeavour we continue to pursue.

Meeting the Tiwi

In January 1705, three ships cleared the Dutch East India Company's (VOC) port at Batavia (now Jakarta). Maarten van Delft was in command. His mission was to explore and chart the northern coast of the southland. There was mention of a possible gulf that was thought to penetrate deep into the interior but, more importantly, van Delft's voyage was part of a larger effort by the Dutch to counteract 'the fossicking, spying and writing of the well-known English traveller William Dampier.'

The Dutch feared that the English had designs on the land we know as Australia, as well as what is now New Guinea. They wanted to be sure that, if there was anything worth trading, they would get their share of the spoils.

Crewed by Dutchmen as well as sailors from islands now forming part of Indonesia, van Delft's small fleet sailed through bad weather via the Timor Sea until the second day of April when they saw smoke on the shore of a large unknown island. By the time the voyage ended in July, the Dutch and Indonesian sailors would have explored parts of Bathurst, Melville and Croker islands, as well as the Cobourg Peninsula. Over that time, van Delft and his men had several first contact experiences with Indigenous Australians. The original journals of the expedition are lost and it is difficult to establish exactly what happened and where through the only surviving account, a summary written by a VOC clerk. However, recent research has given us a clearer picture and also identified the first known European acquisition of First Nations artefacts.

The expedition's first encounter with the people of the south-land took place three weeks after the Dutch had reached the north Australian coast and the territory of the Tiwi people. This meeting did not go well, as recorded in the surviving account—'some natives were met by our men on April 23rd, who did not indeed retire, but nevertheless ran together toward an eminence, and with all sorts of movements and gestures attempted to drive our men from the land.' The Dutch did not retreat and were attacked with spears. In the fight, a 'native' leader was wounded by musket fire.

Another incident, this time with the Iwaidja, took place on the mainland towards the eastern side of the Cobourg Peninsula.

The Dutch had established good relations with the locals, inviting them aboard their ships, exchanging presents and food. But when the ships prepared to leave 'after having conversed with these people for weeks, eaten and drunk, been aboard, examining all things in admiration, having received presents, and on their part had regaled our men with fish and crabs', two sailors were attacked, seemingly for their clothes or possibly other items they carried. The Dutch were perplexed and horrified; 'the nature of these folk is foul and full of betrayal', they wrote, though it is possible that the visitors may have been seen to be departing without exchanging the appropriate amount of goods in return for the hospitality they had received.

Like most European navigators of the period, van Delft was under instructions to bring home anyone who wished to accompany him: 'Our men might also easily have taken and brought over to Batavia with them two or three of the natives who daily came on board,' but the skipper of one of the ships, following out his instructions to the letter, would not allow them to be taken without their full consent, 'either by falsehood or fraud'. Whether this was a Christian act of decency or of simple practicality is difficult to tell, but according to the account 'as no-one understood their language, nothing was to be done in the matter, consequently they remained in their own country.'

It is likely that van Delft sought to make up for his failure to comply with his VOC orders to bring back some Indigenous people by providing some unusually detailed observations on the lifestyles and appearance of the people encountered. The Dutch noted that the men went naked and were often decorated with ceremonial scars while the women covered 'their privy parts with leaves or the like.' The Tiwi ate 'sparingly and moderately' and appeared to live exclusively on fish, roots and vegetables rather than birds or other animals. In terms of technology:

[they had] neither Iron nor anything like minerals or metal; for a stone which has been grounded serves as their hatchet; have neither houses nor huts, and occupy themselves with fishing by means of harpoons of wood, and also of little nets, and putting out to sea in little vessels made of the bark of trees, which are so fragile they have to be shored up with cross-beams.

The friendly relations between the two groups included the Dutch giving presents of clothing, knives and beads, probably in exchange for artefacts as well as food. The Dutch National Museum of World Cultures holds some Tiwi clubs and throwing sticks almost certainly obtained by van Delft's expedition. There may well have been other items, now lost or forgotten in an obscure museum or archive collection.

The Dutch also witnessed a large night-time gathering of perhaps 500 men, women and children 'round several fires among the bushes'. But, mainly interested in possible trade opportunities, they lost interest when they saw that 'nothing however was seen in their possession of any value.' This was around mid-June and was by far the largest group to be reported at this time, suggesting that the gathering was of great ceremonial significance.

Continuing to follow instructions, always a good practice for skippers of the demanding VOC, the Dutch left for the Cobourg Peninsula looking for the fabled passage into the interior. At one location 'a tiger was met with' and, while the little fleet was anchored near Maria's Island, the inhabitants attempted to tow one of the VOC ships. They met with no success and so began to work on the anchor itself. This also proved ineffectual and they returned to the land. It is not clear whether the intention was to bring the ship to the shore or to drag it away. The Dutch also landed on Greenhill Island for water before returning home in August, with crews much depleted from 'severe sickness, principally fever, acute pains in the head and eyes, and above all, dropsy.' Van Delft died four days after reaching Macassar.

Apart from updating charts of the area made by earlier VOC navigators, the voyage had not been what 'Jan Company', as the corporation was colloquially known, would class a success, with the loss of sailors, together with many of the valuable logbooks and charts. Worse, much worse, there was no new potential for trade with those the Dutch now considered of 'rude and barbarous character' and with a 'malicious disposition'.

Like many other encounters between new arrivals and Indigenous Australians, those of 1705 remain contradictory and puzzling. They were collisions of utterly different groups of people with almost unimaginably diverse histories since humans first left Africa.

A Mystery Island

Norfolk Island is forever associated with the dark history of its penal establishment, beginning in 1825. But that unhappy institution was the second European settlement on the island. The first began when Governor Arthur Phillip sent some soldiers and convicts from Port Jackson to establish an agricultural base for growing food for the colonists of New South Wales. It was also hoped to cultivate the native flax plant for sail making and to turn the unique pines that grew there into masts for Britain's mighty navy. Few of these hopes were realised and the Norfolk Island story would take some very unexpected turns.

When James Cook visited the island in 1774 during his most famous voyage of discovery and acquisition, he found it uninhabited. The colonists sailing from Sydney aboard HMS *Supply* landed there in 1788 and were surprised to find bananas growing, together with dogs, rats and other plants not indigenous to the island. They also found ancient human remains. Whose were they? It was over two centuries later that the puzzle began to be solved, though archaeologists still refer to Norfolk as a 'mystery island'.

Some pieces of the historical jigsaw were found in 1995 when a team of archaeologists began excavating in sand dunes at Emily Bay. They found the evidence of a pre-1788 structure. It turned out to be a Polynesian house and prayer site. They also found stone tools, including razor-sharp basalt adzes and knives, as functional as they were perhaps a thousand years before when they had first been chipped from volcanic rock. Islanders had also been finding these chopping and cutting implements for years, but it was not until more excavators arrived in 2022 that the pre-colonial presence of an unknown early people could be confirmed. Evidence of another Polynesian occupation was also found in the Kingston and Arthur's Vale Historic Area (KAVHA).

It seems that Norfolk Island had been a significant Pacific settlement. But beyond that, little is known, to science at least. But to many Norfolk Islanders, descended from the Pitcairners who moved to the island in the 1850s, the finds were validation of their Polynesian heritage and status as the Indigenous inhabitants of the island. Their story began with a notorious episode of naval history.

This chapter of Norfolk history began in 1789 when William Bligh, either insensitive to or unaware of the grievances of his crew, was forced to leave his ship. Whatever the rights and wrongs of the mutiny might have been—and they are still debated today—Fletcher Christian led some of the *Bounty* sailors in setting Bligh and his loyal seamen adrift in the ship's launch. They were a long way from anywhere and it seemed like it would be a fatal voyage. But through exceptional seamanship, Bligh's crew managed to sail and row their small boat around 6000 kilometres to safety in Timor. William Bligh later became the fourth governor of New South Wales, where he would have another contentious encounter with those under his command in an episode known as 'the Rum Rebellion'.

Meanwhile, Fletcher Christian and his fellow *Bounty* mutineers sailed into a different history. They went firstly to Tahiti, revelling in their freedom from what they considered naval servitude and enjoying the relaxed island life, vastly different from that of eighteenth-century Britain. Knowing that the navy would hunt them down, most of the mutineers and their female Tahitian companions fled to distant Pitcairn Island in the south Pacific where they established a safe haven. After several generations, and eventual discovery by the British authorities, it became clear that life on isolated Pitcairn was no longer sustainable and most of the families living there relocated to Norfolk Island in the 1850s where they formed the basis of the Polynesian-identifying community in island society.

For the present-day descendants of these Pitcairners the ancient Polynesian presence on 'Norf'k Ailen' is a strong link with their ancestry and ideals of self-determination. They don't need the science because they have their own powerful traditions about where they come from and who they are today. Arthur Evans is an elder whose great-grandmother came from Pitcairn at the age of three years old. Speaking of his Polynesian ancestry in 2022 he said:

> Even though Australians and New Zealanders are interested in our Bounty history, I'm not. I am interested in my Polynesian history. The most important history on Norfolk today is that of the Indigenous people, and that is us. There was the British arriving here, that's part of the oldest history, but it is not part of our history. If we ever asked about the buildings here, family would say, 'Oh, that's just the convicts.'

While Pitcairners are clear on their identity and that of their forebears, the early Polynesian settlement on Norfolk is still an enigma. Where those people came from is not known for sure, though they probably sailed from East Polynesia through the Kermadec Islands, perhaps as early as 1150AD. They were likely part of the great seagoing expansion of the Lapita ancestors of the Polynesian people into the Pacific that began around 1100, or even much earlier according to some sources. These adaptable people colonised the 'Polynesian Triangle' of islands as far north as Hawaii, south to New Zealand and east to Easter Island. Their seafaring craft and sailing skills were impressive. Those who made their transient home on Norfolk, as we now know it, remained there for around three centuries. Then, it seems, they abruptly departed, leaving only the few traces so far discovered. Where did they go? Perhaps by wind, current and stars to another mystery island in the vast Pacific Ocean. Perhaps elsewhere. We may never know.

A Peaceable Possession

The Australian continent has been home to humans for millennia. The people who first occupied the land presumably made no formal announcements or claims about who owned it. They simply came to it and became part of it. Later comers had different views about territory and ownership.

By the time European navigators began to unpick the puzzle of the unknown south land, the processes of laying formal, legal claims to property of any kind were an established foundational principle of all society—at least, as the Dutch, French and British navigators knew society to be. Following this principle, James Cook and his men in HMB *Endeavour* were given the task, among others, of claiming the east coast of the still shadowy continent in the name of the reigning monarch of Great Britain, as the English had come to call their enforced alliance with Scotland, Wales and Ireland.

To claim something, you need to name it. Cook was not the first to bestow names. The earlier navigators of the Dutch East India Company (VOC) were not generally interested in claiming the southland, seeing no opportunities for trade or exploitation. But they had occasionally given names to those parts of the continent they often saw only from their ships or visited briefly in search of water or food. A VOC ship sailed almost 1500 kilometres along the southern coast of the continent in 1627.

The captain named this area Nuyts Land, after the highest-ranking company official aboard his ship. The French also had a long interest in the southland, some even believing an unlikely fantasy that a French ship and crew had landed and lived there as early as the sixteenth century.

In the end, it fell to a man who had once mucked out Yorkshire farms to make the claim that lasted. He did it on an island known to and used by a number of First Nations clan groups. Even if he had been aware of the ancient existence of these people beyond his brief encounter with them, Cook would not have known their names for what he unequivocally called 'Possession Island'. Located in the Torres Strait off the coast of north Queensland, the 5-kilometre square speck was the last landfall Cook would make along the eastern coast during his epic voyage. Here, on 22 August 1770, he made his claim in the name of King George III.

According to the account of the event by those on the *Endeavour*, they saw around ten islanders lined up on the beach, armed 'as if resolvd [sic] either to oppose or assist our landing.' The men strolled off when someone aboard the ship let off a musket. That was how Joseph Banks recorded the incident. But Cook makes no mention of the musket fire, saying only that he, Banks and others landed. They saw:

> a number of People upon this Island arm'd in the same—manner as all the others we have seen except one man who had a bow and a bundle of Arrows the first we have seen on this coast. From the appeerence of these People we expected they would have opposed our landing but as we approached the Shore they all made off and left us in peaceable posession

[sic] of as much of the Island as served our purpose. [original spelling throughout]

In staking this claim, Cook acknowledged any potential Dutch claims to the west coast 'and as such they may lay claim to it as their property' (subsequently struck out by the editor of the journal). He also says that he is sure the *Endeavour* carried the only Europeans ever to visit this coast which 'therefore by the same Rule belongs to great Brittan [sic]'—also struck out during editing. He then 'hoisted English Coulers and in the Name of His Majesty King George the Third took posession [sic] of the whole Eastern Coast from the above Latitude down to this place by the Name of New South Wales . . .' Three volleys were fired onshore, echoed by three from the *Endeavour*. The east coast and, as it would turn out, the rest of the continent had been, according to Cook, more or less peacefully acquired from the original inhabitants.

The oral traditions of today's descendants of those already in possession of the island known as Bedanug or Bedhan Lag tell the tale rather differently. In one version, they say that Cook did not leave his ship. Instead, he wrapped the British flag around a pistol or cannonball and threw or fired it onto the beach. Another story tells of the Gudang people visiting the island, as they often did, and finding a 'cloth' hanging from a stick in the sand. Having no concept of a flag, they promptly put it to good use as a covering. In the lore of another group of Traditional Owners, the Kaurareg, the Elders would growl whenever Cook was mentioned, saying 'Ah, that bloody no good Cook. He never even set foot on the bloody island!'

While Cook is not remembered well in local tradition, the islanders have had some satisfaction from his 'peaceable possession'. When the Kaurareg people made their native title claim in 2001, the relevant entries in the great navigator's journal were used as evidence to support their ancestral rights to the islands and surrounding seas of which Bedanug/Bedhan lag is a part. Their claim was successful.

Castaway

In April 1801 French navigator Nicolas Baudin's expedition was sailing off the south coast of what is now Western Australia. In the spirit of the age, the French were making a voyage of scientific investigation, as well as discovery. They were, of course, also spying on the British colony of New South Wales, though that was not verified until much later. The voyagers hoped not only to find new places and chart new coastlines but also to make contact with any Indigenous inhabitants they encountered. Equipped with his flagship, *Le Géographe*, and *Le Naturaliste*, under the command of Jacques Félix Emmanuel Hamelin, Baudin was originally accompanied by a large group of scientists, artists and gardeners, though many of these became too ill to complete the voyage, five dying. Many of the sailors were also ill at various stages of the extended expedition. One was lost overboard in the wide expanse of the Indian Ocean that Baudin named Geographe Bay.

Or was he?

Timothée Armand Thomas Joseph Ambroise Vasse was born into a bourgeois family in Dieppe, France, in 1774. He grew up and was educated between Rouen, where his father was a legal official, and Dieppe, where members of his extended family lived. During the French Revolution he joined the army, was wounded and later discharged. After a few years as a civil servant, he joined Baudin's expedition as a junior assistant helmsman on the *Le Naturaliste*. Vasse was in trouble with the captain by the time *Le Naturaliste* reached Isle de France, modern Mauritius. Hamelin planned to dismiss him there but had lost so many other sailors through desertion that he was forced to keep the troublesome 27-year-old aboard his ship.

On 30 May 1801, the voyagers encountered Geographe Bay. They landed in small boats and set up camp while the scientists conducted their investigations of the flora and fauna in the area. A few days later, one of the boats was sunk at the Wonnerup Inlet and had to be abandoned. The shore party was rescued but some equipment was left behind. Three days later, Vasse was aboard a small boat attempting to recover the missing items. But once again the small boat was swamped by the surf. The crew members were washed ashore and only saved by a heroic sailor from another boat, who swam through the dangerous waters carrying a rope by which the castaways were able to haul themselves to safety. Except for Timothée Vasse. Said to have been drinking, he lost his grip on the lifeline and sank into the surf. With no further sign of him, Vasse was presumed drowned and Hamelin made sail, apparently without bothering to confirm the fatality. Good riddance, he perhaps thought?

The fate of the unfortunate Timothée Vasse would have been simply another footnote in the long history of lost sailors if not for the rumours. Soon after the return of Baudin's expedition to France, Parisians began hearing stories that Vasse had not drowned but had survived and been cast away on a strange and very distant shore. Baudin himself was dead by now, but the official expedition account, written by the zoologist on the expedition, François Péron, discounted the possibility that Vasse had survived. Yet the rumours persisted and were published in European newspapers. According to these accounts, Vasse lived with the local people for some years then walked along the coast for hundreds of kilometres to eventually be picked up by an American whaler, handed to the British and subsequently imprisoned in England.

No other Europeans are known to have visited Geographe Bay until after the foundation of the Swan River colony in 1829. When early settlers came into contact with the Wardandi (and other spellings) people of the south-west region, they began to hear odd stories. In 1838 George Fletcher Moore was told while visiting the Wonnerup area that Vasse did not drown. With the help of the local people, he was said to have lived for several years and died of natural causes somewhere between present-day Dunsborough and Busselton:

> He seems to have remained almost constantly upon the beach, looking out for the return of his own ship, or the chance arrival of some other. He pined away gradually in anxiety, becoming daily, as the natives express it, weril, weril (thin, thin.) At last they were absent for some time, on a hunting expedition, and on their return they found him lying dead on the beach, within a stone's throw of the water's edge.
>
> They describe the body as being then swollen and bloated, either from incipient decomposition, or dropsical disease. His

remains were not disturbed even for the purpose of burial, and the bones are yet to be seen.

There were other versions of the tale. In one, Vasse was thought to have eventually been murdered. A 'society in Paris' was said to be offering a reward for the recovery of his bones—'the natives know where they are', wrote one of the Swan River colony's early settlers, Georgiana Molloy, in 1841. In another theory, based on allegedly European features observed among Indigenous people around Geographe Bay, it was suggested that Vasse had fathered children with Wardandi women.

Some attempts have since been made to resolve these conflicting possibilities. Among several books and articles on the subject is one written by a family descendant of Timothée Vasse. According to Alain Sérieyx, family tradition holds that the lost sailor did survive and eventually return to France. The book is speculative fiction based on this belief but adds another thread to a fascinating tale.

Whether or not Timothée Vasse lived, pined and died as a lone white man on a continent far from home will never be known for sure. Whatever his fate, his memory is preserved in the name of the Vasse River and the Vasse region of south-western Australia.

Stealing the Bones

Large collections of bones and body parts lie in dark corners of Australian, American and European scientific institutions. They are the remains of First Nations people acquired during colonisation and shipped to medical establishments, private collectors and museums for preservation, study or exhibition. It is thought that 10,000 or more of these corpses or part corpses were sent to Britain alone and possibly thousands more to other countries.

This grisly catalogue, sometimes called 'the first stolen generation', was assembled during the nineteenth and mid-twentieth centuries by a puzzling assortment of individuals with a variety of motivations. Sometimes the impetus was money. Sometimes it was what is now seen as a misguided sense of contributing to the advancement of science. Always it involved simple racial prejudice based on the flawed belief that Indigenous Australians were some sort of 'missing link' between modern and prehistoric humanity.

One of the most active body thieves was William Ramsay Smith, a Scottish doctor who became the coroner of South Australia in the 1890s. He gathered First Nations people's remains from many sources, including asylums, prisons and elsewhere. Skeletons, heads and other body parts were sent to Ramsay Smith's alma mater, Edinburgh University, where his friend, D.J. Cunningham, Professor of Anatomy, further desecrated them in the name of science.

When the body of a popular local Ngarrindjeri man known as 'Tommy Smith' (Poltpalingada Booboorowie) disappeared while under Ramsay Smith's control, an inquiry was established in 1903. Ramsay Smith, or someone under his authority, had filled Booboorowie's coffin with sandbags. He had then dissected the body and sent the parts to Edinburgh. Gruesome evidence was also given of heads kept in kerosene tins and of a going black market body-snatching rate of £10 for a skeleton. Ramsay Smith was reprimanded but suffered no lasting damage to his reputation and continued as the state coroner. He also continued his close interest in the bodies of First Nations people. When he died in 1937, more than a hundred human skulls were discovered at his house.

Ramsay Smith was only one of many bone collectors either trading or acquiring remains for what they usually claimed were scientific, medical or anthropological research. Beneath this delusion lurked the pernicious idea, derived largely from Charles Darwin's theories on evolution, that European culture was the most developed and advanced 'civilisation' in the world. First Nations people were considered to be at the beginning of a hypothetical chain of evolution and so, went the scientific thinking of the time, should be closely studied. Researchers needed body parts to investigate and there was also a morbid curiosity among private collectors for examples of what they considered exotic lifestyles, including skins displaying customary markings, pieces of skeleton—one man's skull was made into a sugar bowl—and, of course, heads. Full skeletons of adults and children were taken from graves and morgues, boxed up and dispatched to waiting recipients across the seas.

Dark as these practices were, even more reprehensible parts of the trade in the bodies of First Nations people depended on frontier violence. In April 1816, a group of Gandangara people was attacked by a military force at Appin, New South Wales. Fourteen or more men, women and children died, including the leader, Cannabayagal. According to an eyewitness, he and two other warriors were hanged from a tree. The soldiers then 'cut off the heads and brought them to Sydney, where the Government paid 30s and a gallon of rum each for them.' When the National

Museum of Australia received three repatriated skulls from the University of Edinburgh, one was that of Cannabayagal.

The unsanctioned removal of remains is a source of ongoing grief and trauma for First Nations communities. Many are anxious to have the remains of their ancestors returned so they can be given proper burials according to law and custom. Ongoing efforts to ensure that stolen body parts are returned to their Country have had modest success. While the Australian government supports repatriation, some overseas institutions have been uncooperative in agreeing to returns. There are also practical difficulties in identifying remains and in deciding on the most appropriate way to honour them, should they be returned.

First Nations communities also have to make difficult decisions about how and where to reinter their ancestors. In Western Australia, the head of the Whadjuk Noongar warrior, Yagan, cut from his body by settlers in 1833, was repatriated following representations by the then prime minister, John Howard. It was some years before agreements could be reached between the affected parties on the most appropriate means of interment, although the body was known to be buried in the Swan Valley near Perth. Eventually, all the body parts were buried together on Country at the newly opened Yagan Memorial Park at an emotional ceremony in 2010.

Even though the remains of Mungo Man and Woman were removed for authentic scientific research rather than the bone trade, their subsequent return to Lake Mungo in 2022 has been difficult for the Traditional Owners and the government bodies responsible for the protection of First Nations heritage.

A cavern in the Jenolan Caves complex (New South Wales), which includes 'the Devil's Coach House', one of many natural features around the country featuring Satanic names and supernatural legends.

2

THE UNSETTLED LAND

A Lost People

Spirits of the rain and enigmatic human figures are found painted on rocks throughout the Kimberley region of Western Australia. The striking Wandjina and the wispy Gwion Gwion figures (once known as Bradshaw figures) survive where some of the earliest humans settled the land. Little is known of the traditional Doolbong (Duulngari) occupants of the area around what is now Wyndham.

The first European known to have visited the area was navigator Phillip Parker King. He briefly explored and charted it in 1819 while searching for a river leading to the inland sea that many believed lay at the centre of the continent. Explorers came by land from the 1830s; in 1886 the government of the colony established a township, naming it Wyndham, after a relative of the then governor of Western Australia. A rush to the gold finds at Halls Creek put the town on the map and it expanded rapidly. For a short while.

The rush soon ended and the town declined until 1919 when a meatworks was opened, sustaining a small but vital pastoral community. An aerodrome was built and suffered from several Japanese air attacks in World War II. When the Ord River development project began in the 1960s, Wyndham became an important part of the regional economy and today is a significant port.

While these events were occurring the Doolboong people disappeared. From the time of European settlement, their traditional lifestyle was increasingly destroyed by the needs of pastoralists and their herds. Disease and alcohol played a role in the eradication of the region's original inhabitants, as did their coercion as workers, imprisonment for cattle killing and forced relocations. Miners and pastoralists murdered Doolbung, Miriuwung and Gajerong people of the region, sometimes in massacres. Bulla Bilinggiin told a researcher in 1974 that 'Dulbung is finished. Everybody died . . . and there was all that Dulbung lot from the coast down from Ningbing, down from Wyndham back this way.'

Sad though this story is, it does not end there. In advance of the 1988 Bicentennial, the Joorook Ngarni Aboriginal Corporation commissioned a group of statues from sculptor Andrew Hickson as a contribution to the process of reconciliation. The larger-than-life steel statues, based on a concept by Elder Reg Birch, depicted a 5-metre-tall male hunter with spear and family, together with native animals and a rainbow serpent. The group represents the lost Traditional Owners of the Kimberley and was intended to be displayed either near Sydney Harbour Bridge or in Perth's King's Park, a precinct containing many memorials. But the statues never made it to Sydney, or even Perth. Instead they were erected facing west at Warriu Park in Wyndham Three Mile where they appear to have been dedicated in 1990 in a ceremony headed by the MLA for the Kimberley, Ernie Bridge. The front of the statue bears the inscription:

> Warriu Park is dedicated to those who prepared us for today.
>   Built by Joorook Ngarni this monument was presented to the citizens of Wyndham.
>   Aboriginal spirits will always survive in this timeless and beautiful land.

Although they may be gone, the Doolbung people are remembered here and through the ancient art of the Kimberley rockscape.

Land of Monsters

Monsters—unnatural creatures—are known around the world. Australia's distances, varied environments and troubled history have produced more than a few monster traditions, including those of First Nations people and the many that have evolved since European settlement.

Malevolent forces are integral to all First Nations traditions. After many millennia of intimate interaction with the land and all that lives in it, a profound spiritual connection between the observable and the supernatural evolved. The stories that express these connections are filled with magical beings. Many of them are monstrous. Arnhem Land is plagued by sorcerers inclined to butcher humans. There are also mermaid-like creatures dwelling in waterholes from where they rise up to snatch and drown passing people, along with blood-sucking wind and star spirits. The Central and Western deserts are the haunt of giant baby-eaters, ogres and flesh-eating babies, as well as the randy Wati Nyiru who pursues the star sisters who make up the Pleiades constellation.

According to Christine Judith Nicholls, these are just a few of the alarming figures she has encountered in her extensive research on the subject. Some of the most frightening may be found in Warlpiri traditions of people-eaters known as Yapan-garnu. One subgroup of this spectral species is the Pangkarlangu, 'huge lumbering bestial humanoids, [which] roam the desert in search of their desired quarry. In their spare time, they fight one another.' They specialise in catching babies and infants who have strayed from the safety of the camp, then smash out the brains of their victims and hang them from the belt they wear for just this grisly purpose. When they have a belt full of babies, they roast them and enjoy a meal of tender human flesh.

Nicholls recounted her experience of Lajamanu artist and storyteller, Molly Tasman Napurrurla, telling the tale to a group of 'deliciously terrified little children at the Lajamanu School', acting out the Pangkarlangu's gory hulking through the desert. As she concluded, these monsters and their stories 'serve a critically important social function that contributes to the maintenance of life: that of instilling into young and old alike a healthy respect and commensurate fear of the specific dangers, both environmental and psychic, in particular places.'

Elsewhere in the country, south-east of the Katherine River, Northern Territory, the Wardaman caretaker of the spirits and regulator of the rules governing everyday life is the Wulgaru. Fashioned from stone, wood and red ochre, the Wulgaru is a shambling mess of twisted limbs, uncoordinated movements and eyes that blaze like stars. Ever since its misbegotten creation, the Wulgaru has menaced the Wardaman people as keeper and judge of the dead and guardian of tribal law, appearing in their oral traditions as a principle of evil.

In one story, a mother is gathering seeds with her young son. A dark cloud passes across the sun and the mother warns the child not to play so loudly in case 'the evil big-eyed one' comes out of his cave and attacks them. The boy takes no notice and his continued noise soon attracts a Wulgaru, terrifying the boy. Fortunately, his mother knows that the only way to deal with a Wulgaru is to simply ignore it and tells her son that the terrible sights and sounds the Wulgaru is making are nothing but the sound of the wind, the shadows of the sun and the cry of the cockatoo. He is calmed and goes to sleep. The mother goes on grinding the seed she has collected into flour, ignoring the creature threatening them. The Wulgaru is enraged, thrusting its horrible face into hers. But she bravely takes no notice and begins to bake the flour she has made from the seeds.

Her son wakes up and tells her that the Wulgaru is still menacing them. She tells him that it is only the smoke from the cooking fire. Now completely incensed, the Wulgaru jumps at the woman, claws outstretched to tear her apart. Snatching up the hot, sticky dough baking on the fire, she pushes it straight into the Wulgaru's face. As it screams and tries to wipe the gooey mess from its eyes and mouth, the woman takes the opportunity to snatch up her son and flee back to the safety of the camp.

Far North Queensland has long been a monster hotspot. Known variously as 'Yowies', 'Quinkans' or even 'Bunyips', tall, hairy creatures and mysterious big cats are a permanent feature of local folklore. The 'Maalan Monster' is the best known of this cryptid menagerie. It is sometimes described as having the body of a man with the head of a pig, and it was sighted running beside moving cars, looking at the passengers inside. Other stories mention a 'huge man with a fur coat on'. Maalan is located in the Atherton Tablelands, a region first explored by Europeans in the 1870s. Mining, timber cutting and, today, agriculture have been the main industries of the sparsely populated area, a classic location for monsters and the ever-growing yarns about them.

Monsters, of whatever kind, are useful beings. While they may have specific tasks to perform, like looking after the dead or bringing rain, they are also helpful for policing the behaviour of children. Through 'bogeyman' stories, children learn about—and adults are reminded of—the many dangers lurking in the bush. Tales like those of the Maalan Monster, and the many similar yarns told around the country, are rooted in the still unsettling mysteries of the environment and are a reminder that we don't really know much about where we live. They are also ideal fodder for newspapers and tourist brochures. We can't do without our monsters, it seems.

Flesh-Shrivelling Curses

The Aboriginal and Torres Strait Islander Commission (ATSIC) was formed in 1990. It was a federal government body tasked with involving First Nations Australians in official processes that affected them. Always controversial, it was abolished in 2005. When Prime Minister John Howard announced the closure of the organisation, a First Nations woman unhappy with the decision laid a curse on him by 'pointing the bone'.

The aggrieved woman was practising a form of magic usually known as 'kurdaitcha'. Thought to have died out by around the middle of the twentieth century, kurdaitcha was generally carried out by a shaman or 'kurdaitcha man'. In some areas, this person wore distinctive shoes of emu feathers, hair and human blood so not to leave any tracks while hunting the victim and so was known as a 'Featherfoot'. Men believed to have broken customary law and so liable to execution could be dispatched through the will of the kurdaitcha man using a pointed bone (or sometimes a piece of wood) as a spiritual spear to direct the appropriate curse towards the victim who, once having heard it, would languish and die.

There were variations in the methods used, but all involved a preliminary communal chanting or 'singing' over the bone before the kurdaitcha man departed with it to hunt down his target. Sometimes this could take years, but whether the sentence was carried out quickly or not, the end result was the death of the transgressor, as sanctioned by the appropriate Elders. It was sometimes possible for the affected person to find another shaman who might be able to lift the curse. If not, the victim's fate was usually sealed.

During the 1930s the Queensland Museum held a large collection of bones, as described in a newspaper report:

The exhibits of death bones or pointing bones at the Museum cover a very comprehensive range. Nearly every tribe in Australia is represented, and the bones are of all types. A grisly interest attaches to some of them, which have actually caused the deaths of the aborigines at whom they were pointed. Many of the bones are made from human bones, others are highly ornamented. There is one from the Burdekin which is tipped at each end with emu feathers, the idea apparently being to disguise its deadly purpose from the victim when it is pointed by the medicine man. Mr Longman explained that the ceremony of pointing the bone varied with different tribes, but in each instance part of the ritual was the uttering of flesh-shrivelling curses which would make the proverbial 'bullocky' blush with envy.

Kurdaitcha was much sensationalised in newspapers and popular accounts well into the 1960s. It was usually treated as superstitious nonsense, the usual mainstream response to complex mythological and spiritual systems that were incomprehensible to the European mind. But medical science provides support for the possibility of what is called 'psychosomatic' death and similar customs have been observed in other cultures. The kurdaitcha tradition remains strong in some First Nations groups, especially among the Warlpiri of the Tanami Desert. There, the kurdaitcha evolved into a haunting evil spirit, or monster, known variously as a Kurdaitcha or a Jarnpa.

The amateur anthropologists Francis James Gillen and Walter Baldwin Spencer collected First Nations customs, stories and other lore between 1875 and 1912. Their work is considered the most authentic and comprehensive of its kind. As well as documenting the kurdaitcha tradition, they were also told of female kurdaitchas, known as illapurinja, a term they translated as 'the changed one'. These were wives given the task of inflicting psychic damage, including death, upon women who had failed to maintain the mourning custom of ritually cutting themselves when a blood or tribal daughter died. After a complicated, secret ritual in which featherdown is stuck to the woman's body with grease, ochre and some of her husband's blood, she is armed with a magically charged fighting club, referred to as a Churinga, a sacred ancestral object. After certain other preparations, the woman departs at night for the camp of the intended victim, ambushing her or, if unable to locate the offending woman, her brother: 'In either case the Churinga is thrown from behind so as to hit the victim's neck, when it enters the body, becoming, as it does so, broken up into a number of small pieces. The victim at once becomes insensible, and remains so for some little time, and, when consciousness is once more recovered, suffers great pain.' The illapurinja then returns to her camp, waiting until daylight to meet her husband who removes her decorations in mutual silence. Certain other procedures are carried out and the husband asks the woman questions, which she must answer without providing any additional information. As with many customs, the purpose of this is to maintain the laws 'to make some women believe that they, or their brothers, will suffer if certain ceremonies are not duly attended to.'

By the time Spencer and Gillen collected this information, the illapurinja custom had faded away from the area they investigated, though it was said to still be practised further east. The anthropologists also gained the impression that the male kurdaitcha custom was 'merely a matter of myth', though various pointing the bone incidents were reported around the country from the 1930s to the 1950s.

The emu-feather shoes said to be worn by the kurdaitcha men in hunting down their victims were probably too small to have been used, except perhaps in a ceremony of some kind. They were part of the broader mystique surrounding kurdaitcha men, adding further to the genuine fear they produced. Ironically, the shoes became souvenir items, as a correspondent to the *West Australian* newspaper observed in 1939: 'The best feather shoes are made in a southern section of the Arunta tribe, and during recent years, since it has been discovered they have a marketable value, a considerable number have been manufactured by the natives and have for some time past been finding their way into museums and curiosity shops . . .'

Lone Graves

Rody Schwamn was an unlucky man. In September 1904 he was struck by lightning and buried near the now abandoned town of Duketon in Western Australia. Fifteen years later, John (Jack) Duke died at the nearby Mulga Queen goldmine and was also buried in the sparse town cemetery.

Rody Schwamn's and Jack Duke's joint memorial reflects the outback ethos of making do with whatever might be at hand.

A rusted and battered billy, wired to a dead tree, preserves the only known memory of these pioneering deaths. It reads tersely:

Dueketon [sic] Cemetery
J Duke
R Schwamn

Lonely and lone graves lie across the Australian landscape. When they are marked at all, the inscriptions are mostly stark nods to obscure lives lost in obscure places. A bare wooden cross, a boulder or scattering of stones, sometimes just a carving in a tree may be all that marks the last resting place of another corpse, many unknown and unnamed. Usually in remote locations, they tell sad tales of misadventure, tragedy, high infant mortality and the heavy toll the land often levied on those who tried to live and work upon it.

One of these small-scale, everyday tales was that of Maryann and Lewis Dayes. They lived around Kelsey Creek, Queensland where Maryann was accidentally shot by her son. She died before help could arrive and was buried beneath a long stone, along with her husband who is thought to have died of a heart attack.

Other stories are also heartbreaking. In July 1854, William Anset's wife, Elizabeth, was buried in what was then the small settlement of Maldon, Victoria. She was twenty-seven. Interred with her was her fourteen-day-old infant son. The dangers of childbirth and childhood on the Victorian goldfields are further emphasised at Tarrengower, where a grave commemorates the first European child to have died there around 1850. A bullock driver travelling with his daughter lost the team in a storm. Leaving the young girl behind he went in search of the family's means of livelihood. When he returned the girl had disappeared from the camp and she was later found dead.

The massive influx of people to the eastern Australian gold rushes of the mid-nineteenth century and the often frantic nature of life for those afflicted by gold fever led to many tragedies. When the Western Australian rushes got underway in the 1890s, the same uncaring madness often took over as hopefuls ventured recklessly into the traditional lands of First Nations people in search of riches. In the remoteness of Mondooma, north-east of Derby, is a well with two burial sites. They are the last resting places of a European prospector and another of Chinese origin. Both were victims of a man known by his skin name of Billitcha, dubbed by the press 'The Wild White Man at Kimberley'. Billitcha was captured by a group of white men in 1889, one of whom described him and his unusual history:

> We had him in our camp for several hours and were very much surprised to find that he is not a half caste, but a white man and from his appearance I should say he is a Norwegian or a Dane. His skin is not at all yellowish like half castes, but has more of a reddish tinge owing to the effect of the sun on his complexion which is very sandy. He is a man about 25 years old, about 5 feet 6 inches high, upright, square build, slightly bow-legged, has a good deal of hair growing on his limbs and body of a very light colour. His hair is of a reddish brown, his whiskers and moustache very sandy, he has rather long features and thin lips. He is

even more shy than the natives and it was more difficult to elicit an answer from him, he only speaks the native language and has the marks or scars of the native on his body.

It seems that Billitcha had been wrecked with his mother as a little boy somewhere north of Colliwee Bay, perhaps twenty years earlier. The couple had been rescued by the local First Nations people and the child was brought up in that community. He had murdered two prospectors before killing the pair at Mondooma and throwing their bodies into the well. Billitcha was an initiated warrior of the Kimberley resistance to colonisation but was reportedly killed by his own people when he attempted to raise a force of other young men.

The great number of lone and lonely graves throughout Australia has inspired individuals and groups to locate, record and research them. They are recognised as important historical markers as well as commemorating the mostly unknown lives and deaths of those buried there. An important aspect of this work is placing names and other details on the graves. The volunteers who do this work will never finish as they are too few and the lone graves too many.

Devil of a Place

The folk character usually known as 'the devil'—as opposed to the biblical 'Satan' and 'Lucifer'—is widespread throughout European lore and legend. In the United Kingdom, many places were associated with one or more stories starring the devil and his predictably wicked ways. Sometimes he wins, sometimes he loses but in any case, the place where the legend plays out is then known as 'the devil's cave' or 'the devil's meadow', and so on. Most early settlers in Australia were from England, Ireland, Wales and Scotland, so when naming unusual places that were new to them they sometimes made use of the devil's name, or a related term. Many of these places have intriguing stories.

According to the lore of place names, 'Old Nick', as the devil is sometimes known, was especially busy in the appropriately named Van Diemen's Land. The notorious convict settlement of Macquarie Harbour was known as 'Hell's Gate' after the dangerous waters of the area, feared by all who had to pass through them. At another convict site, the Tasman Peninsula, there are several natural features considered satanic. One is the Devil's Gullett, described as 'a remarkable cleavage in the rocks facing that plateau, 3000 feet [900 metres] high, on which the great lakes of the island are located and in which many of the rivers rise.' The other is the Devil's Kitchen, a 60-metre cleft in the cliffs through which the Great Southern Ocean forces its seething swells. Tassie also boasts a Devil's Island, a Hellfire Bluff and, of course, the Tasmanian devil.

Victoria has its own Devil's Kitchen at Piggooreet, described as a natural amphitheatre carved by the Woady Yaloak River passing across the majestic columns of basalt. Gold was found there in the 1850s and the area was heavily mined, despite its difficult location, as described in 1864 by a visitor: 'The approaches to it are bad enough, in all conscience. The path is very like one which leadeth to destruction, as the entrance to Satanic dominions should be . . .'. Now a geological reserve, the site is renowned for its natural beauty and the only faintly supernatural feature seems to be the echoing of birdsong, running river or human voices bouncing off the basalt. A small island between Wilson's Promontory and Tasmania is known as Devil's Tower; there is a Hell Hole Creek and Satan has at least one Victorian well, set of steps and gully to his name.

The story is similar elsewhere. Queensland has a Devil's Knob and a Satan's Lair, while South Australia has the imaginative Devil's Punchbowl, a vast circular formation near Mount Gambier and Mount Schanck. Western Australia has a Devil's Creek near Mullewa and Karlu Karlu, the Devil's Marbles, are near Wauchope in the Northern Territory. Many of these places have unsettling legends attached to them, though the story of the Devil's Coach House in New South Wales combines some uniquely Australian elements with those brought here by British settlers.

The extensive cave system now known as Jenolan Caves was first encountered by settlers in the 1830s. It is in the country of the Burra Burra people of the Gundungurra nation who knew it as Binoomea, 'dark places'. It is believed to have been created through a battle between a giant eel-like being and a large quoll. The settlers generally knew the area as the Fish River Caves and told a vague tale of three brothers stumbling on the site while pursuing a bushranger who menaced their stock and used the caves as a hide-out. In the 1860s the government took control of the caves and they were given their current name in 1884, said to come from the Gundungurra word for a high place in the shape of a foot, Genowlan. By then, the complex of caverns was firmly on the early tourist trails of New South Wales.

One of the favourite sights was known as the Devil's Coach House. How and when it got this name is appropriately murky, as is much of the early colonial history of the area. One visitor in 1871 wrote:

> whether there is a legend connected with this place, and its previous use as a coach house by the personage it is called after I could never ascertain; however, judging from the rugged appearance of the flooring, I should imagine it would take his Satanic Majesty all he knew, to drive his coach, no matter how strong, and drawn by whatever team he choose, into this stupendous natural structure.

It seems that the faint legend behind the name was not known in the 1870s but arose later. The story goes that an early tourist, camping out overnight in the wilderness, saw the devil, driving an infernal coach and horses, blaze through the great cleft in the cliff. He ran off in terror to tell his frightful tale and the place became known as the Devil's Coach House. Wherever it came from, the name seems to have been firmly established in the 1850s by which time tourists were already travelling three or four days through difficult country to visit and return from the area.

One hardy group battled through the overnight ride from Bowenfels in 1856. Entranced by the 'innumerable stalactites and stalagmites, of snowy whiteness, glittering around, in endless variety of form and size', they braved attacks by 'an enormous black snake' and torrential rain. Nothing satanic happened but, being tourists, they 'all carried away specimens' of the formations. The caves were also being featured in the Sydney newspapers and such were the depredations of stalactite-hunting visitors that concerns for the integrity of the cave formations were already being aired, though it was not until the 1870s that souveniring was banned.

In 1903, the calcified skeleton of an Indigenous person was discovered in one of the caves. It was, of course, named 'Skeleton Cave' and remains so today. This added further creepy overtones to the stories told to tourists ever since. It has also been suggested that the skeleton represents the displaced Indigenous people of the area and so injects something of their history into the settler legend of bushrangers, convicts and the devil.

Whatever the facts beneath this story might have been, it binds Indigenous and settler lore into a new tradition. In 2023, Gundungurra custodians raised the First Nations flag at Jenolan Caves. It will fly there permanently next to the Australian flag.

A Ghost of Gold

It was the night of the Cinderella Ball at the Coolgardie Mechanics' Institute in May 1898. A big event in those days and much anticipated by all, especially 33-year-old nurse, Elizabeth Gold. Her jealous lover, Kenneth Snodgrass, was not so keen. A married man with children, he could not escort her to the ball but neither could he bear the thought of Elizabeth dancing in the arms of other men. What happened next became known as 'the Coolgardie Tragedy', a story still remembered in Coolgardie history and ghostly tradition.

Elizabeth Farrell from Victoria married Charles Gold when she was a 28-year-old dressmaker in the Melbourne suburb of Balaclava. Charles, 54 years old, was an ex-military man with an impressive record and described himself as a 'widower'. In reality, he was a serial bigamist with at least fourteen children by four other wives. Elizabeth seems to have been unaware of her husband's crimes and, like many others seeking rewards on the western goldfields, the couple moved to Coolgardie where Charles passed away in 1897.

Before Charles died, an old acquaintance named Kenneth Snodgrass had boarded with the Golds. His wife and family were living elsewhere at the time while he established himself in booming Coolgardie. He gallantly undertook to arrange the funeral and administer Charles Gold's estate. After the funeral, he employed Elizabeth as housekeeper in his Bungalow Dining Rooms. Shortly after, the rest of the Snodgrass family arrived in Coolgardie but, unfortunately, the dining room business failed a month or so later.

Now without employment, Elizabeth became a probationer nurse to support herself and found work at the Coolgardie Hospital. The hospital matron was a cousin of Kenneth Snodgrass and one of Kenneth's daughters was one of the three other nurses sharing Elizabeth's hessian and corrugated iron 'camp' behind the hospital. In the circumstances, this close web of relationships must have put considerable strain on everyone involved. Kenneth was also in dire financial circumstances after the failure of the dining business and, on the day of the crime, his house had been repossessed.

That evening, after borrowing a pistol, Kenneth visited Elizabeth at her camp to persuade her not to attend the event. But Elizabeth was determined to go. Dressed in a white ball gown, she left for the dance. Less than a metre from the door of her camp, Snodgrass fired a shot into Elizabeth's left breast, followed by another below her chin. She fell to the ground as he placed the pistol under his jaw and drew the trigger for the third time. He died instantly as the bullet passed through his brain. Elizabeth Gold was already dead, her white dress stained with blood. The murderer and his victim were buried on the same day, just a few feet from each other. Elizabeth joined her deceased husband in his last resting place.

The rough-and-ready goldfields of the west were used to violence, but this was something unprecedented: 'Absolutely the most sensational tragedy which has ever taken place since Coolgardie was discovered by Bayley, eventuated last night at the Government Hospital. As soon as the news became known about town, it created great excitement, as those connected with the terrible affair are well-known in Coolgardie society.' The dreadful news and torrid details were a feast for the press, with a further serving from the inquest and the funerals. A hint of the supernatural appeared very early in the post-mortem conversations about the tragedy. It was reported that on the morning of her death, Nurse Gold had spoken to her work companions about 'a presentiment that something was going to happen. She could give no reason for her forebodings, so they were put down to a passing fit of depression and laughed away'.

It's hard to pin down just when people began to see a figure in a long white gown drifting through the grounds of the old Coolgardie Hospital, but it was reportedly quite soon after the tragedy. At some point in the development of the legend the date of Elizabeth's murder, 31 May, became the most likely night for ghost hunters to encounter the apparition. Today, both the history and the folklore of the Coolgardie Tragedy live on in the town. The ghost of Elizabeth Gold is an essential element of local tourism. The grave she shares with the bigamous Charles Gold was for many years unmarked until local residents mounted two commemorative plaques upon the remains of the original headstone.

In keeping with its wild history and its atmospheric near-abandonment, Coolgardie is home to quite a few spirits reluctant to take their leave. The shade of Elizabeth Gold is perhaps the best known. The sensational manner of her death and the knotted legend behind it make up a compelling yarn that, like other ghost traditions, resonates across the years.

The Obliging Dead

When Miss Frances Lynch retired in 1953, she was said to have been the longest serving postmistress in Australia. She had looked over the mail in a tiny office in Toowoomba's last link to the pioneering past, the Royal Bull's Head Hotel at Drayton, for forty-five years. Frances had also lived in the building all her life and was one of a fast-fading generation of people who remembered the nineteenth century. She died in 1958 and soon joined an impressive array of venerable ghosts haunting the historic building.

The Bull's Head was built by entrepreneur and reputed ex-convict Bill Horton in 1848, later gaining its regal addition. As well as providing decent food and accommodation, the hotel included a packhorse mail service and, later, a coaching depot, making it a vital hub in the postal communication system of the time. Bill and his wife, Sarah, operated the business until he died at the age of fifty-seven in 1864; 35-year-old Sarah died the following year. Both deaths were unusually young, even for the mid-nineteenth century. In 1908, Sarah Horton became the first recorded apparition in what was to be an expanding cast of creepy characters haunting the hotel.

Since Sarah Horton's first posthumous appearance—wearing the nightdress she is usually said to have on—the Royal Bull's Head Inn has accrued a motley collection of supernatural visitors. In 1870, a recently married nineteen-year-old drover named John Hannay left after a session at the hotel to go home to his wife. They found his body at his stepfather's property. He had unaccountably chewed some tobacco laced with arsenic.

The same year saw a second tragedy connected with the inn. A vagabond carrying a few drinks too many was given a sofa for the night. According to the landlord, the stranger only drank three more glasses of grog before retiring. Next morning the landlord went into the room where the man was accommodated,

> and found him lying on the floor with his throat cut, and dead, the jugular vein being severed in two. He was a young man, middle height, dark complexion, and dark curly hair. There was a magisterial inquiry held on the body. The name of the unfortunate man did not transpire.

There were other deaths at the hotel. A Chinese man suicided in one of the hotel bedrooms by swallowing throat lozenges spiked with strychnine. He may or may not be one of the extensive roll call of unsettled souls in the place. Visitors and residents have also reported the sound of a crying baby unaccountably coming from the well at the rear of the building; a man in a top hat; objects unaccountably moving; unexplained footsteps; and strange smells. All in all, the many hauntings at the Royal Bull's Head Inn have attracted the attention of ghost hunters.

Paranormal investigators have taken a strong and long interest in the old hotel and its resident spirits. In 2013 one group spent a night there. Using the latest ghost-detecting technology, together with antiques and music of the period (said to trigger paranormal manifestations), the investigators sought to determine what, if any, level of spiritual energy and activity they might scare up. There was more ghost hunting in 2016 and the owners of the property, the Queensland National Trust, have a partnership with a local ghost-tour operator taking visitors through the place on selected evenings. Business looks to be brisk: 'Book Now If You Dare' proclaims the website.

Ghost stories of one kind or another are part of the global stock of folklore and legend. Australia has its fair share of these tales, and more. Few areas are without an old building, cemetery or other site that does not have a good haunting. There's probably one near you. Whether the events said to lie behind the stories are historically accurate is often debatable. In the case of the Royal Bull's Head Inn and its ghosts, those of Sarah Horton, the suicide of the 'unfortunate man' without a name and Miss Lynch, the long-serving postmistress, can definitely be linked to the place. But according to one researcher, the poisoned drover—or drovers—and the suiciding Chinese man stories are unconnected to the inn. Over time, they have become associated with the building through the Sarah Horton tradition, though the first recorded instance of this is not until more than forty years after her not especially dramatic death. It is likely that the crying baby in the well is another example of this process.

This happens a lot in folklore and, in an important way, is the point. Ghost stories allow us to maintain a connection with those parts of the past we wish to remember. In this case, it is the pioneering story of the inn itself, the hardy types who built it and ran it, those who died there (actually or not) and the heritage aura of the place as one of the few surviving structures of the much-mythologised pioneering era. The yarns may or may not be historically 'true', but to most people they sound real enough, chiming in with this aspect of our national narrative. 'The Roaring Days' are long gone. They were already legend when Lawson, Paterson and the Heidelberg artists romanticised them around the 1890s. But many want to keep them alive today—with the assistance of the obliging dead.

The Haunted Asylum

The Victorian goldmining town of Ararat straggled into being on the traditional lands of the Djabwurrung people in the 1850s. It is said to be the only Australian town established by Chinese people, who struck payable gold in the area. Beginning in the usual goldfields style of a tent town, it developed into a fine regional settlement until the gold ran out and the city, as it later became, began a long decline that has only reversed to some extent in recent decades. Its most notable structure is what was once a mental asylum.

As the population of the colony increased during the gold rushes, so did the number of 'lunatics', as those with mental disorders were then known. An asylum was opened in Ararat in 1867 after several years of building. It was an imposing, faintly ominous edifice that eventually grew into a sprawling complex of more than sixty buildings, housing at its height around a thousand people deemed to be psychologically or intellectually impaired and supervised by more than five hundred staff members. The asylum became a mini community, with orchards, gardens and farm animals, reminiscent of a medieval monastery. These buildings are now said to be among the most haunted in Australia.

The reluctant dead are as much a part of our social and cultural fabric as the living, perhaps even more so with the underground population far outnumbering those still breathing today. Indigenous tradition honours the spirit of ancestors going back millennia. Those people who have immigrated in modern times have several centuries of the dead to remember. Some of these departed are said to be unwilling to pass on and to remain as 'ghosts', 'spirits' or 'presences'. Favoured locations for these unsettled departed are old buildings, especially those with traumatic histories. The site of the asylum at Ararat is an ideal location for creepy tales.

In the early days of gold digging, there was already a supernatural legend in circulation around the Ararat area. People spoke of an apparition known as the 'Headless Horseman of Cathcart'. On stormy nights a figure might be seen riding through the hills towards another mining settlement known as Cathcart. The spectral rider had no face. Who he, or it, might have been, no one seems to have known, but the tale marks the beginning of an extended local haunting tradition.

A newspaper report of 1868 tells the story of a Chinese miner living in Opossum Gully who encountered 'a malignant spirit, which kept him in the bush for 24 hours, and otherwise inflicted on him a great deal of hardship and trouble.' He became lost, returning in a 'very wild and excited state' and talking to a bush he carried, in which he said the spirit was embedded. How reliable or not this yarn might have been, its existence boosted the supernatural aura of the area.

The frights continued in 1881 when a newspaper carried an elaborate, and probably fictional story, of the 'Death Light of Possum Gully'. It featured a 'tall figure with its head crowned with flames, and its eyes like coals of fire. It was dressed in a long white robe, and kept lifting its hands to the skies.' It turned out that this was not a spectre but 'a madman who had escaped from the Asylum. His mania was to believe that he had to sacrifice a young girl and bury her in a lonely spot . . .' Less than twenty years later a phantom was reported in the Ararat Botanical Gardens and in 1906 an inmate suffered the delusion that he was haunted by a ghost ordering him to kill his mother.

But it is at the old asylum that the ghosts run wild. J Ward was the accommodation for the criminally insane and there are stories about hanged prisoners buried in unmarked graves and visitors experiencing nausea, fear and even being bitten as they pass through the quarters. A Nurse Kerry is said to trouble the women's ward; a former superintendent's office is thought to be the haunt of a doctor who killed himself there by taking cyanide. A criminal inmate named Gary Webb, who was incarcerated for many years, committed many acts of self-harm, including three castrations. Visitors to the room he occupied report him screaming at them to 'get out'.

Today, a thriving tourist industry provides access to the site, together with paranormal investigations, historical re-creations and a steady flow of creepy tales to enthral customers. As the authors of a study of the asylum's supernatural traditions pointed out, it is the sort of place where you would expect to find ghosts, being part of a long tradition of unnerving buildings, especially those with a carceral function, including prisons, hospitals and orphanages. Not everyone experiences the creepy sensations and appearances attributed to these places, but for some the traumatic and violent histories of these institutions somehow remain embedded, long after their suffering inmates have passed on.

A Million Spooky Acres

Was there ever a woman known as 'the Pilliga Princess'? According to a wealth of roughly similar stories, there *was* such a person. What's more, she is still with us. Well, her ghost is, at least.

The legend of the princess is tied to the vast area known as 'the Pilliga' or 'the Pilliga scrub', 5000 square kilometres of native forest between Coonabarabran and Narrabri in New South Wales. The scrub is reckoned to be the largest continuous area of native forest remaining in Australia, renowned for the diversity of its plant and animal life, as well as caves, gorges and dramatic views. 'Pilliga' means 'swamp oak' in the language of the Kamilaroi people, who were the custodians of the area when it was visited by the explorer John Oxley in 1818. Settlement and grazing soon began, followed by logging of the forest, a history covered in Eric Rolls's famous book, *A Million Wild Acres* (1981).

In the early 1940s, a major road, the Newell Highway, was built through the scrub as part of wartime defence preparations to better connect Melbourne and Sydney. Until then, the Pilliga was little visited and its isolation contributed to the growth of its spooky reputation. Said to be the haunt of yowies and bunyips, the enveloping scrub is also prone to unusual weather conditions. But it is the long, empty highway that has become the locale of the Pilliga's most intriguing tale.

The basic narrative involves an elderly woman hitchhiking at night along the lonely Newell Highway. She is usually said to be pushing her few possessions in a shopping trolley or pram and to be dressed in a fishing hat and an old army coat. She presents a striking sight as her head of wild white hair is picked up in the headlights of passing cars and trucks, many kilometres away from any settlements. In some accounts, she is a First Nations woman; in others, a prostitute. Stories about her abound, especially among truckies, though many other travellers claim to have seen her, either alive or dead. The 'Pilliga Princess', as the woman became known, was run down and killed in 1993. But the tale does not end there.

As in all the best folklore, there are various explanations of this woman's origins and identity. In one version she left her family in the city after an unspecified domestic break-up. In another, she became pregnant to the man she worked for on a local property and the child was later taken away from her.

Just as the origins of the Pilliga Princess are vague, so are the details of her death. An unusually detailed account comes from a truckie who met the woman during her lifetime and was familiar with the bush camp where she made her home:

> It is thought she ran out onto the road to get a lift , but misjudged how close the Stockmaster cattle truck was, as she ran across in front of a southbounder waving her arms for the northbounder. Note where her camp was—it was at the bottom of a hill at a creek—either way a Semi would be

flat out . . . to keep his revs up to get up the hill the other side. It is always very dark at night in the Pilliga, I have found it only darker in most places in the Territory. So to see her at the last moment, one would have no chances of stopping.

As well as trading on the eerie reputation of the Pilliga scrub itself, this yarn also draws nourishment from the rich lore of haunted highways. Australia has many roads or stretches of road said to be supernaturally troubled or to have been the site of dark doings and fatal accidents. The Stuart Highway, connecting Darwin in the Northern Territory and Port Augusta in South Australia, is one. Others include Mount Victoria Pass, New South Wales; the 'Horror Stretch' along the Bruce Highway between Rockhampton and Mackay, Queensland; and the haunted section of Allison Road near Ulverstone, Tasmania, among others. There is also a suggestion that the Pilliga area is considered a place of evil spirits in Kamilaroi tradition, a link with the occasional identification of the Princess as an 'Aboriginal' woman.

Murky as all this might be, the legend is a persistent one, intriguing travellers, podcasters and the endlessly echoing chambers of social media. Whether she is now a ghost or not, the Pilliga Princess was once a living presence. Her name was Clare Wibson. She died in a trucking accident and is buried in Coonabarabran Lawn Cemetery. Her headstone bears several plaques. One reads, in part:

To the Memory of Clare Wibson
(The Pilliga Princess)
20.3.1993 Aged 55 Yrs

It also gives the basic details of her story. The other plaque reads:

IN MEMORY OF
THE PILLIGA PRINCESS
DIED 29-3-1993
THIS PLAQUE DONATED BY THE
TRUCKDRIVERS ON THE HIGHWAY

The sad story of the Pilliga Princess connects the land, its original occupiers and its subsequent users, blending the factual and the folkloric in a way that hints at the deep unease of post-colonial Australia. Like many folk stories it provides a means of processing and mediating those things that we cannot, or will not, otherwise express.

Dangerous Journeys

Holidays! Time to pack up the car, fit the family in around the bags and hit the road. What could possibly go wrong? An awful lot, going by this tragic tale about a young married couple driving an aged great-aunt across the Nullarbor Plain to attend a family reunion in Perth.

It is mid-winter and about halfway across the empty plain, great auntie dies. Not wanting to share the rest of the long journey with a corpse, they roll the body into a tarpaulin, move the luggage from the roof rack to the car and strap the bundle to the roof rack. They drive on through the night, eventually arriving in Albany around 3 am. Exhausted and unhappy, the couple decide to get some sleep before reporting the death. They book into a motel and leave the car parked outside their room with the body still tied to the roof rack. In the morning, they come out of their room to drive to the police station but are horrified to discover that the car has been stolen, along with great auntie. No trace of the car or the body has ever been found.

This story was old when it was told in the early 2000s. The events it describes are said to have happened in many places around the world. It was told in Australia and the United Kingdom around the mid-1960s. Folklorists have been collecting versions of the yarn in the United Kingdom since 1960, with the events described said to have taken place sometime during World War II. The tale was still alive, so to speak, through the 1980s and was known in the Scandinavian countries, in what was Yugoslavia, in Switzerland, Italy, Latvia, Germany, Poland and throughout the United States.

Such a widespread story. Could it be true? If it is, the undignified disappearance of the body happened in many places and at many different times. The story is thought to be derived from eighteenth- and nineteenth-century tales of stolen corpses, or possibly from even earlier European legends, though the more recent versions are probably of post–World War II origin.

Many versions of the story feature a grandmother rather than a great-aunt as the unfortunate main character. The elderly relative usually dies as the travellers cross a border of some kind. In the Western Australian case, the border is the vast Nullarbor Plain, but in versions from other countries it is often the political boundary between two countries or states. The setting, also like many other modern legends, is well and truly in the ordinary, with parents, children and an elderly woman going on holiday in the car.

The persistence of this legend, together with its broad spread and age, has led to a good deal of speculation about what it might mean. Theories include the possibility that it is related to the youth-orientation of contemporary society, with the consequent rejection and disguising of ageing, together with the moving aside of the aged. Another view, related to the earlier legends, not very convincingly links the story with cannibalism, while yet another theory suggests that the legend is about an ancient and universal fear, the return of the dead—which is why the aunt or granny is never seen again, because she is safely out of the world of the living.

A more likely possibility is that the story, at least in its best-known recent versions, has more to do with the modern custom of the family automobile holiday, an activity that frequently, easily and quite quickly takes us to out-of-the-way, foreign or otherwise unfamiliar places. The possible dangers of such places include breaking down in the middle of nowhere, not knowing the local customs and practices in order to summon help, and other dark fears. Most, if not all the many renditions of this story have the family overseas, or at least far away from, their familiar territory. Again, in such circumstances, the apparently ordinary can suddenly turn troublesome, with the result that the deceased has to be bundled up and carried hidden.

Whether you find these possible explanations convincing or not, the story was one of the most popular holiday horror stories heard around the world. Like some other modern legend themes, it was even incorporated in a number of movies, including *National Lampoon's Vacation* and a strand of the plot seems to be part of Steinbeck's novel *The Grapes of Wrath*. In a book titled *The Piano Players* (1986), novelist Anthony Burgess claimed to have invented the story in the 1930s. Wherever it came from and wherever it has been, people have found the yarn compelling enough to tell and retell down the decades. Despite its likely European origins, it is an unsettling story well suited to the long distances and isolation of this continent and its many borders.

Sister Rosa O'Kane, a Queensland nurse, was one of twenty brave volunteers who arrived at Woodman's Point quarantine station in Fremantle to nurse returning soldiers sick with Pneumonic Influenza ('Spanish flu') in December 1918. She and three of her fellow nurses paid the ultimate price in their heroic efforts to relieve the suffering of others.

3

HEROES AND HEROINES

The Great Rescue

The New South Wales village of Gundagai flooded several times before the 1850s. Evolving from the 1830s as a vital transport link across the Murrumbidgee River on the main route between Melbourne and Sydney, it was a thriving community of around eighty buildings. Despite warnings from the traditional landholders, the Wiradjuri, the settlement had been laid out on the flood plain. On the night of 24 June 1852, this wilful mistake led to disaster.

Heavy rains had fallen for weeks, forcing torrents of water down the Murrumbidgee. Complacent residents and travellers were taken by surprise as the flood rose rapidly, destroying buildings and forcing desperate rescue efforts. One boat attempting to save a family was swamped, drowning five children and one of the rescuers. Wherever they could, people clutched to trees in hope of surviving the raging waters. A survivor provided an account to the *Sydney Morning Herald*: 'As night drew in the unavailing cries for assistance all around became fearfully harassing. Crash after crash announced the fall of a house and the screams that followed the engulphing [sic] of those who clung till the water attained its greatest height, about eleven o'clock at night . . .' Some were swept away; some died from exposure as they shivered in the branches under the bright light of a full moon. Many were rescued by four Wiradjuri men. Long Jimmy, Tommy Davis, Jackey (or Jacky Jacky) and Yarri (or Yarra). Their skill and bravery saved the lives of sixty-nine people.

Yarri used a traditional bark canoe to save people, one by one, paddling to them and ferrying them to safety time after time in the frail craft that could only carry two. Using a rowing boat, Jackey rescued another twenty lucky souls as the water carried most of the town away. When the flood receded, most of the buildings had disappeared, along with at least eighty to a hundred men, women and children from a population of around 250.

Newspaper reports painted a grim picture of the aftermath: 'At every step you see someone lamenting the dead. Here and there the sorrowing remains, of what three days before was a large and thriving family.' As well as being an eyewitness to the disaster, the writer of this account had himself been rescued from a tree by Jackey.

The scale of the disaster, still reckoned to be Australia's worst flood in terms of lives lost, provoked angry responses and the government eventually relocated the town to its present, higher site. It was more than another twenty years before Yarri and Jackey were recognised for their bravery with engraved breastplates and life pensions paid by the citizens of Gundagai. Tommy Davis also received a brass breastplate, but Long Jimmy seems to have been completely forgotten.

In 2017, after years of fundraising, the Wiradjuri community, together with descendants of flood survivors, erected a memorial to the event. Melbourne artist Darien Pullan was commissioned to create a life-sized plus bronze representation of Yarri and Jackey with a bark canoe.

> Erected in memory of all the men, women and children who perished in the Great Flood of June 1852 when the Murrumbidgee River at Gundagai broke its banks and turned into a raging torrent, destroying the original town on the river flats. Listed below are the details of 78 people who are known to have lost their lives in the disaster. The number of victims was much higher, but their names will never be known as they were only passing through the town when they were caught in the flood.

The sculpture stands at the corner of Kitchener and Sheridan streets and has become one of Gundagai's tourist sights as well as a monument to the bravery of the four Wiradjuri rescuers. After lengthy petitioning, Yarri and Jackey (who later changed their names to James McDonnell and John Morley), were finally honoured with national bravery awards in 2018.

Floods, along with other extreme weather events, continue to trouble the country. The devastating inundations in New South Wales, Victoria and Queensland during 2010–2011 and, it now seems, almost every year since, have left lasting consequences—social, environmental and financial—for the many people affected. As well, recent bushfire seasons are among the worst ever experienced and there are few years in which some part of Australia is not in drought, often severe and long-lasting. These events look likely to continue and to increase in scale, severity and frequency. Whether they are the result of natural cycles or human activity—or something of both—fire, drought and flood will endure as primal features of the Australian experience.

The Boundary Rider's Wife

In the colonial era and for some time after, poetry was a wide-spread and popular form of self-expression and communication. When we read old newspapers, diaries and archives, it's hard to escape the impression that almost everyone was scribbling verse about their work, their troubles and bush life in general. Much of this vast archive of rhyming poetry is rough-and-ready rather than accomplished. But that is not the point of it. The ballads, as most of them are, provide hasty snapshots of life on the run. They tell stories that are often humorous, or intended to be, and make use of colourful, not necessarily vulgar, language. Overall, they give the modern reader an insight into the realities of life at the time, and probably were one way that those who wrote them, read them and often passed them on by word of mouth or in handwritten form coped with their precarious and basic lives.

Little of this verse is about women and their lot. An exception is a poem of 1898 that is not only a cut above the usual bush jingle in its style but is about the experiences of an outback wife and mother. We don't know who wrote it, quite possibly a woman, although it was usually difficult for women to have their work published in that period. A little like Lawson's famous short story, 'The Drover's Wife', 'The Boundary Rider's Wife' is a rare account of the lonely lives many rural and regional women endured when their husbands were away on long journeys checking fence lines.

I'm the wife of a boundary rider,
And we live on the Barcoo Creek.
Our wage is the station ration,
And twenty bob a week.
We are fairly well contented.
But I hope not all my life
Will be spent on a dreary station,
As a boundary rider's wife.
They say I should never be lonely
With six healthy girls and boys,
They say that my life's complete with
So many domestic joys.
Do they reckon the cost, I wonder,
For the keep of six lusty weans;
For you cannot indulge in fancies
On an out-back station's means.
There's never a school for the children,
And we never a sermon hear.
But we toil from the week's beginning
right up to its ending drear.

With seldom a break in the routine
Of this desolate daily life—
The life on an out-back station
Of a boundary rider's wife.
There are missions to save the heathen,
There are millions spent in strife,
There are armies who preach salvation,
And sing of a better life.
But the road is dark and dreary.
And the way with trials rife;
So they leave to God the saving
Of the boundary rider's wife.

The hardships of this life were too much for some. A boundary rider's wife threw herself under a train as it ran down the hill towards the Muddy Creek bridge in south-west Victoria, in 1884. Others found less tragic ways to escape.

In 1907 boundary rider James Maslin sued for divorce from his wife, Christina. The grounds were, as usual at this period when divorce was a difficult and expensive process, 'misconduct' with another boundary rider on the station near Gulnare, South Australia, where they all lived. Christina had left a 'wealthy home' to marry James in 1891. They had six children, five surviving and aged 10 to 16 years of age when James drove Christina to the Gulnare railway station in February 1907, for her holiday trip to Adelaide. She never returned, as outlined in the trial documents:

> He received from her a letter which stated she had no inten-
> tion of returning, and in reply to a subsequent communication

from him she wrote that she was ashamed to go back. Witness came to Adelaide, and three times in May and June saw his wife in King William Street. She would give him no reason for leaving home, and no information regarding her conduct or her place of abode. She refused to return with him.

It was claimed that Christina had 'improperly conducted herself' with Michael Brown on various occasions and that the pair were living together at Port Adelaide.

The Supreme Court Justice hearing the case commented it was 'a very sad one. Respondent had left an affluent home, where she had apparently been comfortable, and had gone to live with a boundary rider. There was no accounting for such vagaries.' After the intimate details of the Maslins' marriage and separation were thoroughly aired in the press, together with claims and counterclaims, the justice found the allegations against Christina and Brown proven. Such humiliation—as it would have been in those days—was the cost of Christina's escape from her life as a boundary rider's wife.

Posties

Australia's first postmaster was not appointed until 1809. By then, the mails had become so chaotic that the government was compelled to attempt some degree of regulation. Ex-convict and wealthy entrepreneur Isaac Nichols was charged with collecting incoming mail from ships and storing it at his office in Sydney. He published lists of addresses and the recipients had to come to his office to collect their letters and parcels. There was a fee of one shilling for a letter and up to five shillings for parcels. These expensive charges added further to the fortune he had already accrued, though Isaac's profitable sinecure ended in 1825 when the government assumed responsibility for postal services. A few years later, the first 'posties' began delivering mail in Sydney and an Australian icon was born.

Postal delivery services soon spread throughout the colonies but the lack of roads and the state of those that did exist meant that mail runs were not for the faint-hearted. In the 1870s, First Nations man Koolbiri, known as 'Mailman Jimmy', carried the post across the Nullarbor Plain between Eucla in Western Australia and Fowlers Bay in South Australia, a distance of over 350 kilometres each way—on foot. Although there were then no roads between the two settlements, Koolbiri completed the journey more speedily than a horse. It took him two weeks each way, carrying only mailbags and living off the land as he went. He was paid in tobacco.

In very different terrain on the other side of the continent, Thomas Bridle was the carrier of mail through the Snowy Mountains settlements. In August 1879 he found himself in deep trouble.

I started from Mr Harris's place, about nine or ten miles [16 km] from Kiandra, and two and a half miles [4 km]down a mountain by the falls of the Tumut River. In this place rain frequently falls when it is snowing half a mile higher up the hill. When I commenced my journey in the morning, snow about nine inches deep had fallen during the night, and was still falling. With a pair of snow shoes, a break stick, and two mailbags on my back, I trudged up the hill, the snow becoming deeper every few yards, and by the time I got to the top of the range that divides Tumut from the Monaro district, I was floundering along, sometimes up to my knees and at others to my armpits in the snow, which varied in depth from 3ft to 8ft [1 to 2.5 m], according to the ground.

Rain had fallen on the snow, making it soft as Thomas struggled on, his snowshoes frequently clogging in the icy slush. After about five hours of this, he fell through a deep drift into a mountain stream, breaking one of his snowshoes. He still had ten kilometres to go and only seven hours of daylight left. Tired, hungry and wishing he had turned back, the determined postman decided to try to speed up his progress by following the river:

On reaching the stream I got along very well for a few hundred yards though the water was covered with half thawed snow, and I could not see the bottom, but all at once I dropped into a hole up to my neck. I got out, emptied my gum boots, and carefully felt my way along a little further, when the water became completely bridged over with snow, and I had to leave it and struggle through the snow, which by this time began to get a crust on it. A freezing wind was blowing, the ice hanging to my clothes and whiskers made me heavy, and I became exhausted and could not make sufficient exertion to keep myself warm—when I tried too hard I got cramps in the thigh joints. I knew that to lie and rest on the snow would insure [sic] death by freezing, and my only idea was that when I could go no further I would burrow a hole under the snow to get out of the frosty wind.

Despite his circumstances and deteriorating condition, Thomas managed to reach the home of a local settler where he was thawed out with ice water to prevent frostbite. He was lucky and he knew it. The settler 'certainly saved my life, as he has done the lives of several others. I was 13 ½ hours in the snow, and two men had perished in the same place within the last few years.'

The experiences of Koolbiri and Thomas Bridle might sound exceptional, but a detailed description of Australian mail runs before and during the 1890s highlighted the dangers faced by many mailmen, noting that 'unhappily, it is no uncommon occurrence for the Australian press to chronicle the death of a mailman.' Most were not that unfortunate, but those who delivered mail in the High Plains country of Victoria had a few close shaves with the hereafter. Thirteen-year-old Dicky (Richard) Gow had an accident with his horse while delivering mail to Dargo and Omeo in 1876. Lying on the ground with his leg broken in two places, he managed to get up and hop after his mount, catch it and reach up far enough to drop the stirrup down low enough to drag himself back into the saddle. The papers, with their customary taste for exaggeration, claimed Dicky had struggled after his mount for a mile (1.6 kilometres), but Richard's father later wrote to the local press to correct the record—he had only hopped after his horse for half a mile. Hardly worth mentioning!

Conditions improved in the twentieth century as colonial postal services became a national responsibility after Federation, but the job could still be demanding. Bruce Dennis delivered the mail on horseback around Gundagai, New South Wales, from 1950 until his retirement in 1985. When he died in 2022 at the age of 94, the community remembered his six-day-a-week service 'come hail, rain or shine', on his memorial plaque. He was also remembered as a cherished local character. As in many places, it was the custom to leave the postie a bottle of beer at the mailbox on Christmas Eve. After delivering the post, Bruce would empty the bottle. Then he continued to the next one, and so on, until he finished his shift at 2 pm by falling off his horse. 'The whole town loved him, and everyone knew him,' recalled one of his friends.

By the time Bruce began his career as a mounted postman, the mail was also being delivered by women. The Post Master General's Department, or PMG, employed females generally as clerical workers rather than posties until the male labour shortages of World War II forced the organisation to take on women as deliverers. The first in Victoria were Margery Garvie and Jean Baxter in the town of Terang from early 1942. Even earlier, in 1941, Brisbane had a Post Office women's auxiliary training to replace men on active service. During the war, women also drove trucks to clear mailboxes, or 'pillar boxes' as they were then known, and trained to replace male telegraphists. Today, your local postie is employed by Australia Post and is as likely to be a woman as a man—but do they receive a bottle of beer at Christmas?

Hell

Susie Cone's war was over before it began. The thirty-year-old Gippsland nurse sailed to Europe on the 'old tub' *Wyreema* with 47 other women of her calling in November 1918. They reached Cape Town in South Africa just as the armistice ending the conflict was signed. Susie wrote in her diary that it was 'a terrible disappointment for everybody. We all expected at least to get to England.' The nurses were sent back home. 'This old tub and her load are bound for old Aussie once more,' she wrote with a mixture of regret and relief. Susie and her companions could not know the peacetime horrors they would face when they reached Western Australia.

The plague that would kill more people than the Great War reached the west on the homeward-bound troop transport ship *Boonah*. Around three hundred returning soldiers were sick with the 'Spanish flu' as the influenza pandemic was then known. A quarantine station was hurriedly established at Woodman Point south of Fremantle where Susie was one of about twenty nurses who volunteered to tend the sick. It was dire from the start: 'About 10am the boys began to come up from the jetty. Our tents and hut were soon full. Poor lads were in a terrible plight. Filth and dirt all over them, terribly sick.' The nurses and doctors had no drugs or clean clothing for their patients, and could only wash them and try to make them comfortable. Three soldiers died on the first day. More soon followed. 'This place is hell,' she wrote, 'nothing but dust, sand and flies and sickness.'

It was not long before the nurses caught the disease. Sister Rosa O'Kane, twenty-eight years old, died in December, followed by Ada Thompson, Hilda Williams and Doris Ridgeway. 'Such a dear little girl,' Susie wrote of Doris Ridgeway's death. Only a week later, Susie contracted influenza. She was ill for a week but recovered and continued to nurse the 330-or so sick soldiers.

Conditions at the station were basic and the nurses had to live in tents quite a distance from their work, forcing them to walk back and forth along a dusty track in the heat of the Western Australian summer. The authorities controversially cancelled Christmas and even though the nurses were given the day off and a dinner that was 'a scream', they were deeply unhappy with their treatment by the officials in charge.

The Woodman Point Quarantine Station was established as early as 1876 when a large area of bushland was set aside for the buildings, which were erected from 1886. The facility was mainly used to quarantine people infected with plague and other transmissible diseases and to screen immigrants deemed to be at risk of carrying dangerous infections. Unusually for the era, the station featured a crematorium, possibly Australia's first. Today, Woodman Point is a recreation camp and heritage site.

By the time Susie Cone's service ended in late January 1919, she was the last of the *Wyreema* nurses left at the quarantine station. Gratefully, she packed her bags for home—'too good to be true,' she wrote. When the influenza crisis ended, 27 soldiers and four nurses had died of the disease. Around Australia it is estimated that possibly 40 per cent of the population contracted influenza and that between 10,000 and 15,000 may have succumbed to the disease.

Susie Cone is commemorated on the Glengarry War Memorial and on the Rosedale Shire Honour Roll in Victoria. Rosa O'Kane and Hilda Williams are buried at the quarantine station. At Rosa O'Kane's grave is a memorial commemorating her extraordinary bravery and sacrifice. The inscription begins with two simple words—'For Valour'. It applies equally to all the *Wyreema* nurses and the others who served at Woodman Point during the desperate months of the influenza outbreak.

Ambitions of the 'Fair Sex'

In Australia, the right of women to vote is today taken for granted. It was not always so and the fight for female suffrage in Australia was long and bitter. Agitation began in the 1850s, when the British government granted the right of representative government to the distant Australian colonies. Momentum grew slowly but firmly into the 1880s when international struggles for political reform began to influence local thinking. The temperance movement in the United States, the United Kingdom and Australia was strongly supported by women. It began as a stand against the destructive powers of alcohol but quickly became a force for women's political rights and an important part of a broad push for reform that included other Christian groups, suffragists and committed individuals from many different backgrounds.

Catherine Helen Spence was a pioneering journalist, social reformer and Australia's first female candidate for political office, yet she is little known by the public today. Catherine was born in Scotland in 1825 and emigrated with her family to South Australia in 1839, becoming a governess and teacher, further educating herself through extensive reading. She was the first woman to write and publish a novel set in Australia, but it was not until her third work of fiction in 1865 that her name appeared as author. Spence later moved to journalism and non-fiction books and had a successful career espousing social, political and educational reform issues. She was influential in the Unitarian Christian Church and developed into an effective public speaker on the many issues she championed, despite strong prejudices against women taking high-profile roles in civic debates and discussions.

In the 1890s the short, white-haired woman with a Scots accent threw her influence behind the female suffrage cause and in 1897 became the first woman to stand for a political office in Australia. Spence ran for one of the ten seats for the colony of South Australia at the Federal Convention leading up to the referendum on the federation of the colonies. She did not win but polled well, an indication of her public standing. For the rest of her life, she continued her advocacy for women's rights and the other causes. She never married but managed to find the time to raise three families of orphaned children during a long and influential life. At her eightieth birthday celebration, South Australia's Chief Justice referred to her as 'the most distinguished woman' Australia had known. In her speech, Spence said 'I am a new woman, and I know it. I mean I am an awakened woman . . . awakened into a sense of capacity and responsibility, not merely to the family and household, but to the state . . .' When she died in 1910, the press called her, affectionately, 'The Grand Old Woman of Australia'.

South Australian women had gained the right to vote and stand for parliament in 1894. When the Commonwealth was established, they and most other women in Australia gained two new rights. Not only could they vote in federal elections, they could also stand for federal office. This was the first time in the world that women had won such significant dual rights. Despite this breakthrough, women did not necessarily have the right to vote in state elections. This was not fully achieved until 1908. Technically, Aboriginal women also had these rights, though were probably unaware that they did. After Federation, Aboriginal and Torres Strait Islander peoples lost the right to vote in federal elections, and did not recover it until 1962.

While South Australia was first in the world to enfranchise women in 1894, it was not until 1902 that women were allowed to vote and stand for election. In 1903 Vida Goldstein became one of the first Australian women to contest a parliamentary seat. A prominent suffragist, Goldstein was born in Victoria in 1869, following her mother into the movement and becoming an effective advocate for what were then often considered the more radical aspects of women's suffrage. Well educated, tall and articulate, she would later have a high-profile international activist career, a factor that might have contributed to her relative obscurity since. A federal electorate in Melbourne is named after Vida Goldstein and a statue commemorating her life and work is scheduled to be unveiled in Melbourne in time for International Women's Day 2025.

Two other women also stood as independent candidates for the federal Senate in 1902—Mary Moore-Bentley (also Mary Ling) and Nellie Martel, while Selina Anderson (later Siggins) stood for the House of Representatives. This was the first time women had stood for any national parliament anywhere in the British Empire. Although none was successful, they opened the way for women to vie for parliamentary seats at federal and state levels. But it would not be until 1921 that a woman was elected to any Australian parliament. It happened in Western Australia, with a shock win by only 46 votes.

When new members of the Western Australian Legislative Assembly gave their maiden speech, the tradition was that there would be no interruptions from either side of the House. When Edith Cowan gave her maiden speech that convention was ignored. She was jeered and heckled by the males in the chamber. Reactions elsewhere were also unfavourable, as the *Age* newspaper put it:

> Were political office to become the ambition of the Fair Sex, and were standing for Parliament to become the latest craze of fashion, there would be many dreary and neglected homes throughout the country sacrificed on the altar of political ambition.

Elected in her sixtieth year, largely through her well-deserved reputation for good works, Edith Cowan's 'indomitable courage' withstood these and other insults. She introduced two private member's bills to improve the lot of women and both were passed. But she served only one term after being relegated to the unwinnable third place on the Nationalist (forerunner of the Liberal party) ballot paper for the next state election. She stood again in 1927 representing the Women's Electoral Lobby but was unsuccessful.

The trailblazing efforts of all these women and their supporters assisted Western Australian Dorothy Tangney and Tasmania's Enid Lyons to become the first two women to be elected to the federal parliament in 1943. It is said that when the two new members arrived in Canberra to take up their seats in (old) Parliament House they found that there were no female bathrooms.

Almost Sir Lancelot

In 1911, Lance de Mole was carrying out an engineering survey in rural Western Australia. Although few roads allowed a comfortable drive at that time, Lance found those in the west were unbearable bone-breakers. Being an inventive bloke, he turned his mind to creating a better, smoother way of getting around. What he came up with was revolutionary.

Lance—short for Lancelot—Eldin de Mole was born in South Australia in 1880 and moved with his family to Victoria where he was educated, later becoming a draftsman involved with mining and engineering projects around the country. Always tinkering with ingenious devices, his new idea was to use 'chain rail'—similar to caterpillar tracks—beneath an armoured vehicle to lay a continuous metal track for carrying heavy loads across rough ground. This sturdy machine could be steered and reversed as necessary and was, Lance thought, ideal for use in warfare. It was the first military tank.

There was no war in 1912, but few doubted that one was coming. Lance drew up plans for his idea and sent them across the seas to the British War Office. In 1913 he received a polite rejection. Disappointed, he nevertheless declined a suggestion that he submit his idea to the German consul. But he had not given up.

World War I began in 1914 and it quickly became apparent that it was like no previous conflict. Cavalry charges were mostly displaced by thundering artillery, with trench networks, muddy fields, festoons of barbed wire and blasted buildings on a barely imaginable industrial scale. A manoeuvrable vehicle that could carry the large weights of materials needed to fight such a war through mud and over devastated trenches would be a game changer.

In 1915, Lance again sent his plans to the War Office. This time the British were prepared to take a look if he could send them a model. Lance had the model made but did not have the money to get it to the United Kingdom. But he had another bright idea. If he enlisted in the Australian Imperial Force (AIF) he could be posted overseas and get his model to the War Office in London. Actually, it probably wasn't that great an idea, so it was just as well that the 37-year-old inventor was rejected as medically unfit.

Meanwhile, the British had been working on the same idea as Lance. They came up with the 'tank', originally the code name for the research and development project, and their first lumbering effort, known as the Mark 1, went into action on the Somme in 1916. The first tanks were crude, but they worked—mostly—and were popular with the ground troops who could gain much needed cover from them during an advance.

Not surprisingly, Lance was unhappy with these developments. He felt the British had ignored his design in favour of their own, which, he claimed, was inferior. Now even more determined, he had a bit of luck. He came into contact with Harold Boyce, a lieutenant in the 10th Battalion, invalided back to South Australia after being wounded at Pozières. Boyce, later to be lord mayor of London and a baronet, took an interest in de Mole's invention and facilitated his enlistment as a private. Lance was able to travel to London and demonstrate his model to the relevant committee, which commended it to the Tank Board, where it was promptly lost in the traditional bureaucratic manner. Six weeks later, having heard nothing despite sending letters and telegrams to the board, Lance got leave and went back to London. He eventually located his model in the basement of a government office and his letters in a pigeonhole. Neither the model or his correspondence had gone to the Tank

Board. A week or so later, Lance was shipped off to France to take his chances fighting the rest of the war.

Lance survived and was back in London in 1919 where a royal commission was sitting to make decisions about awarding the originators of various inventions used in the war. A number of people claimed to have invented and developed the tank. Two were successful in their claim, but Lance was not. The commission did note his work and later agreed that he 'had made and reduced to practical shape, as far back as the year 1912, a brilliant invention which anticipated, and in some respects surpassed, that actually put into use in the year 1916.' But it was not his design that the British used. They acknowledged that Lance's work was ahead of its time and had 'failed to be appreciated'. Although Lance could not receive an award, he was asked to submit a claim for his expenses in developing and promoting his idea. Ultimately, Lance received almost £1000 and was made an honorary corporal, the last rank he had held. He was also appointed a Commander of the Most Excellent Order of the British Empire (CBE), just one step below a knighthood—almost Sir Lancelot.

Having received at least some recognition and compensation, Lance went home, became an engineer in the Sydney Water Board and continued to tinker with various inventions. Still keen to serve his country, during World War II he came up with an artillery shell that could be fired towards enemy aircraft where it would burst to create a screen of wires held by a slowly descending parachute. His idea was well received in Australia but when it was passed to London it was, like his earlier attempt, rejected. The British said that they had already tried something similar and found it 'impracticable'.

Lance de Mole lived until 1950. His tank model is in the collection of the Australian War Memorial.

Anonymous No Longer

Edith Emery's eventful life is a story of constant renewal. As a newcomer to Australia in the 1930s she brought with her much-needed medical skills, yet she was not allowed to practise. Undaunted by this, as well as personal and global turmoils, she married, bore children and retrained as an architect. She made a significant contribution to residential design yet was, until recently, almost unknown.

Born in the wrong place at the wrong time—in Austria, 1909—Edith Wellspacher studied fine arts as a teenager but then decided on a medical career. She graduated as a gynaecologist from the University of Vienna just as Adolph Hitler's Nazi party came to power in Germany. Nazi troops occupied Austria in 1938 and Edith was forced to resign her medical post. Opposed to fascism, she and her boyfriend, Max, were forced apart when he was arrested and later sent to concentration camps.

Fortunately, Edith heard of a teaching position for someone trained in the fine arts approach she had studied in her youth. The job was in Tasmania. At that time, it was still possible to leave occupied Europe and Edith took a ship down under. On the voyage she met an Englishman who worked in Sudan. She and John Emery fell in love, pursuing their romance through letters between Sudan and Tasmania. He eventually proposed, though Edith still felt loyal to Max, whom she had promised to wed if he survived imprisonment. He did, but Edith eventually decided to marry John. After a honeymoon in Tasmania, she returned with him to Sudan, where she soon became pregnant. Her life then descended into chaos as she was forced by circumstances to return to the nightmare she had escaped less than two years before.

On medical advice, Edith left Sudan for France, where her son was born in 1940. Her relationship with a British citizen allowed her and the baby to be accommodated in a hospital in the east of France. Here, she was able to help out medically and as a translator. But this congenial arrangement came to an end after only a few months and mother and son had to move to occupied Paris. There, they were under the authority of the Gestapo and could be arrested at any time.

But, once again, fortune favoured Edith. She was able to return to John in Sudan through a prisoner swap arrangement. A second son was born in 1944 and four years later the family was living in Tasmania. With her medical qualifications unrecognised in Australia, Edith studied architecture and became the first qualified female sole practitioner in the state. She designed houses for clients with modest budgets, lived quietly and died in 2004 at the fine age of 94. She wrote her autobiography and a book on her Asian travels but remained unknown outside her family. That changed nearly twenty years later.

Architects Mat Hinds and Poppy Taylor stumbled on plans Edith had drawn for a friend's Hobart home. The plans revealed a powerful architectural sensibility and attention to detail unusual in suburban home designs of the 1950s. Intrigued, the architects continued to delve into the puzzling obscurity of Edith's architectural work. They discovered that for many years she had worked with eminent Tasmanian architect Esmond

Dorney. His acclaimed and innovative house designs are now thought to have benefited from Edith's unacknowledged input at a critical era in the evolution of Tasmanian domestic architecture. As Mat Hinds observed after researching Edith's work: 'what ended up happening with Edith's work is that she caused a leap to occur but anonymously.'

The chance recovery of Edith Emery's life and work reveals a strong personality who handled discrimination and difficulties with a set of strong social values at a time and place when women were expected to take a back seat other than in the home. Anonymous no longer, she is now seen as an inspiring figure for female architects, acknowledged through the Edith Emery Award for Residential Architecture of the Australian Institute of Architects.

War Widows

Major General George Vasey had a distinctive way with words. As brigadier in command of the 6th Division's 19th Infantry Brigade in Greece during the desperate days of 1941, he told his men: 'Here you bloody well are and here you bloody well stay. And if any bloody German gets between your post and the next, turn your bloody Bren around and shoot him up the arse.' Not surprisingly, his soldiers called him 'Bloody George' and held him in high regard.

Vasey's tough-talking exterior camouflaged a more compassionate heart. He went on to command the Australian forces in what is now Papua New Guinea. After contracting malaria, he was returned to Australia where he visited the widow of one of his men. Shocked at the poverty in which she lived, Vasey later talked about the experience with his wife, Jessie. He asked her to 'stick to the war widows and when I come back you shall have every atom of help I can give you.' Vasey was then sent back to New Guinea to take up his command, but his plane crashed and he, along with all on board, was lost in 1945.

Now a war widow herself, Jessie Vasey formed the War Widows' Craft Guild in Victoria. Members were taught handicraft skills that allowed them to make goods for sale to supplement the less-than-generous pensions they received from the government. The guild quickly developed into a national organisation of women in receipt of pensions for the loss of their husbands on active duty, from war-related causes or as interned civilians. Widows from both world wars were admitted. Under Jessie Vasey's leadership, the guild advocated for adequate pensions and other improvements to entitlements, having some early success in 1947. The organisation also provided a valuable social and emotional support system with the motto:

> We all belong to each other.
> We all need each other.
> It is in serving each other and in sacrificing for our common good that we are finding our true life.

Jessie Halbert was born in Queensland in 1897. She was well educated there and graduated with a Bachelor of Arts from Melbourne University in 1921. The same year she married George Vasey and joined his life and career as a professional soldier. During World War II, like many women, she worked with the

Australian Comforts Fund, and she was also a founding member of the Australian Imperial Forces Women's Association in 1941.

Known for her striking hats and strong views, which she articulated very effectively, Jessie advocated for the economic independence of war widows, and it became her life's work. In 1949 she accused the government of spying on the widows: 'I know of many cases of war widows being trailed by Government agents . . . and being reported to the Repatriation Commission if they have boy friends. Without being consulted, their pensions are stopped.' She was going to continue 'nagging' the government for an increase in the pension to equal the basic wage, also saying that 'the Government gave de facto wives a better deal than war widows, and no questions were asked about the conduct of de facto wives when they received pensions and allowances.

The following year, Jessie continued to speak out. Hearing that the Menzies government was not going to increase pensions by the amount she thought necessary, she was 'horrified' and put her case forcefully through the press directly to Prime Minister Menzies:

I have spent my time, health, and money in a long campaign to make brutal politicians realise a war widow is a human being. Mr. Menzies pretended to listen. He promised the war widow great things when he was campaigning for the general election. We pinned our last hopes on him. But it now appears he intends giving us less than Mr. Chifley did . . . Two years ago I was the leader of an enterprising band of war widows. Today many of them are broken women, psychiatric cases who have spent their husbands' gratuities and deferred pay. Some are getting desperate. The widow trying to clothe and feed her two children on £4/17/6 a week is living in constant anxiety. All I can do now is to live in the hope that Mr. Menzies will respect his promises.

Despite this advocacy, pensions for the widows were only marginally increased.

In the 1950s, Jessie and the guild developed an accommodation scheme for widows in distress, taking advantage of the shared funding available under the *Aged Persons Homes Act* of 1954. The Vasey Housing Auxiliary, as the company was known, was able to house hundreds of war widows in Victoria and elsewhere.

Jessie continued to lead the guild up to her death in 1966, receiving deserved honours and acclaim. Her dedicated work was an important part of a larger movement of organisations, such as Legacy, working for the benefit of those harmed by war. In 2020, the War Widows Guild of Australia became Australian War Widows Incorporated, 'looking to modernise and consolidate ensuring that there is always a service to look after War Widows in need and advocating on behalf of all War Widows to the National Government.'

The Gumboot Tortoise

An unusual memorial can be seen in Victoria's Beech Forest. It takes the form of a plinth of bush rock with a small plaque attached. Crowning the rock is a carving of a single gumboot. The memorial honours the memory of a local potato farmer,

Cliff Young. While Cliff's spuds were undoubtedly excellent, he is celebrated here for another reason.

In 1983 an 'ultra-marathon' footrace was launched between the large Westfield shopping centres of Sydney and Melbourne. The course was almost 900 kilometres and attracted many fine and very fit athletes. Most of them were on the younger side of life, but Cliff Young was over sixty when he signed on to the challenge. The unlikely contender nevertheless went into serious training on his farm, his program consisting mainly of chasing stray cattle while wearing gumboots.

This novel approach was considered by almost everyone to be a bit of a joke, especially when Cliff stumped up to the start line of the marathon wearing his work boots, overalls and without his dentures, which, he said, tended to rattle when he ran. The press and public loved this apparent stereotype of an amiable bush yokel, and Cliff became an overnight media sensation in the days before such oddities could 'go viral' on the internet. Everyone loved him for having a go, though none gave the potato farmer a chance of winning, let alone finishing, the gruelling race. But he had a secret weapon.

Born in 1922, Cliff grew up in the tough depression years of the 1930s. He took up marathon running during his mid-fifties in 1979 and ran some respectable but unspectacular times in several races. By the time of the 1983 marathon, Cliff had developed a unique running style, subsequently known as the 'Young shuffle'. At first, this got him nowhere. He started badly and was well behind on the first day. The competitors, including Cliff, stopped for a mandated six-hour sleep break. Cliff woke up after only two hours thinking that he had slept for six. He got up and, feeling fine, shuffled on. And on.

With his energy-saving technique and a dogged refusal to give in to the need for sleep breaks, Cliff ran for five days. He not only completed the course but beat everyone else by a whopping ten hours, said to have taken two days off a previous record for the run. The tortoise became a fabled hero, especially when he refused to take the prize money, splitting it evenly between the runners-up, who, he said, had worked as hard as he had himself. A six-day race in Colac was named after him and he was made a member of the Order of Australia in 1984 for his achievements in long-distance running.

Cliff's subsequent running career was uneven, though he made a world record run in a race in 2000, then approaching eighty years of age. Undoubtedly fit though he was, the years inevitably caught up with him. Cliff suffered strokes and cancer in the last five years of his life and died in 2003. His legacy is a lingering affection in the popular consciousness, propped up by a telemovie in 2013 and by several younger marathon runners taking up his 'Young shuffle'.

In 1983 aged 61 Cliff won the inaugural 875km Westfield Sydney to Melbourne Ultra Marathon in five days, fifteen hours and four minutes becoming a national hero.

He trained on his farm chasing cattle in gum boots and started the race wearing the unusual footwear which became part of his national image.

Cliff`s peculiar style, labelled the "Cliff Young Shuffle", has since been adopted by other ultra-marathon runners.

For many years Cliff was a familiar sight around the district as he trained or "shuffled" along the local roads. He went on to run more that 20,000 km over his competitive career.

The plaque on Cliff Young's memorial reflects his standing in his local, as well as the national, community:

Dedicated to the memory of Cliff Young
Potato farmer and athlete from Beech Forest.
8/2/1922 – 2/11/2003

Initiated by the Beech Forest Progress Association

Rodney Ansell was the colourful real-life character who inspired the fictional Mick 'Crocodile' Dundee. The film story of Crocodile Dundee ended much less violently than Ansell's troubled life.

4

RATBAGS AND REBELS

'The Only Female Prisoner'

The mob on Beverstone Road, Gloucestershire, was a good 100 strong, according to the special constables sworn in to keep the peace on 26 November 1830. The rioters brandished pickaxes, sledgehammers and sticks, and were on their way to break a threshing machine on Jacob Hayward's farm. Four magistrates were trying in vain to dissuade the mob from carrying out their plan. 'Be d—d if we don't go to Beverstone, and break the machine!' came a cry from the mob. The angry speaker was a woman.

Elizabeth Parker was a gap-toothed prostitute in her early twenties who worked around Tetbury, about three kilometres east of Beverstone. When the mob, trailed by the constables, reached Hayward's farm she took a leading role in the job they were there to do. Witnesses saw her wielding a sledgehammer and, along with many of the men, putting it to effective use on farmer Hayward's threshing machine.

The farm workers and their supporters were trying to rescue their livelihoods from the triple threat of parish tithes, grasping farmers and the newly introduced threshing machines replacing their labour. The 'Captain Swing riots' ravaged southern and other parts of England in the winter of 1830–31. The consequences for those who followed the mythical leader, known as 'Captain Swing', were often dire.

It didn't take long for police to round up many of the rioters and they were tried at the local Quarter Sessions in December. The twenty-three men on trial with Elizabeth produced character witnesses, though no one spoke for her. In the course of the proceedings, the young woman was clearly identified as one of the leaders of the mob. In sentencing her, the chairman expressed the indignation of the law and his gender: 'A woman, the only female prisoner, who had, by violent language and by every means in her power, been active in stimulating her companions to acts of outrage, and had even personally assisted with a large sledge hammer.' Riot leaders were likely to be hanged or transported if found guilty. Elizabeth was among those condemned to be sent to Australia for seven years. But she received royal clemency, presumably because she was a woman, and was released a few months after the trial. Many of the other Beverstone rioters were discharged, though others also identified as leaders received sentences of seven or fourteen years' transportation.

Elizabeth did not stay clear of the courts for long. The following year she was back on a charge of stealing from the parish clerk and assistant overseer of the poor, Daniel Cole. After a few drinks in a local inn, the couple had spent half an hour or so together in the backyard of the pub. Next morning, Cole found that all his money was missing. Elizabeth apparently passed one of Cole's conveniently marked notes in a shop, leading to her arrest, at her mother's house. The constable sent for Cole, who came and identified Elizabeth as the thief. She tried to dissuade him from the accusation without success, then cried, 'Oh, don't take me, and I'll send for my mother, and she will sell everything she has to give you back your money.' But Cole proceeded with his charge against her.

At the trial, Cole claimed that he had not paid Elizabeth anything during their intimate half-hour at the back of the pub though, oddly, he had given her a shilling while she was on remand awaiting trial. Whatever did or did not happen, the woman was predictably found guilty. The judge took an especially dim view of the fact that Elizabeth had recently benefited from royal clemency and transported her for life, an extremely severe sentence for the relatively minor crime she had committed. Nor was the judge impressed with Daniel Cole's motivations and refused to allow him the usual practice of waiving the expense of the prosecution.

Daniel Cole was a man of substance and property and so was allowed to vote. Although he had won the case, Cole's reputation was badly smirched, not only with his employer but, presumably, with his wife. The intricacies of this intensely local relationship went even further. He had been one of the witnesses against Elizabeth when she was earlier tried for machine breaking, giving damning evidence that he had seen her smashing the threshing machine with the sledgehammer.

While Elizabeth had evaded transportation for that offence, this time she sailed for Van Diemen's Land aboard the transport *Frances Charlotte* in 1832. Surviving the hulks and a cholera outbreak that afflicted the ship before leaving port, she disembarked at Hobart some months later with the other ninety-nine convicts aboard. She went straight into the Cascades 'female factory' along with most other female transports. There, women were allocated to one of three classes of prisoner— the well behaved; those who committed minor offences; and, the third class, women who had been transported twice or committed other crimes during their sentences. All classes worked up to twelve hours a day. The first class cooked and oversaw other tasks, including the hospital; the second class made and mended clothing, while the third, 'crime class', did the washing and spun wool.

Rules were harsh and strictly enforced: 'Females guilty of disobedience of orders, neglect of work, profane, obscene, or abusive language, insubordination, or other turbulent or disorderly or disrespectful conduct, shall be punished by the superintendent with close confinement in a dark or other cell, until her case shall be brought under consideration of the Principal Superintendent.' These and other regulations were frequently broken by Elizabeth. She got drunk, neglected her work, went missing, received stolen property, assaulted a constable and was caught in compromising situations on several occasions. These infractions led to her being demoted at times to the third 'crime class', with periods of solitary confinement and hard labour. Elizabeth's record was not especially bad among those of the other refractory women convicts but it meant that she was not granted a conditional pardon until after 1845. And then she disappeared from the record.

Only one woman was ever transported for a Swing offence. Elizabeth Studham (Studdam) was born in Monckton, Kent, in 1810. Twenty years later she was found guilty of setting fire to a haystack or thatched outhouse during the Birchington poorhouse riot of late October 1830. She was committed to Maidstone Gaol in December and transported to Van Diemen's Land, arriving in October 1831. Her record there was like that of Elizabeth Parker: she also gave birth to two children by different fathers in 1834 and 1836. After several men were refused permission to marry her, she eventually wed James King, father of her second child, in 1843. Elizabeth's troublesome conduct meant that she did not receive a conditional pardon for her Swing conviction until 1845. At some point after that, she moved to Victoria and died there aged 64 in 1874.

Like so many of history's nobodies, Elizabeth Parker and Elizabeth Studham came to Australia as part of the great mass of barely known people who all gave something to the future.

Genius or Fool?

The man who is known to history—mostly—as Robert Lyon Milne was 'an enigmatic character who defies easy analysis. It is tempting to conclude that he was either a great genius or a great fool, or perhaps both.'

This was historian Bob Reece's assessment of the strange life of a man who went by several names. Even after extensive research, historians have not been able to pin down exactly who he was or where he came from. But we do know a fair bit about what he did in a momentous life that saw him active in the United Kingdom, Mauritius, New South Wales, Victoria, South Australia and Western Australia between 1829 and the late 1850s.

Aged around forty and going by the name Robert Milne, this man makes his first recorded appearance in the fledgling Swan River colony in 1829. He was a person of substance, with a servant and the servant's family attending him. It wasn't long before he changed his name to 'Robert Menli Lyon', the middle and surname being anagrams of 'Milne' and 'only'. In the colony he represented himself as someone with a military background, an officer, of course. He was granted over 1200 hectares of land in accordance with the arrangements for distributing Indigenous land to settlers. Milne apparently gave this grant away, though he received another almost as large in a better farming location. He also purchased land around the colony and energetically operated a boat-carrying business along the Swan.

Clearly a man on the make, Milne soon became a notorious figure. He assailed Governor Stirling and the government in London, the local courts and individuals with complaints, litigation and suggestions about a range of issues, especially the need to deal fairly with the local people now known as the Whadjuk Noongar. As with his business and other activities, Milne pursued this cause with intensity. As the tensions between the Noongar and settlers rose, he pleaded for recognition of the realities of colonisation. 'You have seized upon land that is not yours. Beware, and do not, as a people, add to this the guilt of dipping your hands in the blood of those who you have spoiled of their country.' This, delivered at a public meeting, and his other spoken and written statements, made Milne widely unpopular. But his arguments did have some effect, especially in relation to one of the colony's most tragic incidents.

Three Noongar men—Yagan, Dommera and Ningina—were captured after a series of attacks by colonists and Noongar. They were to be executed. Surprisingly, given his local reputation, Milne convinced the authorities that it would be better to convert the Noongar to Christianity than to fight with them and that the men should be spared execution and placed in his care.

> I urged that they were guilty of no crime but that of fighting for their country. We call their deeds murder, so might they ours; but the fact was that they had a right to make war after their own manner.
>
> Besides, they were now prisoners of war; and to put prisoners of war to death, in cold blood, was contrary to the law of nations and usages of war.

Together with two military guards, Milne and the reprieved Noongar men spent five or six weeks in isolation on Carnac Island. It was an extraordinary moment in intercultural relations. The exiles had nothing to do but exist and speak with each other, unhindered by distractions or antagonisms. Milne learned much of Noongar language and custom and came to believe that he was close to being able to negotiate a treaty. But one night, the Noongar men took an unattended boat and escaped. Yagan would later be treacherously killed by a young settler for the reward that was offered.

Milne was embarrassed but persistent. He continued to advo-cate for Noongar rights and for a treaty. In 1834 he published another of his many contributions to the *Perth Gazette*, in which he stated that 'the sooner the national rights of the Aboriginal inhabitants are recognized by some regular deed or charter, the better it will be for them, and the British colonies in this hemisphere.'

These events and Milne's passionate defence of Indigenous rights made him even more unpopular, if that were possible. After yet another of his many disagreements, he was expelled from the Agricultural Society, the main civic institution in the colony. Mortgaging his holdings, he sailed for Mauritius in 1835. There, he employed his deep knowledge of Greek and Latin as a professor in a local college and continued to pursue Indigenous rights and other interests. He became involved in a financial venture supposed to assist British emigrants wishing to travel to Australia. Then he moved to Adelaide where, sometimes styling himself 'Captain' and sometimes referred to as 'Reverend', he tried to set up a bank.

These ill-judged schemes collapsed and Milne went to Sydney where he tried to establish a mission to protect First Nations people. This, too, came to nothing and he returned to Adelaide where he purchased property and spent some time in debtors' gaol following his financial disasters. By 1853 he was on the Ballarat goldfields hoping to repair his finances and the following year, in Melbourne, he floated a utopian scheme for a new colony on the Murray River. There was some local support for this, but the government in the United Kingdom was not interested.

Never one to stand still, Milne went back to Adelaide to develop his land for industrial use. Admirably, the profits were to be given to First Nations people. But again, this venture was a flop. He also failed twice to be elected to the colony's House of Assembly, then went to England to develop a proposal for a railway in South Australia. The promised finance dried up when an English railway tycoon went bankrupt and Milne was again left holding a collapsed scheme.

By then, aged around sixty, Milne dropped out of public view. Historians have tracked him down to London where, in 1871, he was living in cheap lodgings. Robert Milne, or whoever he was, died in 1874. He left his Australian lands to a 'dramatic agent' of Surrey and his remaining cash to a dozen other people, leaving not enough to cover his burial costs.

Who was this man? His many names, identities and diverse activities are as perplexing today as they were to his contemporaries. Another early Swan River settler, George Fletcher Moore, wrote in his journal after a visit from 'Lyon' on 26 April 1833:

> In the evening Mr. Lyon, the writer of those essays about the natives in our newspapers, came here on some law business. I do not know what to make of him. He is either a much *better* or much *worse* man than he seems. He is either somebody in *disguise* or incog[nito], or else he is a very great *hypocrite*. He is said to have been a man of *war* (in the 42nd Regiment); [and yet] his words are the words of a man of *peace*.

Moore reflected on other contradictions of his visitor, including his aversion to litigation while frequently engaging in it himself, and pretending to be a simple man yet one able to make persuasive arguments and with an impressive knowledge of languages and religious works:

> —yet this man has been a common or uncommon boatman plying on the river here. A great financier, he proposed an admirable scheme of a bank, which was to enrich us all: the *only difficulty* in which was that the Govt. was to lend us £100,000!!! I think he must be some schoolmaster gone crazed or somebody, in short, touched in the attics . . . [original emphases].

'Great fool', 'great genius' or 'touched in the attics'—whatever and whoever Robert Milne might have been, he was a visionary proponent of a treaty and a leader in defending the rights of First Nations people, recognising the wrongs done to them and trying to do something about it.

A Convict Transformed

If even some of the stories told about—and by—William Sydenham Smith are true, he should have joined the ranks of bushranger celebrities. From his humble beginning in 1815 to his death, Smith's life was remarkable, even by the standards of colonial bad men. Yet, there was a further surprising twist to his story.

In 1829, Smith was transported for life by the Somerset Assizes. He was thirteen or fourteen years old and had stolen a handkerchief. The dark-complexioned, brown-eyed boy arrived in New South Wales aboard the transport ship *Layton* in November 1829 and joined the large convict population of the colony. After helping to save the lives of several people on Norfolk Island, Smith was freed, but in 1838 received another three years' imprisonment for assaulting the Superintendent of Hyde Park Barracks. At some points he adopted the aliases 'William Turner' and 'Gips(e)y Smith' and under these names came to feature frequently in the courts and prisons of three colonies.

By the 1850s Smith was a prisoner in Van Diemen's Land, but he escaped by boat to Victoria in 1852, just in time to begin plundering the gold diggers and shopkeepers of their hard-won earnings. Several criminals were known as 'Gipsy Smith' in this era but there was no mistaking this bushranger. He became a conspicuous character on the Victorian goldfields, sporting a red sash around his waist through which were stuck a couple of pistols, a classic bandit outfit.

Despite his high profile, Smith was hard to catch. But in 1856, he and some accomplices were finally taken by police in a hut at Mount Ararat. The bushrangers were armed with two double-barrelled guns, two Colt revolvers and a couple of pistols, 'all heavily loaded'. There was a struggle, during which Sergeant McNa(u)ty was shot dead by one of Smith's companions. When brought to trial the following year, 'Turner', the name under which Smith was charged, was described as 'one of the most hardened ruffians in the colony' and 'a man possessed of immense physical power and has the air of a daring and desperate man. He has twice succeeded in escaping from the police after capture, on one occasion inflicting severe injuries, after a desperate encounter, upon the trooper who was escorting him to Castlemain [sic].'

His court appearance was a celebrity occasion, as reported by one newspaper: '"Gipsy Smith" and his bush-ranging companion Haines at the City Court yesterday morning collected a full house, and every available place in court was occupied. "Gipsy" was unquestionably the "Hon" of the day, and on being escorted from the station house to the court he seemed to take a particular delight in displaying his irons, and clanking them as much as possible.' While waiting to appear in the dock, Smith enthused about the quality of his prison breakfast compared with the food he received in the hulks and refused to change out of his prison uniform, preferring to 'take his chance in it' rather than wearing everyday clothes. The murder charge against him was dismissed and he pleaded guilty to manslaughter. He was found guilty and at his sentencing gave a further account of himself, expressing remorse. The judge was seemingly moved by Smith's statement, enough to comment 'that he was still possessed of some feeling', but nevertheless sent him back to what is now called Tasmania for fifteen years' hard labour on the roads, the first two years to be spent in irons.

After serving some of that sentence, Smith was in court again in 1864 to answer for his 1852 escape from Van Diemen's Land. He gave a carefully cleansed account of his life. He claimed to be 'a free man' and had only been in trouble twice before: once with his original conviction in England; and secondly with the eight years he had just served at Pentridge, from which 'He had just come out after having been lying in a cell for eight years, until he had nearly lost his senses, and directly on coming out he had been taken and put into another cell.' If he was sent back to Tasmania 'it would not be long before he was away again, if a boat was to be got. Many in court knew him as a tidy boat-steerer. It was in a boat that he got away before.' Since the age of eleven, 'he had not had one hour's liberty, except what he had dragged out through the fire.'

Despite this heartfelt, if rambling, plea, Smith was returned to Tasmania. 'Ah, well', he sighed, 'I will soon see about getting out of it'. And he did. Just two years later, he received a conditional pardon from the Tasmanian Government and was given a ticket-of-leave to live and work in New South Wales. Just how he managed such a trickster-like transformation is still something of a mystery. His criminal career—the real one—included numerous escapes from custody, including from the notorious Port Arthur; a trail of violent behaviour that saw him narrowly avoid a murder charge, as well as numerous armed robberies. His claims to have saved several lives while in custody in different prisons seem to have been mostly verified.

In the end, it was Smith's version of his life that became the dominant narrative, as a newspaper profile of the old lag noted in 1866:

The extraordinary career and character of a man, who appears to have had no special disposition for vice beyond being of a somewhat violent temper, has lately come under our notice, writes the Melbourne correspondent of the Ballaarat [sic] Star. The account vividly illustrates the fatal effects of the beginning of a criminal career, and the difficulties that beset the return path to virtuous conduct and to honest industry and still, more surprising is it that any man could undergo the accumulated sentences, and retain any respect and manliness, and suffer the moral contagion of so many years, and yet retain wholesome sentiments and healthy feelings.

William Sydney Smith, as he was then styling himself, was now around fifty, with the scars of a violent life across his face and tattooed arms, along with three injured fingers. But he was still in a reasonable physical shape and able to work. A son of the prominent firebrand, preacher and politician John Dunmore Lang took the reformed ruffian into his pastoral business, entrusting him with cattle droves from New South Wales to Victoria.

The slow wheels of the convict system continued to move in Tasmania, Victoria, New South Wales and England. In 1868 Smith was given a pardon 'on condition that during the remainder of the term of his sentence, he does not return to the United Kingdom of Great Britain and Ireland.' William Smith did well in his new life and was eventually put in charge of a pastoral station, a considerable responsibility. He spent his remaining years as a useful member of colonial society and died in Melbourne Hospital in 1879, a remarkable example of a convict not only reformed but, apparently, transformed.

Red Ribbons and Bright Gold

The glint of gold has always cast a spell. Enchantment struck again in Victoria during the 1850s. Tens of thousands of ordinary people abandoned their jobs, countries and sometimes their families to journey to far-flung places with strange names. They came from across the world—from China, the United Kingdom, Europe, Canada, America and South Africa—fusing into an unprecedented mixture of hopeful people scrambling together for the elusive metal. Almost overnight, tent and shanty settlements appeared near heaps of mullock tossed up from a warren of holes. This seething mass of overoptimistic humanity had to be regulated by a colonial government unprepared for the task. It did not go well.

To pay for the considerable costs of administering the goldfields, the government set a licence fee to be paid by all miners. The fee was set at thirty shillings a month and, if a miner could not produce a valid licence on demand, the fines were high. The goldfields police quickly became notorious for the overbearing way they carried out their duties, including 'digger hunts' at all times of the day and night to snare miners without a valid licence. The police were also disliked for the brutal way in which they sometimes treated those without the funds to pay what was at the time a substantial amount of money. It was not long before serious unrest among the diggers turned into active protest.

One of the early signs of trouble was a 'monster meeting' of miners in December 1851. Fifteen thousand diggers were said to have attended and refused to pay the licence fee demanded by the Victorian government. By August 1853, the government's continued refusal to hear their case drove the miners to form various advocacy groups, sometimes in opposition to each other. Eventually, a reasonably unified protest movement emerged. Its many members wore red ribbons to display their defiance of the authorities and threatened to refuse to pay the full amount, meaning they would be gaoled, filling the prison and clogging up the administration of the licensing system. They also started a petition to convey their views directly to the governor in

Melbourne. The petition would eventually carry many thousands of names (just two were women) and stretch for 13 metres. It began with a statement of the miners' complaints: 'That in the present impoverished conditions of the Gold Fields the impost of Thirty Shillings a Month is more than Your Petitioners can pay as the fruit of labor [sic] at the Mines scarcely affords to a large proportion of the Gold Miners the common necessaries of life.'

The petition went on to air more of the diggers' complaints, including understaffing of the licence issuing offices and the 'Squatter Land Monopoly' that barred miners from investing in property. The quality of the goldfields police, 'Armed Men (many of whom are notoriously bad in character),' was highlighted, along with allegations that goldfields commissioners 'have on various occasions Chained non-possessors to Trees and Condemned them to hard labor [sic] on the Public Roads of the Colony.' The petitioners argued that this was 'contrary to the spirit of the British Law which does not recognise the principle of the Subject being a Criminal because he is indebted to the State.'

Based on these grievances, the miners asked the governor to reduce the licence to ten shillings a month, reduce fines and generally reform and streamline the system. They also asked to be allowed to buy small parcels of land. The final request was 'To direct that (as the Diggers and other residents on the Gold Fields of the Colony have uniformly developed a love of law and order) the sending of an Armed Force to enforce the License Tax be discontinued.'

Despite its impressive size, reasonable arguments and relatively modest requests, the petition was rejected. The number of demands it made reflected the many different views and interests of the multicultural hopefuls on the goldfields. Some of these, including the main leader of the Red Ribbon movement, George Thomson, had been Chartists, members of a British movement demanding political and social reform. They brought the call for proper representation to the goldfields' movement. The American diggers were strong on the principle of no taxation without representation, and there was a general desire for access to the lands as the chance to make a fortune, or even a living, from the goldfields faded away with dwindling finds. Every miner disliked the police, referred to as 'Joes' or 'traps', who oppressed them. When news of the petition's rejection reached the miners, ten thousand marched on the Ballarat gold commissioner's headquarters, and 'the excitement at Bendigo was most intense. Almost every digger had the red ribbon in his hat, as token of a favorable [sic] disposition to the reduction of the license-tax.'

The marchers massed beneath a banner devised for the movement. It featured four images: a crossed pick and shovel and a mining tool known as a 'dolly', representing the miners; a bundle of sticks tied together, an ancient symbol of unity; a set of scales symbolising justice and the law; and an emu and kangaroo. Outnumbered by the miners, many of whom were armed, the commissioner said he could not accept their refusal to pay more than ten shillings of the licence fee but would take their demands to the governor—again. This time, Governor La Trobe established an inquiry that recommended lower licence fees, voting rights for diggers with an annual licence, and access to land allotments.

The Red Ribbon movement was reformist rather than revolutionary, seeking to bring about change by peaceful, democratic means, or 'moral force', as Thomson and many of his followers would have put it. But the presence of armed men in their ranks hinted at more radical views on the goldfields. On 3 December 1854, a relatively small group of miners would hoist a new banner behind a rude circle of logs 'to defend our rights and liberties', as they saw them. The battle at the Eureka Stockade left more than twenty miners and five soldiers dead.

From this ferment of protest and insurrection came political reform in Victoria, as well as the origins of 'free selection', the process by which those with little money after the gold rush ended were able to 'take up' a parcel of Crown land on very favourable terms, eventually owning it as long as they made 'improvements'. Although the Victorian government did not pass the main legislation required for free selection until the 1860s, agitation to 'unlock the lands' can be traced to the petition of the Red Ribbon movement.

You Can't Wipe Out Carr-Boyd

It is difficult to know where to start with the eventful life of the man who used the pen name 'Potjostler'. Perhaps his death in 1925 is the best way to introduce one of the great characters of the bush, 'a frightful exaggerator and an incurable romantic', as an obituarist who had known William Carr-Boyd wrote of him. Potjostler had also been many other things in his long life—a prospector, explorer, stockman, a noted singer and exponent of gum leaf playing, and a journalist writing in many of the newspapers that flourished in nineteenth-century and early twentieth-century Australia.

Born at sea in 1852, William Henry James Carr-Boyd arrived in Hobart with his English parents. His father was a classics teacher. The family later moved to Queensland where, at an early age, he began working on stations. He joined the Palmer River gold rush in the early 1870s and his well-developed skills as a bushman, together with his eloquence, later saw him as second-in-command of an expedition through country beyond the Diamantina River. His beginning in journalism was a breezy account of the expedition and frontier news from 'Out in the Never-Never Country'. It casually mentioned fatal conflicts between settlers and local people, laced with the usual racist attitudes and language of the time.

Carr-Boyd's reputation as a bushman continued to grow on the Queensland frontier. In the late 1870s, brothers Cornelius ('Syd') and Albert Prout set off from a station near Windorah, Queensland, with another man named Baker. They had heard First Nations stories about a large river that ran somewhere beyond the unknown horizon and went to find it, despite warnings of the dangers involved. They did not return. In 1880 Carr-Boyd led an expedition in search of the men and

> . . . found at Prout's camp the remains of Cornelius, also a skeleton of one horse with its bridle on, tethered to a tree. A pint pot was found on which was scratched: 'Two days without water, C. Prout.' The diary of Cornelius also was found at the camp, but Carr-Boyd said it was lost on the way in . . . His watch also was found, a photograph of his mother, and a few letters. Traces of Albert and Baker were never discovered. Some time afterwards horses belonging to them were discovered alive some distance from the camp.

The Prouts died not far from water that would have saved their lives, a poignancy reflected in a popular commemorative poem on the events by Mary Hannay Foott, 'Where the Pelican Builds Her Nest'.

A few years later, Carr-Boyd was second-in-command of an expedition exploring the Cambridge Gulf area of Western Australia. The Carr-Boyd Range south of Kununurra was named during this journey, though relations between the man himself and the expedition leader, W.J. O'Donnell, were strained. After making several solo side trips, probably to look for signs of gold, Carr-Boyd convinced a reluctant O'Donnell to let him and a First Nations guide ride for Perth. Ten days later they returned, Carr-Boyd sick with dysentery and scurvy. They made it safely back to their starting point at Katherine then Carr-Boyd headed for Melbourne. There, he complained he had been libelled by one of the expedition's sponsors, who had published a letter accusing him of drunkenness, desertion and generally poor behaviour. Carr-Boyd claimed £5000 in damages. He lost.

Returning to the west, Carr-Boyd spent the next few years prospecting with some success and was one of the first diggers at the Coolgardie find. Always restless, the prospector, explorer and sometime pastoralist drifted through the remote regions in search of gold, pegging claims, developing his reputation as a campfire entertainer and teller of tall tales. He even helped expose one of the world's greatest liars.

Louis de Rougemont (Henri Louis Grin) was a Swiss chancer and fantasist who wrote about searching for gold and pearls, flying wombats and other preposterous things. His yarns became wildly popular in the 1890s, with many people believing them. Many also didn't, including Carr-Boyd. While visiting

London he was interviewed about his views on the stories de Rougemont spun about his supposed thirty years' residence with the Western Australian First Nations peoples, a place and peoples Carr-Boyd knew well. The journalist began by describing the bushman as 'a striking figure, lean almost to gauntness, bronzed on face and hands, not with the transitory tint of a long sea voyage, but with a colour permanently burned in by years and years of tropic and semi-tropic suns. The face is lined with suffering and the shoulders stoop, though the man was built for activity and hardihood, and dangerous enterprise.' Carr-Boyd, by then a justice of the peace and member of the Royal Geographical Society, went on to demolish de Rougemont's fantasies by providing anthropological detail of First Nations customs and rituals completely lacking from the imposter's accounts. 'It takes one to know one,' as the saying goes.

Carr-Boyd's versions of his own adventures were often exaggerated but authentic in their settings and details, as recognised by his contemporaries. A rival journalist even celebrated his yarns in shaky verse:

My name's Carr-Boyd,
And I've been destroyed
By the blacks in this land who thrive,
But I'm so strong-willed,
Whenever I'm killed,
It makes me the more alive.
I've lived on grass
In the Bulli Pass,
Where I the sea-serpent saw;
They may wriggle and dance,

But they haven't a chance,

When my long, long bow, I draw.

I've been speared and shot,

I've been served up hot,

On toast, but I wasn't annoyed;

Though you blow out my brain,

'Tis labor in vain,

For you can't wipe out Carr-Boyd.

In 1917 the ageing adventurer visited America, probably to look into to his mining interests. There he threw money around and dressed eccentrically in a white pith helmet and a suit with twenty-four pockets. What these were for also remained a mystery. The celebrated old timer reportedly took little food but 'drank hugely of rum, because he said the molasses in it kept him alive.'

The rum kept William Carr-Boyd this side of eternity for a few more years, or perhaps sent him there. He died in 1925 leaving a widow, four adult children and not a lot more. His legacy was a richly adventurous life and an often-recalled legend that only faded with the last of his generation.

The Legend of Galloping Jones

In the first decades of the twentieth century a controversy raged through the columns of the press. Country and regional newspapers, and sometimes city dailies and weeklies, were filled with passionate articles and correspondence about a topic of vital interest to many of their readers. Who were the greatest rough riders of the golden past?

Before the incursion of proper roads and railways, large tracts of the eastern states were connected only by rough tracks and droving trails. Almost everything depended on horses. The men who knew how to train and handle these essential beasts often became famous in their day and some quickly passed into legend as the frontier succumbed, slowly, to motor transport, trains and, eventually, aeroplanes. As that hard-bitten generation faded into what we now call retirement and its often foggy recollections they conducted the equivalent of a pub argument through the press.

Who was the greatest buckjumper, the toughest drover? Who were the crack riders; who were the best fighters? These arguments were part of an even larger conversation that included debate about the fastest shearer, the deepest driver of shafts, the worst shearers' cook and so on, all contributing to the mythologising of what were often called 'the Roaring Days'. Long forgotten today, back then certain names were presented and vigorously promoted at length and with details of tallies shorn, depths sunk, miles fenced and wild horses broken. One name that featured frequently in these debates was 'Galloping Jones'.

The origins and early days of John Deacy (Decy) Jones remain obscure. He began to make a considerable name for himself in northern Queensland by the last years of the nineteenth century. The tales told of his exploits grew even larger by the time they made the newspapers of the 1920s. But even allowing for the usual exaggerations of oral tradition, his lurid life was emblematic of the idealised bushmen of Australian legend.

According to one yarn, Jones gained his nickname in a race-track 'ring in'. He was riding a horse that had been inexpertly converted from its natural appearance through the application of boot polish and the gluing on of a tail extension. Halfway through the race, the glue on the false tail began to melt, along with the boot polish. The heavily backed horse was revealed to all as a fraud. Knowing what outraged punters were likely to do to the jockey, Jones wisely kept riding out of the track. From that time he was known as 'Galloping Jones'.

Whatever the truth of this tale might be, it heralded the lengthy entanglement with the law that was a feature of Jones's life. A frequent pub brawler, he was charged with assault and resisting arrest in 1925 and again in 1927. In court, his occasional alias of 'Alex Brown' was recorded and he was frequently in trouble for failing to pay maintenance to his estranged wife.

As well as punch-ups in pubs, Jones used his fists in boxing tournaments. In 1926 he lost a bout to a younger and fitter man, going down for the count. He was balding by then and his 'face showed signs of former battles'. By this time there was a certain mystique around the name of Galloping Jones. The indefatigable collector of bush lore and legend, 'Bill Bowyang' (Alexander Vindex Vennard) remembered him as one of the 'horsemen of the past':

A reckless daredevil rider of the old-time type is 'Galloping' Jones, well-known in the Charters Towers district. He has also travelled with Skuthorpe and I never heard of the horse that threw him. He is just as much at home perched on the back of an outlaw in a station paddock as he is in a show ring. Old timers who watch him, go back in thought to the great horsemen of thirty and more years back. There are few buckjump riders like Jones in Australia at the present time.

This was widely syndicated to other newspapers, as was a more general piece focusing on the famous horseman Lance Skuthorpe and others, though also mentioning Jones as one of best buckjump riders of past glory days. In reply, a correspondent named 'Stirrup' wrote:

> I don't know much about the horsemen of the past, but if anyone can introduce a better buck jump rider than 'Galloping' Jones, now working out Muttaburra way, I'd like to be introduced to him. He is the last of the old devil-may-care reckless horsemen who will jump on any thing that can buck, and I have yet to hear about the horse that has thrown him. There's nothing flash about Jones, and I don't suppose you could persuade him to get into a ring with tailor-made riding togs, but, if he did so, he would make most of these rodeo champions look as silly as a wet hen.

Probably in his fifties during the 1930s, Jones was making a living in travelling equine displays popular at agricultural shows. In 1933 at the Sydney Showground, he was described as a 'hardy, bow-legged Australian'. The following year, the ageing but still active horseman was at the Newcastle show, amazing audiences by riding the unbroken 'King of the Ranges'. His 'handling of "Devil Devil"' was a 'revelation to those among the spectators, who, by virtue of an occasional mount on an aged hack, had considered themselves as horsemen of high order.' Around this time someone cemented Jones into immortality by naming a racehorse after him.

By 1940 even the city papers were being informed about the legend. 'Yeralla' wrote in to say that Jones was 'known far and wide throughout Queensland' and that there was not a finer horse-breaker in the country. Unlike lesser mortals, Jones scorned the usual methods of roping horses and was said to be 'possessed of an uncanny faculty, which enables him to go into a yard, or even an open paddock, and put bridle or halter on a horse which never before had known the touch of a human hand.'

Bill Bowyang was still reporting on Jones's activities in 1941 and even as late as 1953 the heroic horse whisperer was still thought to be 'going strong' and admired for his brawling. But that was probably the last mention of Galloping Jones in the newspaper columns. He is said to have died at Charters Towers around 1960.

But his memory lived on in the bush. He was celebrated in verse during the 1980s and, before that, him when folklorist Ron Edwards collected traditions about him in the late 1960s and 1970s. In these yarns, Jones is still a great horseman and brawler, drawing with bruiser Treacle McFarlane in a two-hour blood bout. Cattle duffing and horse stealing had been added to his *curriculum vitae*, along with trickster-like escapes from police custody and even a bank robbery, of sorts.

Little, if any, of this can be verified, of course: that's the point of bush yarns. They're not about history, they're about myth and that tells us a lot about what people thought and what was admired in a now mostly lost Australia. Apart from a recent book referencing Jones in its title, and what you have just read here, Galloping Jones has gone the way of the great Australian legend. His evolution from one of any number of hard drinking bushmen into a fabled horse-breaker who outwits the cops and talks or fights his way out of awkward situations shows how legends are born and how they live on—for a while, at least—until they are no longer deemed relevant.

A Poet of the Kerb

Most of the people and events celebrated by Paddy Collins are now long forgotten. He is not remembered at all by the general public, even in Sydney where the last 'poet of the kerb' eked out the final years of his life.

Patrick Francis Collins was Irish and probably born in 1863, according to his own not-necessarily-reliable account. He was in Queensland during the 1880s, then Victoria and, finally, Sydney, where he was for some time a teacher at a public school in Surry Hills. He was married—probably—and fathered several children. Between the 1890s and 1930s, Paddy Collins documented disasters, murders and topics of public interest in ballads. He had his verses printed and sold them at a penny a time wherever he could, at football matches, in the streets and wherever people gathered, such as the famous 'Speaker's corner' in Sydney's Domain. Stan Ewing remembered Paddy as his primary school teacher around 1912 or 1913, where he was famous for frequently disappearing behind the blackboard to take a nip or two from a hip flask. Stan also recalled later seeing him at the Sydney Cricket Ground, crying out 'a Penny for a poem'.

Paddy was a poet of the people, one of the very last survivors of a tradition of cheap street literature that stretched back to the seventeenth century. When news was hard to come by, the streets of the United Kingdom and Europe were filled with people often known as 'broadside sellers'. They sold printed ballads about the news of the time, especially executions and scandals, to a public anxious to hear about the latest murders and highway robberies. An early form of newspapers, these street ballads carried on into the nineteenth century but were practically extinct in the United Kingdom by the time Paddy came along at the end of the tradition in Australia.

Street verse is not the place for great poetry. It is a simple recounting of a version of what was happening, often written to a well-known tune for those who preferred to sing it. Paddy churned out his verses in the style of the broadside hacks of London and other cities. He wrote about many things, always from the point of view of the common people. In a poem celebrating New South Wales Labor premier Jack Lang, Paddy observed that he was unlike other politicians who 'only crawl and cringe':

> Our politicians are black crows,
> They'd pick your eyes and bleed your nose.
> Indeed, they are the workers' foes
> Without the slightest doubt.

He also wrote on the twelve members of the Industrial Workers of the World (IWW), or 'Wobblies', who were imprisoned on arson and conspiracy charges in 1916. After the return of a Labor government in 1920, the charges were the subject of a royal commission, leading to the release of eleven of the Wobblies. One, Donald Grant, served an extra year before release and later became a federal senator. Paddy hailed the victory:

> Rejoice! You fellow working men,
> Your comrades are set free,

Who have suffered for these long years
In want and misery;
Locked up within grim prison walls
Surely an earthly hell,
The anguish that they have endured
None but themselves can tell.

Paddy's known ballads dealt with anything that he hoped would appeal to his buyers. There were obituaries to noted figures, including writer Henry Lawson, opera singer Dame Nellie Melba, boxer Les Darcy, racehorse Phar Lap and the alcoholic rabble rouser, politician and newspaper proprietor, John Norton:

A brilliant man has passed away.
John Norton was his name;
He made the tyrants shake with fear.
The cowards blush with shame.
For wowsers, quacks and hypocrites
He had no time at all,
He hated cant and humbug,
And those who cringe and crawl.

A disaster was always good for sales. Paddy wrote about the Mount Lyell mining disaster of 1912, the wreck of the north-west Moree mail train in 1926 and the sinking of the collier *Galava* in 1927, among many other, now mostly forgotten tragedies.

World War I was a boon for Paddy. He turned out rhymes on naval battles, the death of Lord Kitchener, the heroic Australian troops in battle, the Kaiser and even on the debate over six o'clock closing of pubs, a topic close to his own heart.

Some of his ballads share the attitudes of many Australians of his time. He wrote sexist and bloodily jingoistic poems, as well as racist mock minstrel verses, and one ballad called 'Keep Australia White'. Yet he was sympathetic to the fate of First Nations bushranger Roy Governor, gaoled in 1923 for shooting a policeman:

> Although he's black and loves the bush,
> Remember, he's a man!
> Let the law makers treat him now,
> As lenient as they can.
> He's a human like ourselves—
> There's none of us divine;
> So treat him as an equal now,
> Don't draw the colour line!

Paddy did have some competition in his fading line of work. Jack Bradshaw, a small-time bushranger, was also a scribbler of verses. He wrote mainly about himself and his alleged exploits as a young bushranger in the colonial era, but he also knocked out ballads on similar topics to those favoured by Paddy and hawked them on the same streets. Bradshaw and Paddy Collins both died in the 1930s. Their passing ended a centuries-old tradition of social comment and protest spanning the United Kingdom and Australia.

The Death of Crocodile Dundee

In 1977, the nation was enthralled by an epic outback survival story. Northern Territory buffalo shooter Rodney Ansell lived off the land for seven weeks following the capsizing of his motorboat. With only his rifle, knife, a few cans of food and his dogs—one with a broken leg—the bushman kept himself and the animals alive by hunting wild cattle and buffalo, drinking their blood when no fresh water was available and avoiding the crocodiles by sleeping in trees.

The media dubbed the usually barefooted Ansell a 'modern day Robinson Crusoe' and he became a national and international celebrity. He seemed to typify the ideal of the Australian bushman—tough, independent and anti-authoritarian. His story became the basis for a feature film that would sweep popular Aussie bloke comedian Paul Hogan to international fame and fortune. Released in 1986, *Crocodile Dundee* was a clever, tongue-in-cheek yarn that played some of our most cherished myths for laughs.

Not averse to basking in the reflected glory of the media glare, 'the barefoot bushman', as Ansell was dubbed, played up to it for a while. But it seems that other Top End folk, equally tough and independent, came to see him as a boaster, or 'skiter' in Australian slang. He became increasingly disconnected and pursued a number of unsuccessful business ventures as well as a financially disastrous conflict with the Territory Government that forced him to put down 3000 feral buffalo. Following the end of a marriage that had produced two sons, a depressed Ansell became addicted to methyl amphetamine and made heavy use of marijuana.

In 1996, he began a relationship with a woman who suffered from a paranoid delusion that the Freemasons were kidnapping, torturing and ritually slaughtering children. She was also a heavy user of drugs and as Ansell's livelihood faded away, the couple developed a shared delusion. By 1999, they reached a point where their fantasy consumed them. A series of trivial and unconnected incidents led Ansell to an intersection on the Stuart Highway and a deadly shootout with police.

What brought Ansell to this fatal rendezvous was the presence of a small group of bow hunters in the area and his inability to contact either of his two sons. The hunters were not locals and to Ansell's paranoid mind that made them ominously suspicious. He and his partner suspected the men were really Freemasons who had Ansell's sons in their sights. Still unable to contact his sons, neither of whom was in any danger, Ansell finally decided to act. He attacked the hunters, David Hobden and Brian Williams, temporarily blinding one and wounding the other. A neighbour came to see what was going on and he was also assaulted. As Ansell disappeared into the night, the neighbour reported the incident and local police officers armed themselves and swung into action.

Twelve hours later, on the morning of 3 August 1999, Sergeant Glen Huitson and Constable James O'Brien formed a roadblock at the intersection of Old Bynoe Road and the Stuart Highway. Trucks and cars were halted as police sought to catch the gunman. But Ansell was not driving. He had come across country and was now lying prone in light scrub about forty metres north of the roadblock. His beard and hair were wild; he wore a green jumper and was carrying his 30.30 repeater rifle. At about 10.30 am he began to use it.

The first shot badly wounded bystander Jonathan Anthonysz. He fell to the ground, screaming. O'Brien returned fire from his pistol, Huitson called for Tactical Response Group backup then grabbed the shotgun. While O'Brien tried to pin Ansell down, Huitson fired twice through the closed window on the driver's side of the police car. O'Brien heard Ansell fire again and Huitson fell down. The rifle bullet had ricocheted from the top of the driver's door and caught him in the abdomen.

With two wounded people and two unarmed civilians in need of protection, O'Brien picked up the shotgun. He called on Ansell to surrender but he only yelled back: 'You're all dead.' The policeman then began a three or four-minute gunfight with Ansell. He feared that he would run out of ammunition before the Tactical Response Group arrived. When they did, Ansell rose from his cover and aimed his rifle directly at them. Seizing this opportunity to take better aim, O'Brien, as he later recalled:

fired two rapid aimed shots at the gunman's head and upper torso area. I saw dust come off his clothing and the gunman dropped back down into the prone position. I was unable to tell whether he was injured or not as he was still moving and seemed to be in his original shooting position. I fired one more shot at the main body area and the gunman stopped moving.

The man who inspired the character of Mick 'Crocodile' Dundee died in a hail of shotgun pellets. His body was riddled with thirty entry wounds and three exit wounds. One pellet tore into his aorta and he died from loss of blood. Sergeant Glenn Huitson, a family man, was near death and died shortly after his arrival at Royal Darwin Hospital. The wounded civilian lived but underwent major surgery. In bringing down his findings on the killing of Rodney Ansell, the coroner concluded:

The contrast between on the one hand, the healthy man who appeared in television and magazine articles, and, on the other, the man who opened fire on 3 August 1999, could hardly be more marked. By the instrumentality of his chosen drug of abuse, Ansell had rendered himself emaciated (53 kg at the time of his death) and so addled of mind as to believe fantasies that a child would dismiss with contempt. His pointless destructive actions caused immediate agony, and permanent disablement and suffering to the men he wounded, David Hobden, Brian Williams and Jonathan Anthonysz. Sgt Glen Huitson, the man he killed, was an admirable police officer of proven courage and resource.

Rod Ansell and Glenn Huitson died on the Stuart Highway, a vital road link between the north and south of the continent and a route deeply embedded in the history of the continent. It is named after John McDouall Stuart, the first European to traverse the continent from south to north and back again in 1861–1862. A decade later, the Overland Telegraph (OT) line followed the same route. Stuart and the 'OT' effectively employed one of the 'superhighways' along which First Nations people travelled from north to south more than 60,000 years earlier. The road is often colloquially referred to as 'The Track' and has a dark recent history of unexplained disappearances and murders.

During the 'Great Depression' of the 1930s, families of unemployed workers were often evicted when they were unable to pay their rent. Like this family in the Sydney suburb of Redfern, their belongings were thrown onto the street.

5

TROUBLED TIMES

Rights and Wrongs

Dissenter and political activist Reverend Thomas Fyshe Palmer arrived in New South Wales aboard a transport ship in 1794. Convicted in Scotland of sedition for facilitating publication of a pamphlet on political reform, he was given a seven-year sentence to be served with several fellow activists, known as the 'Scottish martyrs'. Palmer and his friends considered themselves gentlemen political prisoners and so refused to work as other convicts did, bringing them into direct and continuing conflict with the colonial administration. After angry exchanges with the authorities, the martyrs were allowed to manage themselves as long as they did not draw on any government resources or services.

At first, Palmer and his companions established a collective farm to supply themselves with food, then branched out into shipbuilding and other ventures, including beer brewing. The enterprising, if troublesome, convicts quickly discovered that there was little business activity in the colony in which the officers of the New South Wales Corps were not deeply engaged. Palmer wrote home:

> the officers have monopolized all the trade of the colony. They suffer no one but themselves to board any ship that may arrive. They alone buy the cargo and sell it at one, two, three, 400 and even 1,000 per cent profit. They have set their faces against my friends and me. A message has been sent me to pull my hat to the officers, or I should be confined in the cells and punished.

Palmer's years in captivity were tumultuous. It was a crucial time for the struggling young colony, in desperate need of more food than could be produced around Sydney and under the control of the compromised officers of the New South Wales Corps. Hundreds of settlers occupied land along the Hawkesbury River, cleared the bush and planted crops, mostly maize, then known as 'Indian corn'. They accessed the life-giving waters and destroyed the edible plants usually called 'yams' growing along the riverbanks, leaving the Dharug people of the area without sufficient food. The Dharug considered that the settlers' corn crop was fair exchange for the loss of their larder and carried off the ripened grain. The settlers saw this as theft and a cycle of Dharug raids on farms followed by reprisals soon developed.

In May 1795, settlers sent urgent messages to the Parramatta barracks of the New South Wales Corps, fearing that the Dharug were about to attack them in force. William Paterson, a member of the New South Wales Corps, was acting governor of New South Wales at the time and he immediately sent a group of more than sixty soldiers to the area. Their orders were to disperse the First Nations population. The soldiers, accompanied by several settlers, found the Dharug camp at Richmond Hill and opened fire, killing possibly seven or eight people, one a baby. Six were captured, including a woman. According to Palmer, bodies of the Dharug were hung 'on gibbets', meaning that they were hung up in public, probably on trees, as a warning against further resistance. This pattern of bloody reprisals was, as Palmer also observed, one of 'unparalleled severities' and the conflict of which it was a part raged on until 1816.

The Richmond Hill event was the first recorded incident of official armed attacks on First Nations peoples in Australia. Its causes and consequences would be repeated across the country well into the twentieth century, at first by military units and, from around 1850, by new forces that would have a devastating impact on First Nations peoples and their ways of life. At this time, colonial governments adapted methods used to police the frontiers elsewhere in the sprawling British Empire. This involved forming armed semi-military units of First Nations peoples commanded by European officers. These groups typically operated along advancing frontiers where local people attempted to resist colonists. Their mission was to police conflict between the original inhabitants and the newcomers. They frequently did this by crushing any who defied the newcomers. In Australia, these regulators were usually known as Native Mounted Police.

Between 1849 and 1904, a Native Mounted Police force was maintained by governments in New South Wales and, after separation, in Queensland. This body recruited First Nations men, usually from areas far from where they would operate to minimise potential sympathy for those they were policing. The men, sometimes only boys and some of whom had survived similar massacres, were uniformed, armed with rifles and paid a fraction of what a white policeman would receive for similar duties. They established camps, mostly in remote areas, and used their tracking and bush skills in the service of the government that employed them.

Recent historical and archaeological research has revealed little-known information about the operations of the Queensland Native Mounted Police. The unit went about its work in much the same way as the New South Wales Corps at Richmond Hill, hunting down and firing indiscriminately on small groups of men, women and children. It is thought that the Native Mounted Police, led by European officers, made hundreds of such attacks, murdering possibly 60,000 people.

Native mounted police units elsewhere in the country conducted similar operations. Evidence of these atrocities is often difficult to trace in official records without intensive research, but historians have found enough to broadly confirm First Nations oral traditions about these events, even if the exact numbers of casualties are difficult to pin down: estimates vary widely, depending on methods used and the approach of different researchers.

Frontier massacres are a profoundly emotive issue. Those carried out by First Nations troopers are especially difficult, for descendants of both those involved and those who died. Descendants of officers involved may also be especially troubled by revelations of what their ancestors did, as David Marr wrote in his *Killing for Country: A family story*. There is also a reluctance among the broader community to acknowledge that such incidents occurred. Despite a growing volume of evidence about such events, there is little broad agreement about the numbers of incidents and the numbers of people involved, or about what should be described with the formidable word 'massacre'.

How many people have to die for an event to be considered a 'frontier massacre'? There is no agreed definition, but many researchers in this field consider that 'a colonial frontier massacre is defined as the deliberate and unlawful killing of six or more undefended people in one operation.' This number may seem small, but the reason for using it is that First Nations peoples typically operated in small groups and the loss of even a few is considered to have 'a devastating impact' upon them. But whatever definitions are used and whatever the exact numbers involved, we know that serious attacks against First Nations peoples were carried out by official forces from very early in colonial Australia's history.

The last recognised massacre of First Nations people by officials was at Coniston, Northern Territory, in August 1928, when possibly 200 Warlpiri, Anmatyerre and Kaytetye people were killed in several related attacks. Other attacks against First Nations peoples were also carried out by individuals and groups not under government control. Reprehensible though these private acts were, it is those enacted by legally constituted government forces that raise difficult questions about the intentions and integrity of governments.

The Devil Himself

On 2 July 1880, railway goods guard Jesse Dowsett wrote to the traffic manager at Benalla. It was a few days after the siege at Glenrowan, where the Kelly gang had planned to attack a police train from Melbourne. Jesse Dowsett had a compelling tale to tell about his part at Glenrowan. He began with some details of the police special train and his job:

> I was told by Station Master at Benalla on Sunday not to go far away from the Station as it was likely I would have to run a Special with Police to Beechworth as the Kellys had shot a man. Afterwards was told that no special would leave till arrival of Special from Melbourne as that would not arrive till about 1am I went home to get some sleep, the Special came from Melbourne with Guard Bell in charge. Guard McPhee went on the Pilot Engine about 4.50. I was called and told that the Kellys were fighting at Glenrowan.

Dowsett quickly dressed and found his railways department issue revolver, 'a Splendid Breech loader'. He jumped aboard the engine of the police special:

> We arrived at Glenrowan about 5.26 am my attention was attracted by hearing some dreadful screams from a woman proceeding from the hotel. I went up in the bush a bit and then crawled on my knees to within about 40 yards of the house when I could see a woman with a baby in arms crying

out not to shoot her child. As soon as I could see that it was not a lure to entice some of us to our death I called softly to her to come this way, come to the Police, thinking that would give her confidence. She turned towards me and at that moment the Police in front of the place fired very heavily in response to some shots from there. I caught the child and the woman, who was Mrs. Reardon a Platelayer's Wife, and ran down to the station and put her in the Carriage where Mrs. O'Connor and another Lady were.

Returning to the fight, Dowsett dodged from tree to tree and linked up with Sergeant Steele and Constable Kelly who were covering the back of the crude building known as a 'hotel', where the bushrangers were holed up with their hostages. The two policemen and Dowsett expected the bushrangers to break out from the hotel to their horses:

As the firing came from the back window pretty quick I thought they would rush from there and called out to the Police why not shoot the horses who were tied up there? Kelly shot one who fell at once. I fired at another, hit him, he reared up breaking away from the fence. We still returned the fire from the house when all at once as I heard the thud of a bullet on the tree where I was. On looking back I saw what seemed a tremendous big black fellow with something like a blanket on him. This would be about 6.45 am and the morning being hazy or else the smoke from the guns hanging about made him look a deal bigger than he was. I called to [Constable] Kelly to see who that was and somebody called out twice to him but the strange figure still advanced on us and all at once fired several shots at us. 'It is one of them! Scatter boys for cover', says someone. I fired a few shots at him but he stopped in a clump of saplings about 50 yards from us.

Undeterred, Dowsett began crawling through the scrub to a fallen tree, about 30 metres from the hulking apparition:

I emptied my revolver at him as he seemed to be sitting down. As I laid down to reload I saw Constable Kelly not far behind me and said to him 'see if you can hit him with your rifle.' He fired his rifle and I told him where he hit the tree, just missing Kelly, who seemed to keep behind the clump of saplings. He fired again and I said 'he is hit.'

He came out in to the open and walked straight for us, firing away and taking the fire from the Police quite cooly. I thought he must be mad, for he would hit his helmet with his revolver which sounded like a cracked bell, and saying 'you can't shoot me you b— dogs.' As he still was walking towards me I gave him four shots for the centre of his body. And hearing, in fact almost seeing them, jump off his body I felt very queer. I said 'this must be the Devil himself.'

The 'Devil' was now behind the fork of a large fallen tree, with Dowsett at the other end of the trunk, close enough for a conversation. 'You had better surrender', Dowsett said. 'Never while I have a shot left', replied the bushranger. Dowsett rested his revolver on his end of the tree 'and pulled straight for his head only fifteen yards off'. As the bullet bounced off the armour, Dowsett called out 'how do you like it, old man?' Kelly rose and fired back: 'How do you like that?' The bullet flew close to the guard, 'singing as it passed.' At the same moment Sergeant

Steel, a man with a grudge against the outlaw, emerged from a tree behind the bushranger and fired two shots, 'very low.' Ned Kelly fell to the ground as Dowsett ran towards him:

> Sergeant Steele got hold of his hand and I wrenched the revolver, one he had taken from the N.S.W. Police, out of his hand, it going off as I did. Constable Kelly who was almost up at the same moment and clearing the head gear off [Ned]. Sergeant Steele at once called out 'it is Ned himself. I swore to be at your death.' He exclaiming 'that's enough, I have got my gruel.'

The fallen outlaw was taken to the railway station where the rest of his armour was removed—'it weighed 97 lb [44 kg], the head piece alone 23 lb [10 kg].' Dowsett helped the doctor as he 'probed' Kelly's many wounds. Police Inspector Sadleir wanted the captured bushranger to signal those still inside the building and tell them to surrender. 'How do you know they are there?', Kelly asked. Dowsett confirmed that the bushrangers were still firing from the back window, to which Kelly responded 'Yes, one of them [or?] the others must be away or you would be shot down like rotten sheep when you rushed me.'

A conscientious railway guard and conspicuously brave man, Jesse Dowsett then took the Benalla train away from the action. He needed to get on with his day job—boarding the 6.10 am to Euroa in time to carry out his guard responsibilities on another train leaving there at 3 pm. The firefight at the Glenrowan Hotel raged on long after he left and he regretted that, after he finished his shift, the Benalla train was late and he 'could not get back to take part in the finish.' He signed off by thanking his employer 'for supplying me with an excellent weapon which enabled me to perform my part with some little credit to the Railways to which I have the honor [sic] to belong.'

Cutting Cane

Queensland celebrated the 100th anniversary of its separation from New South Wales in 1959. The founding of a new colony was a significant moment in modern Australian history and the centennial was commemorated in various ways throughout the state. At Innisfail in north Queensland, the Italian community erected a memorial to the pioneers of sugar industry.

Usually known as 'The Canecutters Memorial', it was designed by Renato Beretta and made of the same marble the great Michelangelo preferred for his work. The impressive edifice has a theme of water and sea creatures, accompanied by human figures of workers, topped with the dramatic figure of a canecutter, stripped to his shorts and wielding a cane knife. It celebrates the contribution of Italian immigrants to the sugarcane industry and the importance of that industry to the development of the colony and, subsequently, the state. Those economic successes came with a large human cost.

The first commercially successful sugarcane operation was established near Brisbane in the early 1860s and the industry grew rapidly. Labour was needed to carry out the hard and dirty work of harvesting the cane. There were not enough workers in the colony and so the system of indenturing South Pacific Islanders was introduced. Ships sailed mainly to Polynesia and Micronesian islands and recruited men to work in Queensland under an indenture arrangement. Islanders were expected to work for three years and could then either stay on or leave. While this seemed fair enough to begin with, as with the indentured labour systems that had operated in colonial north America, abuses quickly arose. Islanders unwilling to enter into contracts were often kidnapped or simply deceived into travelling to Queensland, a practice that became notoriously known as 'blackbirding'. When the workers arrived they were likely to experience slave-like living and working conditions. This abusive industry continued until 1906 when Islanders, many of whom by then had families and homes in Australia, were deported under the 'white Australia policy' of the day.

Italians came to Queensland from the 1850s and worked in developing industries, including timber, mining and sugarcane farming. Larger scale immigration schemes were organised in the 1890s and more Italians went to work in the sugar districts. Unfortunately, locals saw them as a threat to employment and there was strong opposition from the trade unions, frequently expressed in racist forms. Most of those who came were younger, unmarried men, leading to a large gender imbalance. Many Italians married Islander and First Nations women, further inflaming the racist opposition to them as 'aliens'. Despite this unwelcoming environment, Italians continued to escape from the poverty afflicting their homeland, coming increasingly from southern Italy. When the colonies were federated in 1901, Italians were officially accepted only as 'white aliens'.

The restriction of immigration to the United States in the 1920s brought another generation of Italians to Queensland, joining those who had pioneered the sugarcane industry and who by then were significant owners of cane plantations. Italian community facilities were opened as Italians became an economic and social sector of importance. Italian-Australian culture was an adaptation of what immigrants had known back home, with religious activities, sports, music and dance and related activities often pursued through Italian clubs. This continued into the 1930s, although the growth of fascism in Italy led to tensions within the Italian communities in Australia. When war with Italy came, many men of Italian descent were interned as enemy aliens, in some cases even while their sons were serving in the Australian armed forces.

Discrimination against Italians continued after the war as new waves of settlers arrived through mass immigration programs. This time, many women came, usually as 'proxy brides', restoring the balance between the sexes. Recollections of the era tell of the shock of adapting to the Queensland environment, to the snakes, the mosquitoes and the heat. The hard and dangerous nature of sugarcane work included exposure to Weill's disease, a potentially fatal sickness that barefoot cutters contracted from the urine of the rats in the green cane fields. Burning the green crop before cutting only became a regular practice in the 1950s and 1960s, reducing the risks for the cutters. Luigina Torre, a post-war immigrant, remembered:

[my husband] had the rats' fever, from the cane . . . because the first year he came, when he cut the cane, they wouldn't burn the cane, it was green and so snakes, rats inside, rats, you know? . . . The first cane cut he did, he did it under the rain and in the water, for all six months. It was always, always, always raining. And . . . you know it was dirty, there were animals, there was everything, it was ugly inside, it was hard, very hard, it was a hard job.

From the 1970s, mechanisation reduced the need for human labour in the cane industry. By then, Italian culture in north Queensland, and beyond, had become a greatly valued part of community life.

When the Canecutters Memorial was built, its terse inscription made no reference to the troubles and hardships within the Queensland sugar industry. It was a simple acknowledgement of the presence of those who had come before by those who were still there:

To the pioneers of the Sugar Industry
Donated by the Italian community of Innisfail District on
the first Centenary of the State of Queensland
1859–1959

The memorial also bears an inscription in Latin—UBI BENI IBI PATRIA—which translates loosely as 'wherever you are happy you are home'.

We Gave Them Hell

June 1931 was a bloody month in the Sydney suburbs of Bankstown and Newtown. The Great Depression was grinding onwards in seemingly unending misery for many. The unemployment rate would reach almost 40 per cent in inner-city Newtown by 1933 and things were not much better in the more distant Bankstown. Many working people lost their jobs and were forced to rely on government sustenance programs for food. These relief measures, known as 'the susso', were difficult to access and tightly policed. Even if workers and their families were successful in obtaining the susso, it did not pay their rent.

In these circumstances, many landlords began to evict tenants. In Sydney, a form of guerrilla warfare developed between radical trade union members of the Unemployed Workers' Movement (UWM), the police and bailiffs working on behalf of landlords. Defaulting renters were usually issued with a quit notice and if they did not vacate the premises by the due date they received a visit from the bailiffs, usually accompanied by police. Their furniture and other belongings were thrown into the street and they were ejected; the doors were sealed with new locks. Families were forced into the tent cities and shanty camps that had sprung up in marginal spaces, getting by as best they could. Some decided to fight back.

When a family was to be evicted, members of the UWM would turn up on the day. They let the bailiffs enter the house then, as Daisy McWilliams remembered her eviction many years later:

> When the place was empty of everything, the bailiffs called the children and myself to come outside. Then something happened. The members of the Anti-Eviction Committee each grabbed a piece of furniture on the street, pushed the bailiffs aside, and dashed into the house.
>
> The people surged forward, and women and children all helped to put the things back. It had taken three men hours to evict us; it took less than ten minutes to return the furniture into the house . . . We waited for something to happen, and looked through the window, and to our surprise we saw the police and bailiffs walking away to their cars.

Eviction confrontations did not always go as well as this one. At Brancourt Avenue, Bankstown, the tenant was a member of the UWM. He and his comrades fortified the house destined for a visit from the bailiffs with barbed wire and sandbags. Expecting trouble, the police turned up in force early on the morning of 17 June 1931. They attacked the house, firing into the building and wounding two defenders. The police won, of course, and arrested seventeen people, including a First Nations man, for resisting police. They were sentenced to hard labour.

At Newtown the following day, a two-storey house in Union Street was the scene of another battle. Dozens of police attacked, again firing into the building. The UWM defenders were prepared this time and hurled a volley of stones at the police, injuring many. Local people swarmed into the street in protest, some attacking a police patrol van. The *Sydney Morning Herald* described it:

> The most sensational battle Sydney has ever known was fought between 40 policemen and 18 Communists ... All the defenders were injured, some seriously. Bullets flew, one man was hit. Entrenched behind barbed wire and sandbags, the defenders rained stones weighing several pounds from the top floor of the building on to the heads of the attacking police, who were attempting to execute an eviction order. A crowd hostile to the police, numbering many thousands ... threatened to become out of hand ... When constables emerged from the back of the building with their faces covered in blood, the crowd hooted and shouted insulting remarks.

These events were celebrated in a popular ditty of the day:

For we met them at the door,
And we knocked them on the floor,
At Bankstown and Newtown,
We made the cops feel sore,
They outnumbered us ten to one,
And were armed with stick and gun,
But we fought well, we gave them hell,
When we met them at the door.

After these violent scenes, the state Labor government of Jack Lang introduced a moratorium on evictions, and legislation providing tenants with some protection. The threat of eviction remained, though. At least people in New South Wales were better off than those in other states: they received the highest level of susso in the country—three times more by 1932 than Victoria's unemployed were given.

By the mid-1930s the economic situation slowly improved. But it was not until the Great Depression faded into World War II that work, or military service, became available for many struck by unemployment, poverty and the trauma of suddenly having to depend on the state and charity to live.

Memories of the Great Depression, its hardships and its repressions endured across generations. It may be one of the reasons that home ownership in Australia increased from around 50 per cent at the start of the 1950s to its peak of around 70 per cent from the late sixties to the early 2000s. The children of the depression era saw what happened to those without homes and, aided by the rise in prosperity following World War II, took the opportunity to buy instead of rent. 'The Great Australian dream' came true for many. There has been a slight decline in home ownership since then to 66 per cent, most significantly affecting younger Australians. As the 2023 Intergenerational Report put it: 'The decline in homeownership is most significant for younger age groups. Home ownership fell by 18 percentage points from 1981 to 2021 for those aged between 30 and 34, and 17 percentage points for those aged 25 to 29.'

The Battle of Brisbane

It is known as a 'battle', though it was really a series of riots between Australian and American troops. The violence was serious enough to leave one dead and hundreds wounded, some quite badly. At the time, and for long after, news of the disturbances was mostly suppressed by the authorities anxious to downplay conflict involving the arrival in Australia of very large numbers of American service personnel from late 1941 on.

The 'Yanks', as the visitors were inevitably called, were led by General Douglas MacArthur, who had overall command of Allied forces fighting in the south-west Pacific theatre of World War II, which also made him the effective military commander of the Australian troops in that region. His headquarters were in the AMP building in central Brisbane, then a sleepy city of around 330,000. Large numbers of Americans, about 80,000 at the time of the riots, put an immediate and unprecedented strain on the city, its facilities and its people.

Adding to the pressure was a broader Australian antagonism towards the American troops. They were better paid, better dressed and, due to better dental care, generally looked better than the average digger. They were also believed to be more attractive to Australian women, as reflected in the catchphrase of the period, claiming that the Yanks were 'oversexed, overpaid and over here'. This perception was sharpened by the American custom of public courting and physical contact with female companions, a practice that outraged many used to the much staider forms of Australian sexual relations.

The riots were centred around two or three blocks in Brisbane where the Americans and Australians could not avoid encountering each other. The Australian 'wet canteen' was across the street from the American Red Cross and cafe, and a few doors along from the 'PX' (the commandeered post office) where Americans could purchase the quality products generally unavailable to the local population. Although American troops could visit the Australian canteen, Australian troops were denied access to the American facilities and had to make do with much inferior premises and conditions. On the next block was a barracks for enlisted American troops, making the relatively small section of the city an American enclave.

In this pressure cooker of prejudices and perceptions it would not be long before tensions boiled over. Predictably, it was alcohol that lit the fuse. Thursday, 26 November 1942, was the important American holiday, Thanksgiving. Riots and rebellions often start during or near holidays and festivals as people celebrate and generally relax, sometimes a little too much. On this occasion Private James Stein of the 404th US Signal Company had a drink or three in the Australian wet canteen. He left and made his unsteady way towards the American PX. He met three similarly jolly Australian soldiers in the street, including Gunner Edward Webster, and they began a conversation.

There are various versions of exactly what happened and why, but they all end up with an American military policeman (MP), Private Anthony O'Sullivan, approaching the group and demanding to see Stein's leave pass. Stein fumbled for the document and the MP became impatient and threatening. The Australians, almost certainly in colourful terms, told him to give Stein a chance to find the pass. Unwisely, O'Sullivan raised his baton and it was on.

Australians in the street and nearby hotel rushed to the fray, as did American MPs from their PX. Outnumbered, the Americans retreated, carrying a now insensible Private O'Sullivan and pursued by a large and growing crowd of Australians hurling bottles, rocks and a parking sign into the PX. More MPs and civil police arrived fairly soon and found not only the PX under siege but also the US Red Cross building across the street. By 8 pm it is estimated that at least 2000, and perhaps as many as 5000, soldiers and civilians were battling it out. It was time to pick a side. Australian MPs removed their identifying armbands and joined in. A truck manned by Australian soldiers and loaded with Owen submachine guns and grenades was, fortunately, prevented from reaching the now chaotic scene.

Inside the PX, the Americans armed themselves with pump-action shotguns issued by their MPs. Private Norbert Grant took his weapon and pushed his way to the front door to confront the Australians. He was soon attacked and the shotgun fired—three times. Edward Webster, at the front of the crowd, was killed instantly. Six other Australians were wounded. Hostilities paused briefly, then Grant escaped back into the safety of the building, smashing the butt of his shotgun across the head of an Australian as he went. The American was injured, along with eight others, one with a fractured skull. By 10 pm the riot at the PX and smaller fights elsewhere in the city were over. But not the battle.

The following night, the wrecked PX was heavily fortified as a smaller crowd of around 600 Australians—some with hand grenades, soon confiscated—again gathered outside. Prevented from further action, the rioters surged a block up the road to the AMP building and shouted abuse at General MacArthur. He was not there. Throughout the city, Americans—and some Australian women in their company—were assaulted. There were later claims that several Americans had been beaten to death during the riots though these were never officially verified.

In the post-riot reckoning, American units involved in the violence were posted elsewhere, the PX was moved and the Australian wet canteen was closed altogether. Private Grant was acquitted of the death of Gunner Webster by a court martial that deemed his actions to be self-defence. Assault charges were upheld against five Australians, one being gaoled for six months.

Official censorship of the events could not stop the 'bush telegraph' word of mouth. Wild rumours about the number killed and Americans using machine guns on the rioters did the rounds, stimulating some smaller disturbances elsewhere in Queensland and even as far away as Victoria and Western Australia.

Neither the Australians nor the Americans came out of these events with any credit. It was mob rule, plain and simple, with innocent people being attacked and deep resentments being channelled into vindictive violence. Meanwhile, a real war raged to the north of Australia. Many of those who fought through the streets of Brisbane during the riots would later serve in New Guinea, where they would be declared heroes.

The Peace Ship

The World Festival of Youth and Students was held at different times from 1947 to 2005. The event was inspired by an anti-war gathering of youth in Prague, Czechoslovakia, after the end of World War II. As that conflict gave way to the Cold War era, the world quickly fell into the ideological blocs we are still familiar with today, with then-Soviet Russia and other communist countries arrayed against the United States of America and other western democracies. The geopolitical stand-off quickly threatened to become a possibly apocalyptic global nuclear war and the anti-fascist peace movement soon adopted anti-nuclear proliferation as a primary focus.

Once faraway Australia became increasingly involved with these global realities through strategic and political alliances with the United States and the United Kingdom, as well as the local testing of nuclear and associated weaponry, a homegrown movement sympathetic to the values of the Festival of Youth soon developed. As well as seeking a more peaceful world, the movement also advocated for Indigenous and Pacific Islander rights.

World peace was not the only aspiration of the era. The 1950s initiated a struggle over civil rights, an issue that also became closely identified with the broader peace movement. This led to some cases of persecution of those perceived to be dangerous left-wing activists. The McCarthy hearings in

America are perhaps the best remembered of those today, but the same conflicts were also played out in Australia, involving artists, musicians and other cultural workers, and First Nations activists, together with trade unions.

These issues were also aired through cultural activities and organisations that included the New Theatre and the associated Unity Dance Group based in Melbourne and headed by Margaret Walker, a classically trained dancer with a strong social and political conscience. The dancers in her troupe performed at rallies and factories with productions designed to highlight the injustices of colonialism. One of the programs was a social and political fable titled *The Little Black Girl*, depicting the refusal of some white girls to play with a black girl and their eventual change of heart.

In 1951, a year of especially intense political struggles, a ship was organised to take Australian activists to the third World Festival (sometimes titled 'Congress') of Youth and Students, due to be held in Berlin, Germany. The passengers included members of the Unity Dance Group, who intended to present *The Little Black Girl* to the large international audience expected in Berlin. The group included Faith Bandler, a woman of South Pacific Islander–descent in her thirties and Wiradjuri man Ray Peckham, then in his twenties. Bandler was to play the lead role in the dance and Peckham, already known as an activist, was also part of the ensemble.

In the politically charged climate of the time, official reaction to the dance plan was swift. The Australian Security Intelligence Organisation (ASIO) began investigations of those involved and Peckham's passport was withheld. Fortunately, the cultural workers had good links with the waterside workers and their union, as well as the Australian Aborigines' League. The Waterside Workers Federation indicated that there would be national industrial action if Peckham was not allowed to leave the country, as he recalled many years later: 'the might of the trade union movement was moving into em. "If Peckham doesn't go on this ship, then this ship doesn't leave this harbour", and "we'll tie up every ship that's in port and round the shores of Australia". Down comes the passport, eh, four hours later! Yeh, that's true.'

Peckham sailed with the dance troupe aboard MV *Australia*, but despite broad community support from across the political spectrum, the delegates were still vilified as dangerous left-wing radicals. The Melbourne *Age* newspaper reported that the farewell of the ship was 'a communist demonstration', a description vigorously denied by a group of Melbourne University students replying to the article:

There were at least 50 students there who are members of various clubs at the University. There were members of the Liberal Club, Labor Club, Australian Overseas Club, Newman Society, Australian Labor Party Club, Students' Christian Movement, Science Club and so on. We were there to farewell the president of the University Students' Representative Council, who is going to Berlin, Mr. Woods Lloyd. He is not a Communist. The three cheers for "the other country," mentioned in the report, were in fact three cheers for "Woodsie." The scene was not characterised by violence but by gaiety. The songs sung were not the Red Flag, the Soviet anthem, and the Internationale, but the University anthem, Auld Lang Syne and Viva La Compagnie, etc.

The newspaper defended its reporter saying that the account 'reflected the general atmosphere on the pier' and that 'members of the Communist party and their supporters attended in force and some of the Communist leaders in Melbourne were conspicuous.'

Leaving these controversies in their wake, the dancers attended the conference, performed there and experienced access to events and activities that would have been denied them in Australia. They returned home with a strong desire to further the cause of Indigenous and Pacific Islander rights. Faith Bandler went on to become a noted figure in various aspects of the movement, as did Ray Peckham. The progressive aims they represented, supported by many in the broader community, helped pave the way to the successful 1967 referendum recognising Aboriginal and Torres Strait Islander peoples as Australian citizens.

The First Boat People

The fall of Saigon ended the already lost Vietnam War in 1975. Australia, as an ally of the United States of America, had been slowly drawn into the conflict between communist North Vietnam and democratic South Vietnam since 1962. Ultimately, more than 500 Australian soldiers died in a primarily ideological conflict that had limited relevance to Australian national security.

But, although the fighting was over, tens of thousands of South Vietnamese people began another battle for survival. Many tried to escape the persecution of the victorious Communists aboard leaky and overcrowded boats, hoping to sail to refuge in neighbouring countries. Mostly they were turned away, spurring men, women and children to even riskier voyages south to Australia.

The first five of what would eventually be around 2000 Vietnamese 'boat people', as seaborne refugees became known, arrived near the Tiwi Islands and were in Darwin harbour by 26 April 1976. The group, including the Lam family and several others, had left Vietnam in a 17-metre fishing boat they named *Kein Giang* and made for international waters. Lam Binh, Lam Tac Tam and three friends were turned away from several countries, but with the help of a partial map and some vague directions from the captain of an Australian ship in Malaysia, motored south for sixteen days and nights.

Darwin was a small sleepy town then; the harbour was deserted and it took the new arrivals several hours to find someone to help them. The prawn fishermen they eventually approached did not believe they could have sailed from Vietnam but gave them cigarettes and ten cents to call the police from a public telephone box. After long-distance arrangements made by the Department of Immigration in Canberra, the five were looked after by the Darwin St Vincent de Paul. It was a year after Cyclone Tracy devastated the city and rebuilding was in full swing. The men all found construction jobs within a week of their arrival.

Lam Binh would later work as a government interpreter. In that role, he was the first to greet twenty-five boat people who arrived in Broome, Western Australia, in May 1977. This group barely evaded the Vietnamese security forces and the group's leader, former South Vietnamese soldier Ng Ba Nghiep, had been forced to leave his wife and three children in Saigon, by then renamed Ho Chi Min City. Other boat people would also have stories of separation, hardship and brutality suffered through their perilous journeys.

At first, there was some concern about the arrival of the boat people. But Australians were weary of the social and political divisions caused by the Vietnam War, particularly over the issue of conscription, and took little interest in its aftermath. The coming of the first Vietnamese refugees received limited coverage in the press. Although it became an issue in the 1977 federal election, the unofficial arrival of boat people did not lead to the prolonged bitterness generated by the politics surrounding later asylum seekers, whose sometimes sinking craft began to arrive from the late 1980s.

In 2001 the Australian government refused entry to over 400 asylum seekers rescued from a sinking ship by the Norwegian freighter, MV *Tampa*. Official policy towards such arrivals changed from one of reception to one of detention. Boat people arriving after that time, including large numbers of Vietnamese, encountered a very different regime. 'Stop the boats' became a political slogan and many arrivals were held in indefinite detention pending relocation or other settlement, a policy and procedure eventually ruled illegal by the High Court in 2023.

Around 1.5 million Vietnamese refugees eventually found shelter somewhere by the mid-1990s. Another 400,000 to 600,000 are thought to have died of starvation, at the hands of pirates or by drowning. Although they did not all come by sea, more than 80,000 Vietnamese, as well as refugees from Laos and Cambodia, were eventually resettled in Australia and now form a distinctive group in some neighbourhoods around the country. Vietnamese food has become part of Australia's increasingly multicultural dining menus and many refugees and their descendants have made distinguished contributions to our society.

There are now few parts of the globe where distressed, aspirational or persecuted people are not seeking survival, sanctuary or simply better lives in countries they believe can provide for these reasonable desires. Australia is one of those countries and although it is, for most, still difficult to reach, the voyages to freedom made by the first 'boat people' showed that it could be done. Those born in the wrong place have few choices but to do what humans have done since the beginning. Move.

Playing with Covid

'. . . don't share cups, you might get Coronapirates!'

Children have their own ways of getting by. Barely known to most adults is their closed culture of games, chants, rhymes and jokes shared in the playground, the park and the street and, increasingly, through social media. It is a world of secrecy, subversion and fun.

For as long as we know, children have been improvising play as a way to learn about the world and to deal with its realities. Many will be familiar with these older games and chants such as 'Ring a ring o' rosy', 'London Bridge is falling down' or 'Oranges and lemons'. In the modern era, children have a lot more to deal with, much of it mediated through popular culture. In the 1950s children reworked a pop ballad used as the theme song for a successful Disney movie called *Davy Crockett: King of the Wild Frontier*. The song reflected the masculinity and violence of the American frontier, beginning with the first verse:

Born on a mountain top in Tennessee.
Bravest state in the land of the free
Whipped his pa when he was only three
Killed him a bear with a hickory tree
Davy, Davy Crockett,
King of the wild frontier

The kids turned it into:

Born on a tabletop in Joe's cafe.
Dirtiest joint in the USA
Killed his ma when he was only four
Used Mortein Plus forevermore.
Davy, Davy Crockett,
The man who is no good

Television jingles accompanying product advertising also generated the playful parodies. One was based on an advertisement for a brand of insecticide:

If there are white ants in the floor,
Borers in the door,
Silverfish galore
Get a Flick man, that's your answer
Remember, one Flick and they're gone.

In the Cold War fears of nuclear extinction this became:

If there are Russians in the floor
Soviets at the door
Communists galore—

Get an A Bomb, that's your answer
Remember: one flash—and they're ash.

Later eras produced ditties on celluloid super heroes:

Jingle bells, Batman smells
Robin flew away.
Wonder Woman lost her bosom
Flying TAA [Trans Australia Airlines, now defunct]

As were popular television shows:

Oh, the Addams family started
When uncle Festa farted.
They thought it very funny
When he blew up the dunny
And landed in the sewer,
A drain of raw manure.
The Addams family—
Blurt, blurt.

The AIDS crisis of the 1980s was dealt with in a cheeky reworking of the lyrics of the famous 'Happy Little Vegemites' jingle, the opening lines of which became:

We're happy little condoms,
We come in packs of six,
You buy us at the chemist and you stick us on your ——

The knife-attack scares that have been a feature of recent years in the United Kingdom and, to a lesser—though still concerning—extent in Australia were greeted with a playground parody of the 'Now I know My ABC' ditty, featuring the well-known lollies marketed as 'Gummy Bears':

ABCDEFG
Gummy Bears are chasing me.
One is red, one is blue,
One is peeing on my shoe.
Now I'm running for my life
Coz the red one has a knife.

In the first years of the COVID pandemic, 2020–22, schools were frequently closed, depriving many children of a major location for socialising and play. Kids found new ways to make sense of the situation and to deal with it. Being at home with parents tended to restrict many of their customary peer expressions and activities. But in parks, playgrounds and streets the same creative needs found necessary outlets. Rainbows, flowers, stars and messages of hope were chalked on walls and pavements; 'spoonvilles' of wooden spoons painted as whimsical characters sprang up in parks and children were able to meet and share, often without prying parents, through internet VoIP platforms, such as Skype and Zoom.

When children did get back to school, they soon adapted their traditional hiding and chasing games. These games, known by various names such as 'Corona Tip' and 'Corona Bullrush', were played in schools around Australia in one version or another. In some, the player deemed to be 'it' was 'infected' with the virus and sought to catch other players and pass it on or all players began with the virus and chased each other in mimicry of the biological spread of the coronavirus.

Children's play and lore are often trivialised and even deliberately restricted in some educational approaches. But their persistence and constructive adaptation to changing circumstances are an important element of childhood resilience. As British artist David Hockney once observed: 'People tend to forget that play is serious.'

Christmas is celebrated in many forms by many different people across the country. The basic format of 'Father Christmas' or 'Santa Claus' bringing gifts for children, as here in 1939, is a relatively recent development of the older tradition.

6

CELEBRATIONS

A Horse of Light

At the top of Yeerakine Rock near the quiet Western Australian wheat-belt town of Kondinin is a simple but evocative steel silhouette of a horse and armed rider mounted on a granite outcrop. As the sun rises, its rays shine through the sculpture, creating a memorable scene. On Anzac Days this dawn display has a special significance, reflecting the early hour at which ANZAC troops disembarked at Gallipoli as part of an ill-fated attempt to invade Turkey in 1915.

Faced with declining numbers at Anzac Day events, the local Returned Services League (RSL) moved the dawn service to Yeerakine Rock in 2015 for the 100th anniversary of the Gallipoli landings. They commissioned the corten steel Light Horse cut-out to commemorate the soldiers and animals of the Light Horse regiments of World War I. Men from the Kondinin district served in those regiments, including the 10th Light Horse, fabled for its exploits at the Nek, in Palestine and in Egypt. Other local men served in various units and their combined contribution to the war had a profound impact on Kondinin, both then and since. The 3.5-metre-high inscription on the memorial reads:

ANZAC
Many men from the Kondinin district
fought in World War I as members of
the 10th Light Horse Regiment.
This silhouette sculpture honours
those soldiers as well as other
service personnel and was
officially unveiled by the
sunrise on Anzac Day.

Settlers began to take up land at Kondinin around 1910, clearing the land and sowing seed in hopes of good harvests to come. But they were soon faced with a disastrous drought over the 1913–14 season, just as the war began. In the initial enthusiasm of the early months, many farmers from the area, like brothers Eustace, Bert and Reg Sykes, joined up. Some left wives and children to run the farms while those without families simply walked off their properties.

Local labour quickly dried up and development of the area slowed, although a primary school and the railway arrived during the war years. These provided a firm basis for the post-war growth of the district and Kondinin. Soldier settlement schemes allowed ex-soldiers to take up blocks of land on favourable terms, though many suffered from physical injuries and 'shell shock', now known as post-traumatic stress disorder (PTSD).

In 2023 a commemorative mural was painted by artist Jacob Butler (Shakey) on the large water tank near the Light Horse memorial. It tells the wider story of Kondinin's soldiers during the war. Noongar man Lewis 'Beaky' Collard served as a frontline runner in France, carrying messages between sergeant and officers. He is shown in the mural leaving the graves at Gallipoli. The Collards are a large and important extended family in the south-west and, like other Noongar families in the area, have made significant community contributions in both war and peace. The town's Community Garden features the 'Six Season Noongar Poles' painted by former resident, Ashley Collard, depicting the six seasons of the Noongar year:

- Birak—season of the young. First summer: December–January . . .
- Bunuru—season of adolescence. Second summer: February–March . . .
- Djeran—season of adulthood. Autumn: April–May . . .
- Makuru—season of fertility. Winter: June–July . . .
- Djilba—season of conception. First spring: August–September . . .
- Kambarang—season of birth: October–November

Although the Light Horse sculpture has only been up since 2015, Anzac Day observances there have grown. Originally intended mainly for local people, by 2023 the memorial was attracting around 150 attendees, including some from other states.

The Anzac tradition is a commemoration of wartime sacrifice and loss, of course. It is full of symbols and messages of remembering and mourning. But it is also a celebration. Anzac Day begins with ceremonies of commemoration at dawn and during the morning. In the afternoon and evening, there is festivity, two-up and sports. Together, this seemingly conflicting but now familiar combination is, for many, a celebration of a potent idea of nation and what has been, for a long time, its preferred form of cultural identity. Whether or not those popular sentiments change in the future, it is likely that Australians will continue to both memorialise and celebrate the events of Gallipoli and elsewhere on the 'one day of the year'.

One Long Party

With its multicultural population, Australia has a rich repertoire of colourful celebrations. Most of these belong to calendars very different to the standard January to December mode of the Gregorian calendar. Feast, fasts and festivals fall at various times on major calendars such as those of Judaism, Islam, Buddhism, Hinduism and other ways of measuring and marking time. Many of these events are observed in private or among their relevant cultural and ethnic groups but others have become, or are in the process of becoming, part of the regular annual schedule of partying.

Perhaps the earliest multicultural celebration to be added to the Australian Gregorian calendar was the Spring Festival associated with the lunar calendar of Chinese tradition. 'Chinese New Year', as the event is widely known, began during the Victorian gold rushes and has steadily expanded around the country as various waves of ethnic Chinese immigrants have arrived. It begins around late January and lasts for up to fifteen days of feasting, socialising, lion and dragon dancing, fireworks and gift giving, all heavily featuring red, the Chinese colour of good luck and prosperity. Many people will also pay respect to their ancestors through traditional ceremonies and, as with the new year traditions of many cultures, will clean and clear the home in readiness for the coming year.

Another new year festival following a similar trajectory into the broader community is Diwali, (also known as Divali and other names), usually translated as 'the festival of lights'. In one form or another, it marks the start of the year on one of India's most prominent calendars and usually falls around November. In one or another of its versions, Diwali is observed by many of the more than 700,000 people of Indian descent in Australia, and by many others. Its colourful combination of clothing, food and festivity, as well as its inclusive character, has seen the event spread around the country as immigrants who follow the lunisolar calendar settle here.

The core of Diwali is an acknowledgement of the reality that light banishes darkness. Symbolically, light deters evil spirits and represents the triumph of good over evil and of knowledge over ignorance. The various stories behind this belief in the traditions of the Hindus, Sikhs, Buddhists and Jains who observe it may be religious or cultural but all reflect these basic notions. For those of other faiths, or none, Diwali is a five-day festival of lamps, vivid and elaborate costumes, special foods and outdoor events.

It isn't necessary to have a formal 'calendar' like those supporting most festivals. First Nations people traditionally measure time by the cycle of the seasons, though religious observances are not necessarily tied to seasonal times. The climatic, plant, animal, insect and astronomical changes observed in different areas of the continent determine the changing of the seasons and, together with spiritual and mythological factors, fix the appropriate time for ceremonies. These vary from various forms of secret-sacred ritual to more public events of the kind usually described in the borrowed term 'corroboree'. In Western Australia, for example, the Whadjuk Noongar of the Swan River region recognise six seasons, while the customary division in the Kimberley is similar to that of the four European seasons. On the east coast, the D'harawal people around Sydney may also identify six seasons, while the Wurundjeri people of the Melbourne region recognise seven regular seasons together with another two accounting for occasional episodes of fire and flood.

There are a great many other moments of celebration on the calendars of other cultural groups. Together with those observed on the official Gregorian calendar—including those on its Orthodox version—there are few, if any, days of the year on which somebody is not celebrating a religious belief, a historical or mythical event or story, harvest time, the beginning or the end of a year, or simply something or someone deemed significant enough to commemorate. When looked at from this point of view, the Australian year is just one long party, ending with the Christmas period.

Keeping Christmas

Dixie is not in America's deep south. It is a locality in south-west Victoria, a bit over a hundred kilometres from Melbourne. The recent population of the tight-knit dairy farming community is only a few dozen over one hundred people. But they do Christmas in grand style.

The small and much-loved Dixie Hall is cleaned and decorated in preparation for the big event of the year, an almost ninety-year-long (or more) tradition known as 'Santa Night'. For 'the social event of the year', every family 'brings a plate, a salad or a dessert, and pays $20 for a feed of cold meats.' There is an abundance of sweet desserts and then, as darkness falls, the moment the kids assembled on the stage have been waiting for. Santa arrives in the Country Fire Authority fire truck with a bulging sack of lollies. He throws them into the crowd and onto the floor, not surprisingly 'the kids go mad' as they scramble for the treats.

On the other side of the country, its oldest inhabitants have developed a new version of the same tradition. When Christian missionaries came to Gija country in the nineteenth century, they introduced the Christmas story. Probably since the 1980s, the Christmas Crows, based on the Gija story of the Eagle and the Crow, have replaced Santa as the gift bringer.

The Catholic Ngalangangpum School Christmas party in the Warmun community begins like many Indigenous celebrations, with a barbie, live music and traditional dancing, known as junba. All the local kids are there, of course, excited for the big event they know will soon take place. Eventually, a four-wheel drive, or perhaps even a helicopter, arrives. Out jump three giant crows. The kids scream with delight and a bit of fear. The big black birds have long, sinister beaks and big round, white eyes. The adults laugh and, soon, so do the kids as the crows start to dole out presents for all. When the fun is over, the crows get back into whatever vehicle they came in and disappear until next Christmas.

Christmas in Dixie and in Gija country are just two of the many different ways Australians have been keeping 'the season of the year' since 1788, and even before. About a month away from landfall in Australia, Sergeant of Marines James Scott recorded Christmas dinner among the First Fleet. He and his veteran soldier companions dined on pork with apple sauce, beef, plum pudding and four bottles of rum. He didn't say if that was four between them or four each.

Since then, the Australian Christmas continued to evolve from this festive fare into dishes more appropriate to the climate. But it was a slow process, as settlers and their descendants were reluctant to let go of what for many, regardless of how irregular their church attendance, was a primal rite of family and community life. Nostalgia for 'home' at Christmas was a frequent newspaper topic in the nineteenth century.

In 1815, Australian-born Captain James Kelly was trying to enter what is now Macquarie Harbour on the rugged west coast of Tasmania. A strong gale and heavy seas heaved the open boat rowed by him and his damp companions into an inlet he named Christmas Cove. No plum pudding for their Christmas dinner, though they did have 'a Glorious Feed' that attempted to replicate the traditional meal, with antipodean adaptations. They roasted two black swans in a large iron pot. They also threw a glass of brandy into the sea while naming their uncomfortable anchorage, presumably after drinking a glass or two.

Later Christmas feasts began to show further evidence of environmental adaptation, with mention of ham and parrot pie, followed by plum pudding for dessert in the 1830s. Twenty or so years later, diggers in the Victorian goldfields had to be satisfied with salt pork and rum. Turkey began to appear on festive tables, succeeding the traditional British roast goose, and the Australian seasonal menu gradually became an amalgam of transported stodge and local wildlife. Tropical and stone fruits became popular from the late nineteenth century, expanding greatly on the dried fruits favoured for the British Christmas. In Sydney in 1890, King Street Arcade featured 'great masses of beautiful flowers at the florists and the magnificent spread of fruit near by—the piles of oranges, lemons, mangoes, pineapples, apricots, nectarines, peaches, plums, cherries, red and white currants, grapes, gooseberries and other fruits—decked with Christmas bush making a picture worth travelling to see.'

The hardest adaptation for most was the heat. Scorching summer was an unavoidable reminder that things in Australia were not as they were in the northern hemisphere at the same time of year. In an era before air conditioning, the wisdom of getting outside hot homes into the bush and onto the beach eventually began to shape the location of Christmas dinner, in whatever form it came. As more and more people of European descent were born here, nostalgia for the old country faded to some extent. Christmas Day picnics and large community or occupational parties became increasingly common in the last half of the nineteenth century, especially as rail travel allowed people to revel away from cities and suburbs.

These changes in diet and location were accompanied by other localisations. Houses were often decorated with greenery cut from nearby bush. The decorated Christmas tree, a feature exported from Germany to the United Kingdom, also began to appear towards the end of the nineteenth century, usually set up in public spaces for all to enjoy.

Christmas fare has continued to evolve. From the 1980s the influence of Mediterranean immigrants saw seafood begin its rise to seasonal popularity and the thirty-six-hour marathons at some fish markets and seafood suppliers established another new tradition. At the start of the twenty-first century, Christmas continues to be a pivotal point on the calendar as a distinctively Australian affair, an extravaganza of homes decorated with intricate and expensive lighting displays, blow-up Santas and other elaborate symbols of the season. In contrast to the austere gift giving of the colonial period, and even the early twentieth century, lavish presents are often exchanged.

And there have been even more recent changes. Like many living customs, Christmas continually takes in new traditions. Singer-songwriter Paul Kelly's celebrated song, 'How To Make Gravy', first released in 1996, has been steadily growing in popularity since then. When the COVID pandemic forced lockdowns across the country, the song's story about a man in prison and unable to get home to his family for Christmas became something of an anthem for the millions in isolation. The prisoner writes his letter on 21 December and, for many, that day is now part of the Christmas season, known as 'Gravy Day'.

Light Up the Night

There aren't too many places around the world where people haven't found an excuse for occasionally making a lot of noise, smoke and flame. Fire festivals of one kind or another—usually featuring pyrotechnics—have probably been around since the invention of gunpowder. For many years, Australians have celebrated our own version of this custom.

The history of Guy Fawkes Night in Australia was derived from the English anniversary of the execution of a traitor who plotted to assassinate King James I in 1604. Guy Fawkes Day, or Bonfire Night, commemorates this 'Gunpowder Plot', as the conspiracy became known. The English custom generally involves bonfires, fireworks, the burning of the 'guy' (an effigy of Fawkes) and a child's begging custom ('penny for the guy') accompanied by the chant: 'Remember, remember the fifth of November.' The day has been celebrated in Australia since at least 1805 when it was enthusiastically and alcoholically marked 'by a mob of juvenile patriots'. As in England, Guy Fawkes Day was associated with sectarian differences between Catholics and Protestants. *The Sydney Monitor* of 1829 complained bitterly of this 'annual insult to all Catholics' and requested the rambunctious 'boys' who observed it to be taken to the police. In the early 1830s, the young Swan River colony included the day in a list of public holidays, calling it exactly what it had been—'Gun-powder Treason'.

As well as religious conflicts, Guy Fawkes celebrations could also be dangerous for revellers. A report from Sydney in 1833 indicates that mishaps with fireworks are not just a recent danger:

> An accident happened to a boy named Ledyard of Upper Castlereagh Street, on Tuesday night last by which his life is despaired of. Having a considerable quantity of gunpowder in his pocket, for the purpose of making squibs,

&c, in commemoration of Guy Fawkes Day, he incautiously mingled with some boys at a bonfire when some sparks communicated to his pocket, it blew up, inflicting serious injuries on various parts of his body.

By the 1860s Sydneysiders were enthusiastically celebrating the occasion by sending up their politicians with some whimsy and spicy comment from one of the city's colourful identities, complete with a topical reference to the imminent visit of Prince Alfred:

A somewhat unusual Guy Fawkes exhibition took place in Sydney on Tuesday last the 5th of November . . . in which the whole of the Ministry were caricatured by dummies dressed up most ridiculously in garbs that bore some resemblance to the Windsor uniforms. Three [?] were in chairs and carried by boys while a few urchins in coloured rags and tatters kept up as much noise and shouting as they were able. The Guys made their appearance in front of the Houses of Parliament shortly after 3 o'clock, heaped [helped] by the Flying Pieman who recited some verses. This is the first time in the colony that Guy Fawkes has been made use of for political purposes and except for this reason the affair would hardly have been worth notice. The verses recited by the Pieman, in addition to the usual nonsensical doggerel, were amusing enough.

The rhyme further satirised politicians, beginning:

Oh please to remember the 5th of November.
Guy Fawkes may be dead,

But we've got here instead.
Six Windsor uniforms all in a row
To carry about for a rare show
When the Prince comes ashore at the end of December ...

In 1905 a new holiday was added to the calendar. Empire
Day was a celebration of the then-extensive global network of
colonial holdings known as the British Empire. Australia was a
mostly enthusiastic member of the imperial 'family' and 24 May
was quickly endorsed as another opportunity for evening fireworks displays. Popularly known in many parts of the country
as 'Cracker Night', it slowly displaced many, though not all,
Guy Fawkes celebrations as an annual fire festival involving the
family and the community in street parties, children begging
for money, bonfires on which old tyres might be burned and,
of course, 'crackers', as fireworks were generally known.

Increasing concerns about injuries from fireworks and the
risk of bushfire in many parts of the country so late in the year
as November led to the eventual extinguishment of Guy Fawkes
and his pyrotechnics. Western Australia seems to have been the
first to ban fireworks (except in supervised public displays), in
1971. Over the next decade or so most of the country gradually
followed a similar path, with a couple of exceptions. The event
was widely and enthusiastically observed within living memory,
especially in New South Wales, South Australia and Western
Australia and was popular in and around Moe in Victoria's
Latrobe Valley during the 1990s.

While Guy Fawkes has been toppled from his fiery eminence
in most of the country by concerns for community safety, the

folk memory of his night still lingers. Lamenting the demise of Cracker Night, a correspondent to the *West Australian* wrote in the year 2000 that 'The vacuum left by the loss of a genuine cultural tradition, a community event of great happiness, was filled by a synthetic, imported newcomer and public fireworks events in which we are more the audience than the participants.'

Although Cracker Night in any of its forms has, officially at least, disappeared from most of the country, the tradition lives on in some form in Tasmania and the Northern Territory. In Tasmania on 24 May or the following Sunday, fireworks, bonfires and related activities are allowed with an official permit. In the Top End, Territorians celebrate the anniversary of their self-government in 1978 and their cherished identity as rugged individualists, quite different to the soft types inhabiting other states and territories, usually referred to disdainfully as 'southerners'. Between 9 am and 9 pm on 1 July, Territory residents and visitors can purchase fireworks that they are allowed to ignite at will between 6 pm and 11 pm. Retailers report that people spend $30–$300 dollars each, sometimes up to $2000. That money goes up in flame, smoke and stink in a few permitted hours of licensed misrule, sharpened by the fact that the Territory is usually already in bushfire season.

Inevitably, there are fires, terrified animals and sometimes horrific injuries. In 2012 an overenthusiastic reveller tried to impress fellow partygoers by inserting a firecracker known as a 'spinning bee' into his rectum—then lighting it. As well as burns to his rear and genitals, his fingers were injured when he desperately tried to withdraw the flaming cracker. As the police Watch Commander at the time put it 'What must have seemed to be a great idea at the time has obviously backfired.'

Hunting for Halloween

She was a young Australian writer at the World Fair in New York, 1940. Leona Deane had a great time there, describing all the impressively modernist international pavilions, including the Australian effort which was 'a really good show, although it was mainly wheat and wool'. She had cocktails at the Waldorf-Astoria, 'the swishest hotel in New York', and enjoyed a show at the music hall of the Rockerfeller Centre Building which included the Rockettes, the most famous 'comedy wenches' team in the world at that time. She did a lot of other things, too—one of which was discovering 'trick or treat':

> The youngsters come round the houses saying 'Trick or treat'— if you haven't a treat for them, they play tricks . . . in the form of soaping your windows, and raising general merry destruction. Small niece and nephew showed me how to hollow out a pumpkin, and cut faces in it; then you place a lighted candle inside and use it as decoration. We had popcorn, marshmallows, nuts and candy for treat [sic] for any youngsters who should ring at the front door; there were quite a few and we all polished off what wasn't given away. The most destruction done in our neighbourhood was to a statue of one of the pioneers, whose face was covered in red paint. This was accounted in the local newspaper as 'the most dastardly deed perpetrated this Hallowe'en.' But ours is a singularly genteel neighbourhood—in the tougher

areas hooligans smash windows, ruin gardens and set fire to things. Oh yes, and break electric light globes.

As we can tell from Leona's bubbly account (she went on to a writing career in advertising and radio) these Halloween hijinks were new to her. But if she had been part of the Scots-Australian community, she would already have known that Halloween was an important folk custom, probably observed here ever since substantial communities of Scots formed around the 1820s. A Halloween ball took place on the Victorian gold-fields at Forrest Creek in 1858 and Halloween continued to be observed by Scots Australians into the twentieth century. The Scots in Perth kept it in 1911 and in 1912, the Bundaberg Musgrave Caledonian Association observed the date with 'a grand social dance' and 'dookin for apples as well as other amusements for the children.'

These events followed the Scots tradition and do not seem to have been especially spooky. But in Kempsey, New South Wales, the tradition was being more broadly observed by 1942 (on 3 November) when it was promised that 'There will be devils, witches, spiders, bats, owls and similar weird things to provoke thrills and screams of excitement. All Kempsey will be out that night.'

None of these accounts mention what is now the defining feature of Australian Halloween, 'trick or treat'. How did this American version of the Halloween custom get here?

The process by which we came to celebrate Halloween with trick or treating may well have begun when the Australian press made much of Leona's visit to an American millionaire's mansion where she saw trick or treating in action, New York style. Her story was repeated in the press in the early 1950s, along with reports of expatriate Americans observing Halloween in Melbourne in 1952. By the 1970s, kids were demanding trick or treat at Halloween parties in Canberra, introduced by the Australian wife of a visiting American academic. A primary school teacher was involved in organising a 'trick or treat in the remote Western Australian town of Dampier in 1972, by which time it seems that the custom was beginning its rise to broader popularity.

A likely part of the explanation for the growth of Halloween in Australia since the 1970s is that primary school teachers, searching for October–November seasonal activities, introduced the custom to their pupils. The popularity of horror novels and movies since the 1970s may have prepared the way for the adoption of such an event, as well as its increasingly spooky character. More recently, the spread of social media and related access to especially American movies, such as *Mean Girls* with its Halloween sequence, is thought to have influenced Australian kids. Manufacturers and sellers of toys, costumes and cards have also been quick to identify a marketing opportunity for an otherwise quiet period of the retail cycle between Father's Day and Christmas.

The last night of the year according to the Celtic calendar, Halloween (31 October) is a popular festival in the Celtic countries, in many parts of Britain and in the United States. It is closely connected with the Catholic and Protestant feasts of All Saints Day (1 November) and All Souls Day (2 November). These two days are known as 'Hallow Tide' and commemorate the lives of past, present and future saints and the souls of the recently deceased. Halloween has attracted criticism from the

Christian church, and elsewhere, in part due to its importance on the witches' calendar, where it is called Samhain (pronounced 'Sow-in'), the Celtic name by which it is still known in Ireland. But there is little evidence of a connection between Samhain and any pagan rites for the dead.

Halloween is now a major annual event, with extensive spooky paraphernalia filling shops and elaborate house decorations on a scale threatening to rival those of Christmas. Typically, hordes of overexcited young children roam the streets on 'fright night' dressed as ghosts or monsters and 'trick or treating'—visiting houses and demanding lollies, or drinks on threat of mischief to the garbage bin or front lawn—threats rarely, if ever, carried out.

Fittingly, folklore provides an added element of potential danger on this night. Urban myths about treats laced with poison, as well as other allegedly true horror stories, have been doing the rounds at Halloween for decades. Consequently, trick or treating tends to be closely monitored by concerned parents and neighbours. Judging by the amount of money spent on Halloween decorations, costumes and the like, as well as the trouble taken to decorate homes, the grown-ups have almost as much fun as the kids.

One Day in September

Kenneth Gordon McIntyre was an accomplished man: Professor of Literature at Melbourne University, then a noted lawyer, a historian, mayor of Box Hill, Victoria, and a Commander of the British Empire (CBE). But his most important claim to fame is in the annals of the Australian Football League (AFL), in particular his role in the creation of one of the country's most popular and spectacular events—the 'one day in September', 'the big dance' or, inevitably, 'the Granny'.

Sporting competitions had occasionally been dubbed 'Grand' in Britain and the term 'grand final' or 'finale', was often used in advertising retail sales, the culmination of theatrical and musical performances and in horseracing from the early nineteenth century. But Australia has the credit for elevating the term and concept to the specialised sporting status it has today, particularly in relation to the evolution of the AFL 'Grand Final'.

The first finals matches to be called 'Grand' were those played in Melbourne in the 1890s. The term was used informally, usually rendered in French as a 'finale', for some years before the first match generally accepted as being a 'grand final' took place. The game, its players and the outcome were already the focus of enthusiastic speculation in pubs, streets and even police stations, with columns of local newspaper space devoted to who would kick the most goals and which teams would be victorious. Little has changed in that respect. In 1896 the 'grand finale' was between Collingwood and South Melbourne was to be played with 'every expectation of an immense crowd turning up to see the great final tussle, and the East Melbourne ground should be well filled.' Collingwood won.

While the winners of a game of football might seem to be a fairly straightforward thing to judge, Australian football leagues have invented or adapted various systems to decide on the 'premier' team each year. Different methods were used by the Victorian Football League (VFL) until 1931, when the first of five systems devised or co-devised by McIntyre was adopted. These were successively refined into different versions over the years until the McIntyre Final Eight system was introduced in the 1994 season. Always controversial, McIntyre's penultimate method was replaced with another in 2000. Ken McIntyre, as he is usually known to footy aficionados, died in his mid-nineties in 2004 and holds a hallowed place in the history and lore of the game he loved.

And which millions more also love.

Australian Rules Football is one of the country's great badges of identity. A homegrown game beginning in the 1850s, it quickly became the most popular Victorian game, generating fanatical loyalties and rivalries between clubs as it rapidly expanded beyond the colony to the rest of the country. Western Australia was the last to join in, in the 1880s, becoming another place where 'Aussie Rules' is played and followed with often more than religious devotion.

Followers see their players as heroes and rival clubs and players as arch-villains. The legendry and lore of the game is vast and ever expanding. It has a distinctive lingo that identifies and unites its fans, players, administrators and commentators, with rhyming terms like 'sausage roll', or simply 'snag' for a goal, ''white maggots' for umpires and a 'mongrel punt' for a badly kicked ball that still moves in the right direction. Traditions of the great day itself include the ritual playing of the match on the last Saturday afternoon in September, the 'one day in September' (since shifted to the first Saturday in October); the parade established in 1977 and the Grand Final breakfast initiated a decade earlier. The on-field entertainments are lavish, with high-profile celebrities often performing popular music hits. After the match, of course, there is celebration by the winning supporters and despair amongst the losers, both emotions treated with the universal cure-all of alcohol.

More Australians are said to attend 'the footy' than any other sport. Whether that is true or not, the AFL Grand Final has become one of Australia's largest and most anticipated public events, attracting up to 100,000 to the annual extravaganza in Melbourne, with millions more viewing the game on television. Other football codes have grand finals of their own, notably the National Rugby League (NRL), with similar enthusiasm from all involved. But 'Aussie Rules', also known as 'aerial ping pong', is when 'the big men fly'. It is a spectacular experience to witness, a highly skilled display of human movement by the players and a profoundly emotional game for its community of followers who frequently attribute to it a sense of local, state and national identity.

For some, it might be even more than that. Novelist Amanda Lohrey wrote about the role of the sacred in Australia's increasingly secular society in *The Conversion* (2023). Interviewed about her work, she observed: 'If you talk to any Victorian and ask them, "What's a sacred space in Melbourne?", they'll most likely tell you the MCG . . . They won't say St Patrick's Cathedral, and they certainly won't say Federation Square, but they'll point to a space which has a long history, a long tradition, which is very heavily invested with the emotions of the community over decades.'

More Than a Meal

In South Australia's Barossa region town of Tanunda, Saturday, 8 September 1917, was 'Australia Day'. It had nothing to do with the First Fleet but everything to do with the war reaching its horrific peak in faraway Europe and the Middle East. Like almost every country town, Tanunda and surrounds had sent its sons away to fight. On the home front a vital part of the support that civilians could provide was through fundraising activities. A newspaper report of the event reflected the inclusive character of the day:

> On Saturday last Australia Day was celebrated, and proved a great success ... it is anticipated that the Soldiers' Fund will benefit to the extent of £385. The procession was one of the best seen in the town, and included the Tanunda Town Band, members of the Tanunda Loyal Lodge, ladies on horseback, cheap jack, Paddy's market, draught horses, cadets, Tanunda school drum and fife band, children of the Tanunda, Bethany, and New Mecklenburg schools, juvenile concert party, decorated bicycles and motor cars, &c.

The main item was a draught-horse race that 'caused amusement, and not a little excitement, as some of the "boys" were not equal to handling their unwieldy mounts and lost their seats. The children's chief attraction was Mr. T. Kelly's donkey . . .'

As part of the activities, the local *Barossa News* published a modest booklet titled *The Barossa Cookery Book*. All proceeds 'other than bare expenses' were to go to the South Australian Soldiers' Fund. Priced at sixpence, the booklet had a cover that proclaimed: 'All these Recipes have been tried and tested, and bear the signature of each Donor as a guarantee of faith.' The book was reportedly 'selling rapidly' at the time, not surprisingly given the charitable nature of Tanunda's Australia

Day. Remarkably, this modest publication is still in print. It was revised in the 1930s when its original 400 recipes were increased to 1000, and today is celebrated, if not venerated, in the Barossa region. The proceeds from the original publication, almost £400, went towards building a Soldiers' Memorial Hall in Tanunda, a popular way to memorialise the war in that period. Community halls like this were erected around the country, and were focal points for local dances, events and other activities. They played—and sometimes still do—a vital role in bringing people together in a shared sense of belonging and local identity. A cookery book can do the same.

'Those Barossa Girls' is a local community history project and workshop business dedicated to preserving and extending the iconic cookbook. Not only are a selection of the recipes to be republished in a companion volume with modern metric equivalents to aid current cooks, but some of the stories of the women who originally donated their family recipes to the cause will be told. Why? Because, as the project leaders point out, the book and the recipes are snapshots of not only a bygone way of life but also repositories of the food traditions brought to the Barossa by early immigrants. As the project website puts it:

> But it's also about the contributors. We have no living memories of the despair, the grief, the loss and destruction of WW1, but these recipe contributors were living it. And they endured. And it shaped their communities and in turn the country we became. These were ordinary women living humble normal lives, yet their quiet stories of commitment, devotion and love deserve to be heard. In 1917 when the world was dark these women were beacons of hope, strength

and light for their families and community. Our project exists for them.

Many of the recipes came from women of German origin. One of the still-popular recipes from the original book is for a yeasted *Streusel Kuchen*, now usually known as 'German Cake'. Its transition from basic slab of German folk food based on fermented potato to a modern fruity delicacy tells a powerful story of a difficult aspect of Barossa history. The cake was a family and social favourite under its original name. But during World War I, anti-German sentiment around Australia forced a name change to 'Yeast Cake'. When the book had a second edition in the 1920s, the editors needed to be sure to stress their patriotism by emphasising that the donated recipes had gone towards the considerable cost of the Tanunda Soldiers' Memorial Hall. As the living memory of both world wars has faded, so the cake has regained its ethnic origins and is now generally known as 'German Yeast Cake'.

Folklorists and food historians point out that recipe books are repositories of information about their time and place, about values and attitudes, lifestyles and technological change. Depression-era cookbooks are full of hard-times recipes, doing more with less, making everything go just a little further. The famous *Country Women's Association Cook Book*, like *The Barossa Cookery Book*, contains the accumulated culinary knowledge of generations of Australian cooks, families and communities. Along with the Presbyterian Mission Women's Union's *PWMU Cookbook* (1904) and several other historical 'how to cook' manuals, it remains in print in an era of fast food and eating out, suggesting that such publications have a meaning that transcends the recipes within. Like many traditions, those associated with food are sometimes overlooked and taken for granted. Yet they are powerful expressions of identity, often written down on scraps of paper, in family cookbooks and in collections of recipes. They are indeed, 'more than a meal'.

In the early days of commercial radio, owners of proprietary radios were required to buy a licence. Many circumvented the cost of both a radio and a licence by building crude but effective 'crystal sets', as in this picture from the 1920s.

7

CREATIONS

Creative Convicts

We're used to thinking about transported convicts as the brutalised victims of an oppressive regime. They certainly experienced plenty of cruelty, misery and violence, but there was also opportunity for many. The criminal transportation system to Australia was a large and long-lasting experience that involved hundreds of thousands of people, not only as prisoners but also warders, soldiers, servants, administrators and their families, all connected somehow or other to the penal bureaucracy of 'the fatal shore'.

When large numbers of people are thrown together, as they were in this system, most not only survived but also practised the enduring creativity of human beings. Convicts sang, danced, wrote, acted, painted, engraved (sometimes feloniously), tattooed and generally involved themselves in the full range of human creativity. We'll never know how much they did because their works were often ephemeral, oral or otherwise transitory, neither respected by the establishment nor officially documented. When they do break into the more or less official records, we usually get a glimpse of hard lives in hard times.

Earning a living from music has always been a precarious activity. This was especially true in convict Australia. In 1848 a group of fourteen fiddlers—folk violinists—had to petition the Van Diemen's Land government to allow them to play unhindered in public houses. While there were no laws against music making in pubs, the police saw it as their duty to supress music because it contributed, they thought, to 'disorder'. The fiddlers said they were trying only to make honest livings by providing the poor labourer with some music and dancing 'after his daily toil'. They claimed that other colonies did not forbid such entertainment and that many of them suffered physical ailments that made it impossible for them to earn a living other than by playing the violin. Whether the petition succeeded or not, music continued to be played by convicts.

One such convict was a Scots fiddler named Neil Gow Foggo. Descended from a musical family, Foggo was born in 1811. He went to sea at an early age and ended up in trouble ashore in the 1830s. Convicted of stealing from his parents, he was transported to Van Diemen's Land and was there until 1841, when he disappeared, stowing away on an American whaling ship. He was only away for another few years until he was again transported in 1844. He spent much of the rest of his life in Port Arthur and other criminal institutions on the island. In these unpromising surroundings, Foggo became an admired performer on the violin as well as a teacher of stringed instruments, not only to other convicts but also to at least one official at Port Arthur, who recalled:

> As a teacher of music, he was remarkably successful. He seemed quite at home in playing any instrument. He carried his music in his head, having an astonishing memory and could write page after page of difficult music as rapidly as a shorthand writer could take down a speech.
>
> I was a pupil of his and belonged to his string band. The ease and facility with which he would write out our various parts used to astonish me . . .

Foggo was a natural musician, inheritor of a rich tradition of Scots folk music. There were also many more formally-educated musicians who played pianos, guitars and other instruments for the respectable revels of Van Diemen's Land society, including for dancing. At this time almost everyone, high, low and in-between, danced. Workplaces, pubs or the streets were the dance floors of the poor, while the better-off classes had their halls and grand ballrooms. In the 1820s, Sydney could even boast a French dancing master.

François Girard (alias De Lisle) was born in Normandy in 1793. He was a soldier and then a teacher of French in England until convicted of stealing watches in 1820, possibly a trumped-up charge designed to rid England of a potential revolutionary. As a gentleman with, it seems, a British officer friend resident in the colony, Girard was given the freedom to do pretty much as he wished and he became well known, and wealthy, as a teacher of the popular dances of the day, as outlined in his advertising copy:

FRENCH LANGUAGE AND DANCING.—M. Girard, of Paris, presenting Compliments to the Families of Sydney, most respectfully informs them that he gives Instruction in his native language, and also in quadrilles, waltzes, Sec. All kind of elegant dances, at Mr. Nott's Academy, 44. Castlereagh street; and those Families, who desire it, may be waited on at their own houses.

After some initial difficulties, Girard established himself in the colony, married, opened a baking business, became a father and embarked on a continually expanding business career that eventually came to include flour mills, quarries, timber, pastoral activities, real estate and shipping. He was an early adopter of the new technology of steam to power his enterprises and was reportedly a founding member of the elite Australian Club. Always a volatile personality, Girard was in a more or less constant state of dispute with the officials and courts of New South Wales over business matters and, he believed (probably correctly), because he was a Frenchman in a British colony. He died aged around sixty-seven in 1859.

Graphic artists of one form or another were well represented in colonial society. Many of them had been convicted of crimes involving artistic skills, mainly counterfeiting and forgery. Joseph Lycett arrived in Sydney with a fourteen-year sentence in 1814. He was soon in trouble for again turning his talents to forging banknotes but his skills, particularly for the painting of Christ Church in Newcastle, New South Wales, led to a conditional pardon and a successful artistic career in the colony. Other transported painters opened drawing schools, took commissions painting landscapes, flora, fauna and, of course, portraits of those deemed important enough.

The colony also had plenty of artisans with high-level etching skills they had perfected in the criminal pursuits that led to their transportation. The best known of these talented creatives was William Buelow Gould. Born in 1801 and transported in 1827, he was a multi-talented painter of portraits, landscapes and nature. His most famous work, *Sketchbook of Fishes*, was produced in the early 1830s while the artist was serving time at Macquarie Harbour in Van Diemen's Land. The fine drawings—some of which might have been by hands other than Gould's—were recognised by the UNESCO Australian Memory of the World Register in 2011. Gould gained his freedom in 1835, married and continued to paint. He later received another prison term for theft and his life ended in alcoholism and poverty in Hobart in 1853.

The Dreaded Tomhooka!

Teasing those unfamiliar with bush life has long been an Australian pastime. Newcomers from overseas or from the cities, often called 'new chums', were regaled with unlikely yarns told with all sincerity by bushies with a wicked sense of humour. An Englishman calling himself 'Cockney' told of his typical experience when he first arrived in Townsville and 'ventured out into the country'.

> Some of us fellows, when we first came from England, had to listen to many wild and woolly yarns from the old timers

we met in those parts. Knowing no better, we believed what we were told. Arriving in Brisbane I secured a job out from Cairns, and the cocky was a notorious hard-case. After I was working for him a couple of days, my nights were disturbed by a noise coming from the direction of the creek, half-a-mile away. I spoke to the cocky about it.

'Cripes, you heard it, did you,' he said, looking real alarmed. 'Why that must be a tomhooka. We've been trying to exterminate them for years, and it's a terrible hard job. They're dangerous beggars, a sort of cross between an alligator, a snake, an' a scorpion. Yaas, the tomhooka has got all their vices an' none of their virtues. His teeth an' tail are sudden death, an' the scratch of his claws is deadly poison. Worst of it is, you can't kill 'em. Their hide will turn a bullet. There was one of the cows in the creek when I first took up this farm, and he was full-grown. We were afraid to go out of the house, an' the suspense was something terrible. Well, we used to take our life in our hands and sneak down the creek, where we fed the brute on all the poisons we could procure. He swallowed the lot of them, concealed in lumps of goat, then he started sneezin' an' gigglin,' an' didn't stop for a bloomin' fortnight. None of us could sleep, so we had to start feedin' the cow on rum, to keep him shikkered. Cost us a lot of money, but at last he got the horrors an' hung himself in the fork of a tree he tried to climb, thinkin' he was an expert high diver.

Apparently, 'Cockney' was inclined to believe this until he discovered that the fearful noise he had heard from the creek was the bellowing of a calf.

This story resonates of the drop bear and hoop snake lies that Australians still enjoy telling newcomers. The 'tomhooka' also has a bit of the bunyip and perhaps the even more unpleasant yarama (yara-ma-yha-who), a vampirical creature that attacks humans from the fig trees in which it is said to live.

Sometimes, trying it on with the new chum backfires badly. In outback Queensland during the 1930s, a young Englishman turned up at an outback station looking for work. The boss was doubtful as he didn't look like a bushman. 'Not long out from England?', he asked. The man agreed and said he'd only arrived a few months earlier but was happy to try any work. The boss decided to give him a go and sent him down to the hut to join the other hands. Billy Marcoochy and another boundary rider decided to have some fun with the raw new bloke and arranged to have him ride the 'outlaw' that no one had been able to break. Word went round and all assembled after breakfast to watch the bucking mount throw the new chum into the dust. They got him into the saddle, with Marcoochy yelling 'Good bye old chap; I'll write and tell your mother you died game.' But then the new hand suddenly yelled for the yard gate to be opened:

The horse immediately made for open country, bucking every inch of the way. Outside of the fence, the rider, as the horse was bucking, kicked off first one boot, and then the other. Then, after giving a brilliant display of horsemanship, he leaned down, picked up his boots, put them on, and then rode the now shivering and sweating animal over to where the squatter was standing. Jumping from the saddle he said: 'Got any more horses to ride, boss!'

The hands and the boss were amazed:

'Darn it all', said the squatter, 'I thought you said you only came from England a couple of months back. Where in the name of jumping wild cats did you learn to ride like that?'

'That's right', replied the new hand, 'I only came from England recently, but I handled horses from the time I was a kiddie until I went with the Light Horse to the war in '15. I stopped a couple of Turkish bullets near the Jordan Valley and was sent to England. Over there the doctors reckoned that the war could proceed without me, so I was sent back to Australia . . .'

'Well,' said the squatter. 'So far as I am concerned you can stay here all your life, and as Marcoochy over there is not such a good man as he thinks he is, you can take his job, I'm going to sack him right away.'

Another spoof was probably old when it appeared in print in 1902. Since then, the tale of the well-dressed kangaroo has been told about a visiting English cricket team in the 1950s and about an Italian team contesting the America's Cup in Fremantle in 1983. This version is about a group of American, sometimes Japanese, tourists being driven through the outback to see the sights. The bus runs down a kangaroo and the driver stops to assess the damage. The tourists are all excited at this bit of authentic Australiana and rush out to have a look. After the cameras have been clicking for a while, someone gets the bright idea of standing the dead roo up against a tree and putting his sports jacket on the animal for a bit of a different souvenir photo. Just as the tourist is about to snap his photo the roo, only stunned by the bus, returns to consciousness and leaps off into the scrub, still wearing the tourist's expensive jacket which also contains his wallet, money, credit cards and passport.

Why do some of us take such great delight in hoaxing newcomers and visitors? Is it perhaps a way of initiating new chums into Australian society? Do we have some deep-seated insecurity that needs to be allayed? Or, as the celebrated historian, the late Manning Clark, once mused, 'Are we a nation of bastards?'

Where's Christina?

Australia's most iconic song, our emblem of national identity is, of course, 'Waltzing Matilda'. The simple ditty that its author sold off for five quid has been enmeshed in myth, rumour and countless speculations since it was created in 1895. There are various theories about Waltzing Matilda's genesis and spread but there is also a human tale of thwarted romance, broken dreams, commercial opportunism and the disappearance of the song's co-creator from its history.

The already-noted poet Andrew Barton 'Banjo' Paterson visited Dagworth station near Winton, Queensland, in August 1895. Also staying on the property was Miss Sarah Riley, whom Paterson had been courting for some years. Their relationship had been difficult as Sarah lived in Victoria while Paterson lived and worked in Sydney and had not yet committed to a proposal of marriage. At the time, Christina Macpherson, the old schoolchum of Sarah and sister of station manager Robert Macpherson was also visiting Dagworth. Paterson and Christina, both aged thirty-one and the children of Scottish immigrants, immediately hit it off, as we might now say.

In accordance with the etiquette of the time and place, social relations revolved around groups taking rides to picnic spots around the country, visiting other properties and self-entertainments at home. Musical items were popular at these events and, as with most respectable young ladies of the era, Christina could play the piano and knew the rudiments of music. She was also learning to play a portable stringed instrument known as an autoharp, useful for travelling and for venues where no piano was available. One evening after dinner at Dagworth, she picked out on the autoharp what she could remember of a tune she heard the band play at a race meeting well over a year earlier. Paterson, although not a musician, was struck by the melody and rhythm, saying that he would write some words to it. According to a later reflection, he then 'grabbed his notebook and penned the first lyrics of "Waltzing Matilda".' The draft was refined over the next few days as the socialising and private performances of the song continued.

It seems that Sarah took a dim view of her fiancé and Christina obviously getting on so well as they collaborated on their joint creation. By the end of the visit, Riley and Paterson's relationship was finished. But so was the song, in its earliest version, at least. It was soon being learned and sung in the district and beyond, growing ever more popular. By 1902 it was 'all the rage here', according to a correspondent to a Queensland newspaper.

Although Christina had put the tune together, she was, by her own admission, 'no musician'. When she and Paterson had finished their joint composition a professional musician, Harry Nathan, was at some point enlisted to write her rough melody down and arrange it in a proper musical form as a 'bush song'. Later, witnessing the rapid rise of the song, Nathan claimed his own arrangement of the tune, with no mention of Christina's originating role. This was the beginning of Christina Macpherson's disappearance from the tale.

In 1903 Nathan's version was published in sheet-music form, the medium of the era for distributing hits. The song now spread even further, attracting the interest of the tea merchants James Inglis & Co., who owned the Billy Tea brand. An astute businessman, Inglis saw the potential of having a hit song to advertise his product. He bought the rights to the lyrics from Paterson's publisher and another musician was engaged to adapt them and the tune into the early twentieth-century version of an advertising jingle. Marie Cowan used Nathan's arrangement as a basis for her own and a minor change was made to the lyric to improve its advertising effectiveness. At this point in the song's history the line '"You'll never catch me alive," said he' seems to have been substituted for Paterson's original, which had the swaggie drowning himself under the coolibah tree. The swagman also became 'jolly'. Again, there was no mention of Christina.

Assisted by the wide availability of the reworked lyrics on packets of Billy Tea, 'Waltzing Matilda' continued its astonishing journey, growing in popularity year by year. Paterson went on with his life, as did the unsung Christina, who never married. During the 1930s a visiting English musician and writer, Thomas Wood, tracked down a version of the song near its birthplace and published an arrangement of it in his best-selling travel book, *Cobbers*. Bob Macpherson's sister was mentioned as the composer of the tune, but not by name. Perhaps irritated by being removed from the history of the popular song, Christina drafted a letter to Wood, giving her version of the song's creation. For some reason, she never sent any of the several versions of the letter she wrote and another chance to have her due acknowledgement was lost. It was not until many years later that Christina's letter became public and a slow process of research by various people gradually brought her back into the picture.

There is a much broader mythology surrounding our national song, but the human story of its creation and dissemination is little known. 'Waltzing Matilda' brought about the end of at least one romance, possibly two. It generated a number of legal claims and counterclaims about its origins, its ownership and its legendry. Harry Nathan, disappointed in his hopes for his arrangement of the song, is said to have drunk himself to death in 1906. Paterson spoke little in public about the song or the circumstances of its creation, apart from a brief reference in a radio interview towards the end of his life. He basically agreed with Christina's account, given in her unsent letter. By then, the song was widely acknowledged as the unofficial national anthem, recorded by artists around the world, sung and played whenever a musical symbol of Australia was required.

Although it no longer has that status, it is still considered by many to be the 'unofficial national anthem'. 'Waltzing Matilda' was, briefly, Australia's official 'national song'. Its tale of a swagman being caught stealing sheep and then suiciding rather than surrender to the representatives of wealth and power resonates with the legends of the bush and our cherished, but inaccurate, belief that we are a nation of independent types who take no heed of uniforms or status. Christina Macpherson's decisive musical role in the making of 'Waltzing Matilda' is still not a central part of the song's creation story. She is now revealed as the rightful—and equal—musical partner of the poet, Paterson.

There is a growing recognition that Christina Macpherson was erased from the 'Waltzing Matilda' creation story. There is currently a strong push for a statue of her to accompany that of Paterson at the forecourt of what seems to be the world's only museum to a song, the Waltzing Matilda Centre at Winton. Perhaps there will be one day.

The Anzac News

In 1915 tens of thousands of Australians and New Zealanders were brought together into the Australian and New Zealand Army Corps—ANZAC. The name has been with us ever since, becoming an iconic, even sacred, word that generations of Australians have related to and whose use is even controlled by Commonwealth legislation. The soldiers of the corps created many of their own newspapers and magazines. These hastily produced publications were often cobbled together on troopships or in camps behind the lines. Some were even created near the front on Gallipoli and at the Western Front as well as in Palestine and Egypt. Some were printed, some produced on spirit duplicators and some were handwritten with the carbon copies passed along from soldier to soldier. The 'trench journals', as they are often called, carried verse, yarns, cartoons, jokes, snippets of news, gossip and hearsay, all jostling together in a lively froth of humour, sharp satire and the occasional critical comment. They provide a unique picture of the realities of active duty life and death, written and drawn by, for and about diggers.

During the Dardanelles campaign, a number of these publications appeared, including the *Anzac Argus*, *The Dardanelles Driveller* and *Sniper's Shots* and, in book form shortly after the evacuation, the famous *Anzac Book*. The 4th Light Horse published *The Bran Mash*, a pun on the usual horse feed. Scribbled in pencil on two leaves of official typing paper with the dateline of 'Anzac Cove, Gallipoli June 15, 1915', it featured a few basic cartoons and poems like 'The Trooper's Lament' in which an anonymous Light Horseman complained of being separated from his 'prad' or horse and having to serve as an infantryman.

> But let me feel just once again me old prad shy an' reef,
> An' you can 'ave me biscuit an' me tin of bully beef.
> MY ---- OATH!!

The Dinkum Oil—meaning the 'truth'—lasted longer than most of the Gallipoli periodicals. When a German aeroplane dropped leaflets over Anzac 'telling Australians and New Zealanders "not to hesitate further but to come in and surrender"', the editors immediately responded with an 'Extra Special Edition'. It included the mock headline 'AUSTRALIANS RUSH TO SURRENDER':

> A German aeroplane passed over Anzac yesterday and distributed a lot of leaflets, advising the Australian troops not to hesitate any longer, but come and surrender. (This is the first bit of true news 'The Dinkum Oil' has published and we thoroughly expect it will be the last).

We have since received the following urgent cables from our correspondents:

Quinn's Post, 2a.m.—Scramble of Australians out of trenches to get into Turkish lines is so great that parapets completely broken down. The scene reminded onlookers of the memorable rush on the canteens in 1902.

Quinn's Post—2.51 a.m.—Dreadful mistake has occurred. The Turks did not realise that the Australians were coming to surrender, and accordingly made a tactical readjustment of their firing line, and our men found the trenches empty. Thousands of Australians are now wandering about disconsolately looking for some Turk to surrender to.

The satire went on say that those attempting to surrender later found a German officer asleep in a trench. 'After having finished remaining beer bottles for him the Australians awakened him and nearly smothered him with kisses.'

Heavy-handed though it might seem today, humour like this became essential to maintaining morale right through the war. In Palestine the Mechanical Transport Services published the *Gamrah Weekly Wail* and the 3rd Field Troop Engineers created the *Palestine Prattle*. *The Kia Ora Coo-ee* was published in Palestine and Egypt by the combined ANZAC forces in Egypt, while the 3rd Light Horse Field Artillery published the *Desert Dust Bin*. Camel Corps journals included *The Cacolet* (after the carrying frames fitted to camels and mules) and *Barrak*. *The Kia Ora Coo-ee* carried verse by a Major Paterson, better known as Australia's most famous poet of the day, 'Banjo' Paterson, including one on a more serious note, titled 'Moving On':

In this war we're always moving on,
Moving on;
When we make a friend another friend has gone;
Should a woman's kindly face
Make us welcome for a space,
Then its boot and saddle, boys, we're
Moving on.
In the hospitals they're moving,
Moving on;
They're here today, tomorrow they are gone;
When the bravest and the best
Of the boys you know 'go west',
Then you're choking down your tears and
Moving on.

On the Western Front the need to express the diggers' view of the war continued with trench newspapers like the 7th Field Artillery Brigade's *Yandoo*, *Digger*, the *Rising Sun* and, later on, the famous *Aussie*. The Australian 1st Field Ambulance periodical gloried in the title *Ghutz*. Other Western Front titles included *Honk*, the work of 5th Corps Ammunition Park, which, in August 1915, carried this brief but evocative piece by Sergeant C. Strong:

Whilst seated one day on my lorry,
Weary and ill at ease,
I saw a gunner scratching
As though he was full of fleas.
I asked him why he was scratching
And what was he scratching for,
But his only reply was a long drawn sigh,
And he carefully killed some more.

Printed 'Somewhere in France', the *Rising Sun* was first published on Christmas Day 1916. Edited by the official Australian war correspondent, C.E.W. Bean, it carried verse like this piece of poetic homesickness by 'Pip':

> I am standing in the trenches with the mud up to my knees
> And I'm thinking of the bushland far away;
> Where we used to gallop madly through the gum and wattle trees;
> And the horse I used to ride—the Dapple Grey.

In the many deprivations of the war, soldiers found solace in even the smallest of comforts. Food, a warm mug of tea or cocoa, a bath, the rum ration or tobacco: these commonplaces of everyday civilian life were at a premium at the front and were highly valued, as their frequent appearance in the Anzac press attested. 'My Lady Nicotine' appeared in *The Anzac Book*, penned by a grateful digger named H.G. (Hugh) Garland, who had been a journalist before the war, and included the lines:

> Her gift is small and seemingly
> Of little value, yet
> It teaches me so charmingly
> To think and to forget.
> So I and those along with me
> In all this dreary scene
> Unite in giving thanks to thee,
> My Lady Nicotine.

Garland was awarded the Distinguished Conduct Medal (DCM) in 1916 but was killed in France in 1918, aged twenty-four.

Not surprisingly, the Anzac newspapers featured many items about homesickness and going home after the war's end. In one of the papers produced during a long voyage aboard the troopship *Port Lyttelton* under the title *Lytteltonik*, one especially enthusiastic digger wrote: 'Australia is the cleanest, sweetest, healthiest, sunniest, happiest, and everythingelsest country in the whole blooming world. Amen!'

A Special Kind of Magic

In 2016, *The School Magazine of Literature for Our Boys and Girls* celebrated 100 years of continuous publication. The original stuffy title disappeared long ago but primary school children in New South Wales and around the country are still entranced by its stories, pictures, poems, games and activities of all kinds. Now known as *The School Magazine*, it is truly an institution. It is both Australia's longest-running magazine and the world's oldest children's periodical.

The magazine sprang into life during World War I at the start of the 1916 school year. Published by the New South Wales Department of Education, the periodical aimed to give kids of that time a regular dose of solid educational information mixed with stories, plays, poems and more—facts trimmed with fun. From the start, it featured Australian authors, such as Mary Gilmore, as well as some pretty heavy prose and poetry from British writers such as Sir Walter Scott, Alfred Tennyson and William Wordsworth, as well as the king of nonsense verse, Lewis Carroll. Today, the magazine still keeps to its central mission of mixing education and entertainment with a lively mix of poetry, prose, songs, pictures, plays, non-fiction, reviews, puzzles and more, often relevant to topical issues such as the environment.

As part of the 2016 centenary celebrations, the National Centre for Australian Children's Literature asked readers past and present for their thoughts and feelings. One woman recalled her mother reading to her from the earliest editions. She read it herself during the 1940s and her grandchildren were still reading it. Another woman who attended primary school in the 1950s and 1960s still had her copies, cherished memories preserved in the special cardboard folders issued to schools for kids to retain their copies. That certainly worked. The folders were funded by local businesses who also advertised through them.

The influence of the magazine went well beyond the classroom. In families where money was too tight to buy books or other publications, the issues provided reading opportunities for everyone. The magazine often featured extracts from works for children, introducing readers to books they might otherwise have missed in the more frugal eras of the past. Immigrant children from non-English speaking countries learned the language through the magazine; so did their parents in some cases.

Especially during the early decades of its existence, teachers found the magazine an invaluable teaching tool. The production and distribution of 'educational resources' is a relatively recent—and welcome—development. In earlier times, these were scarce, expensive and pretty boring. *The School Magazine* gave often struggling teachers materials they could use for instruction, comprehension and development of reading, colouring and other skills.

Even discipline could be inflicted through the magazines. One man recalled his teacher making a disobedient class analyse paragraphs. 'We certainly learnt our grammar', he said. 'You would think that would have turned me off English but I became an English teacher!' As well as punishment, the popular periodical could be used to reward achievement. A woman recalled blitzing her spelling test and being allowed to spend twenty minutes outside the classroom doing nothing but reading the magazine.

The other essential ingredient in the success of *The School Magazine* has been to provide paid opportunities for creativity. Australian writers and illustrators of all styles have been, and are, published in its many pages. Some of the country's most loved and awarded creators have had their work appear, some going on to substantial national and international careers. More than a few of them read the magazine with pleasure during their own childhoods and also found their first publication success in one of its issues. Author and illustrator Sophie Masson was one of these. She recalled her excited absorption in her copies, reading them all the way home from school along the highway, bumping distractedly into telegraph poles as she went.

Today, this educational and creative institution is a thoroughly modern enterprise, appearing in different print, digital and age-group formats each month, together with related teaching and learning resources. It goes to more than 4000 schools around Australia and some people continue to subscribe to it many years or decades after they leave primary school. The kids still love it, too. A young girl said in 2023: 'Your magazine is so cool because you have cool cartoons, crosswords and very good poems. The plays are very hilarious. You have magic tricks that are amazing but quite hard. I really like the puzzling tales. You make the best mag! Keep up the good work!' And a young boy expressed his appreciation of the magazine and looked forward to a future as cherished as its past: 'I love your magazine so much that when I get it I literally read the whole thing straight away. I enjoy reading the magazines over and over again. I hope you continue making wonderful magazines for years to come'.

That is a special kind of magic.

Louie the Fly

You may think that this story is frivolous, but the tale of how we have dealt with one of our most inconvenient insects has involved many state and local government departments and campaigns, the Commonwealth Scientific and Industrial Research Organisation (CSIRO) and the advertising and media industries, as well as a large corporate sector devoted to swatting or otherwise exterminating the buzzing pests. All this activity, inventiveness, entrepreneurialism and creativity has also produced one of our most memorable advertising jingles and the gangster-like figure known to almost everyone as 'Louie the Fly'—'straight from rubbish tip to you'.

Flies have been here forever and have important functions in pollinating plants and recycling nutrients. Many varieties are unique to Australia, others arrived with Europeans. As the cattle and sheep industries grew, so did the fly population, finding a congenial breeding place in the dung, which was rapidly accumulating because the local beetles did not break it down. The irritating, buzzing pests were usually the first thing newcomers complained about and one of the first things they tried to control. The 'Australian salute', a frequent waving of the hand in front of the face was probably the first response, quickly followed by frantic swatting with a few leaves and burning smoky fires. Keeping the mouth tightly closed and speaking as little as possible is also said to be an Australian characteristic and a reaction to the swarming insects.

None of these tactics were, or are, very effective, so attempts to find natural repellents began early, with people trying to make potions from various plants. In the 1870s a German immigrant named J. Hagemann extracted pyrethrum from chrysanthemums and marketed it as an insecticidal powder. The product was sold under the brand name 'Mortein', derived from the French *mort* for dead (Mrs Hageman was French) and the German *ein*, for one—'dead one'.

At first, the powder was sprinkled around. Later it was distributed with a squeeze puffer. But it was in 1928 that a liquid version was developed, together with what was known as a 'flit gun'. Mortein was mixed with kerosene, poured into a small canister attached to what looked like a bicycle pump. Flies were dispatched with the crude but workable aerosol created. This was the most effective form of repellent until the 1950s when the pressure pack ('pak') arrived. So did Louie.

The tough-talking cartoon fly figure originated in the early 1950s with the late advertising executive and author, Bryce Courtenay. But it was not until 1957 that he made his first television appearance to promote Mortein. In 1962 Louie gained a jingle. The song he sang was composed by James Joseph White, and White took out copyright on this alone of all his compositions—a prescient decision, as it turned out: Louie was an instant hit.

While Mortein and other brands of insecticide did provide some protection from the pests, dealing with them was still an uphill battle as the flies continued to breed in their bothersome billions. By the 1960s the flies were not only a nuisance, but also a problem for pastoralists, a threat to public health and a national embarrassment. So was the dung that prevented pasture growing. Something had to be done. It was. The scientists were called in.

Between the 1960s and the 1980s the CSIRO, under the leadership of Hungarian-born Dr George Bornemissza, conducted the 'Australian Dung Beetle Project'. The idea was to introduce the beetles from overseas in the hope that they would consume cow pats and so reduce the number of flies hatching. There was a lot of necessary trial and error involved and funding for the work eventually ran out. But its success in reducing flies, for a while at least, was confirmed in later research, along with other environmental benefits. Research with the beetles was taken up again in the 1990s and, in one form or another, has continued to the present.

So has Louie. Anyone who lived in Australia since the late 1950s and up to the 2010s would have found it as difficult to avoid Louie as it was to avoid the real flies. He was a continual presence on television and other advertising media until 2011. In that year, Louie's keepers conducted a public relations campaign that purported to bring an end to Louie's long flight. The public were invited to vote for the retention of the feisty fly—or else! Two hundred and fifty thousand votes were eventually received in favour of reprieving Louie.

Louie is not only an Australian celebrity, but he is also a star in India where he has been employed in various advertising campaigns, most recently in 2022 when he appeared as an 'all-new meaner, stronger and more menacing avatar: dheeth machhar'. This time, though, Louie is a mosquito, an even more dangerous insect pest.

People sometimes say that Australians have a weird sense of humour. It's probably true that—not withstanding Louie's moonlighting as a mozzie in India—we are the only country with a jingle about a fly as a centrepiece of popular culture, so maybe they're right? In any case, Louie and his song are recognised in the National Film and Sound Archive *Sounds of Australia* registry alongside the earliest recording of 'Waltzing Matilda', sung by John Collinson, Nellie Melba's 'Chant Vénitien' and that other advertising jingle classic, 'The Aeroplane Jelly Song'.

A Crystal Mystery

In July 1932, readers of the Brisbane *Sunday Mail* could have turned to the popular column known as 'Our Wireless Circle'. The column, hosted by 'Proton', began with an enthusiastic endorsement of a 'crystal receiver', as very early radio sets were known: 'The Mystery crystal receiver is so called because I do not know just why it should be so good, and after trying it out for about a fortnight I am more amazed at the results than before. It is without a doubt the best crystal set that I have heard.' Crystal sets were clever but very basic gadgets built by hobbyists with an interest in receiving radio broadcasts for next to nothing and, of course, for the challenge presented by wiring up things called coils, detectors and capacitors. The reward, if you got everything just right, was an often faint but discernible radio signal from one or more stations broadcasting in your area and possibly well beyond. In the days before valve radios were widespread, the crystal set, which required no external power supply, was a popular alternative way to hear music, news, sport and other entertainments on the air. The primitive circuits for constructing the sets varied slightly and gave differing results, but hobbyists—early examples of hackers—experimented keenly with many different combinations in the hope of coming up with the best possible combination of components.

'Proton' thought that his 'mystery' crystal set was better than good, even though he wasn't too sure why. The *Sunday Mail* had often published circuits for its avid readership of radio builders, some achieving 'Australia-wide fame'. But this one was different: 'When you look at the diagram you will note that it is quite a different arrangement from that which you normally see in crystal circuits, but nevertheless it is a simple crystal receiver that will cost only a few shillings, and sufficiently selective to separate all the local stations without any overlap, and bring them in with enough volume to make the reception enjoyable.' The column continued with the technical details necessary to build this piece of proto-electronic alchemy. As Proton wrote, his set was different though that is not readily apparent from the circuit design. What was that difference? He seems to have stumbled on a previously unknown characteristic of the crystal radio. An enduring enigma was born as the design was taken up throughout Australia, and beyond.

Readers of Proton's column were deeply engaged with it and its subject. There was a lively exchange of comment, ideas and occasional complaint through the letters sent to the *Sunday Mail*. These were received with humour and civility and often led to improvements to previously published designs as the many members of the wireless community experimented and reported their results: what stations could be received, or not; a better way to put a crystal set together; how many turns of wire on the coil and other intricate technicalities guaranteed to glaze the eyes of any but the true radio buff. The original Mystery Crystal Set was so popular in Australia that reader feedback eventually led to an improved 'Mystery Plus Crystal Set' for them to build the following year.

In our era of instant communication of everything, the importance of radio has been largely forgotten. As well as its original intended use for communication, broadcast radio became the first electronic technology to bring everyday information and entertainment straight into the family home. Broadcast radio began in Australia during the early 1920s and grew rapidly. Few newspapers did not carry information about broadcast times and programs, advertisements for radios and often extensive columns on the technicalities of doing it yourself.

At first, the commercially produced receivers required to enjoy whatever was sent out on the airwaves were too expensive for the average family, especially with the licence fee required to own a radio at that time. The earlier receiver, or 'detector', popularly known as a 'crystal set', became a favoured way to access the airwaves on a budget. Probably millions of people built these gadgets in those countries where broadcast radio was available, and they were especially popular in Australia where newspapers and magazines frequently carried columns like 'Our Wireless World'. Australians seem to be an inventive and curious people and took to the DIY of early radio with gusto, forming clubs to swap ideas and source the basic components needed to build amplifiers, valve radios and other gadgets, as well as crystal sets. The *Wireless Weekly* magazine began in 1922, others followed, all founded on a growing public fascination with the wonders of the air.

By the end of the 1940s, the era of the crystal set was over, as the more functional valve radio receivers became cheaper and more widely available. Radio was by then a central part of Australian life and leisure and remained so until the advent of television from the 1950s. But many people continued to build crystal sets and some still do today. Electronic supply shops often sell them in kit form as an introduction to electronics and radio technology. But despite all our subsequent electronic sophistication, the 1932 crystal set from the *Sunday Mail* continues to puzzle makers.

One latter-day experimenter in America decided to build his own version of the device to solve the technicalities of its cunning design. Crystal sets of the early era, and usually since, depended on a 'coil', comprising coils of wire wound round a cylinder, together with a long, high antenna. The signal comes into the aerial and is transmitted to the coil, which is 'earthed' to the ground to allow the signal to flow through the circuit. One of the oddities of the Mystery Crystal Set is that, unlike other designs, there is no direct connection between the aerial and the earth. In theory, it should not work. Those who have sought to plumb the puzzles of the set have discovered that it uses a clever, if seemingly inadvertent, technical trick to complete the circuit through the winding of its two coils. With the wisdom of almost a century since Proton's original serendipitous design, the modern maker was able to introduce a few tweaks that dramatically improved its performance, successfully picking up stations broadcasting more than a thousand kilometres from his location in Florida.

Around 2001 Australian enthusiast Ken Harthun had a go at re-creating both models. He used some more modern components, including better headphones, and found the deluxe version was still 'the best simple set I've tried for casual listening on local signals.' But despite better modern technology, the device worked best with its original crude crystal detector rather than the modern equivalent.

Have modern tweaks and original components solved the crystal set mystery? Well, maybe. Crystal-set hobbyists are always experimenting with the gadgets of the past, either to reconstruct them or to improve them. Whatever they might or might not come up with, the humble crystal set brought the delights of radio to many who would otherwise not have had the pleasure.

The 100th anniversary of Australia's first public radio broadcast was on 23 November 2023. The Sydney Symphony Orchestra kicked off that historic moment with Camille Saint-Saëns' 'Le cygne' ('The Swan') from his *Carnival of the Animals* suite. The National Film and Sound Archive celebrated with an online exhibition called 'Radio 100' that ran in five 'chapters' over 100 days, 'providing a carefully curated insight into the pivotal moments, songs, tech and people in radio's first century.' Online users could 'tune in' to hear historic recordings, a podcast and stories from the golden days of radio to the present. They could even leave a recording of their own radio memories, some perhaps about crystal sets.

Wi-Fi

People in Australia have a long history of inventing useful things. The woomera, or spear thrower, and the boomerang are among a long list of First Nations innovations using the materials of the natural world. Since the colonial era, people have used their wits and knowledge to develop, or lay the foundation for the development of, the stump-jump plough and other agricultural implements, refrigeration, the electric drill, the black box recorder, ultrasound and the bionic ear, among many other functional devices.

A good idea is often obvious after someone has had it. One of those was the humble, simple but very useful notepad. It was invented in Tasmania when a Launceston stationer, J.A. Birchall, decided that single sheets of paper were too large and fiddly for taking and keeping notes. He cut the sheets in half and glued them together at the top on a cardboard backing, christening his innovation the 'Silver City Writing Tablet'. Seemingly a 'no-brainer' now, Birchall has the credit for being the first to combine paper, glue and cardboard into something that did not previously exist. It is often the melding of existing technologies and materials that creates valuable inventions.

One particular innovation has profoundly changed the way Australians, and much of the world, organise their lives. The wireless communications technology in our homes and communities—'wi-fi'—was the end result of decades of research, beginning with Guglielmo Marconi's work on radio waves. A clever electronic chip, known as a fast Fourier transform (FFT) processing chip was invented by an Australian and eventually enabled CSIRO scientists to develop the local area networks (LANs) that most of us depend on every day and almost everywhere. It has been hailed as possibly the most important Australian invention ever and is one of the world's most celebrated technological innovations. But we almost lost it.

Nowadays, Wi-fi is a central element of the larger technological revolution generally known as the 'internet'. This electronic communications network is the outcome of the serendipitous merging of several technologies, including the business and personal computer, the World Wide Web and broadband. As the internet and the part of it that most of us are familiar with, the World Wide Web, grew from the 1990s, there was a need for moving ever larger amounts of data as quickly as possible. John O'Sullivan and his fellow researchers—John Deane, Graham Daniels, Terry Percival and Diethelm Ostry—went to work on solving the tricky problem of separating large amounts of data into small packages, transmitting them on a range of radio frequencies and reassembling them into the right order—almost instantly. It turned out that the FFT chip, originally invented in the 1970s by John O'Sullivan for use with radio telescopes, was the means to achieve this apparent miracle.

Patents were filed in Australia and the United States, but by 2002 technology companies were beginning to use the technology in commercial applications without regard to the CSIRO claims to the invention. Polite attempts to get the big companies to pay up went nowhere and the relatively small CSIRO began legal proceedings against the goliaths of some of the world's largest enterprises in 2005. It was not until 2009 that, one by one, the fourteen tech corporations settled through an out-of-court agreement with the CSIRO, reportedly for more than $200 million. The CSIRO then began proceedings against mobile telephone providers who were also using its wi-fi technology without a licence. Eventually hundreds of millions more came back to the organisation after another out-of-court settlement, helping to fund future Australian research and development.

In 2012, John O'Sullivan and his research team were acknowledged and honoured in the European Inventor Awards for 'making the wireless LAN as fast and powerful as the cabled solutions of the time, and is the basis for the wireless networking technology (wi-fi) now used in billions of devices worldwide. O'Sullivan and his team thus ushered in the age of high-speed, always-on wireless connectivity we enjoy today.

Other CSIRO inventions include solar hot water, distance measuring equipment (DME), the 'Siroset' permanent wool-creasing process, polymer bank notes, Relenza anti-flu medication and a range of other genetic, medical and technical innovations.

Another invention has immeasurably improved our lives and originated with research by Dr Douglas Waterhouse into sheep blowfly. The lessons from this work were applied in World War II to protect soldiers in the mosquito-ridden Pacific from the likelihood of contracting malaria from mosquito bites. Known to the troops as 'Mary', it worked, but was not made into a commercial product until the 1960s after the repellent was used by Queen Elizabeth II while she played golf. The Mortein insecticide company saw that the spray was effective and acquired the formula, legally, from the CSIRO. And that was the origin of Aerogard.

The CSIRO had its beginnings in the period after Federation and, under various names, grew into a national body in the 1920s. After developing research in agriculture, forestry, food and fuels, the Council of Scientific and Industrial Research, as it was then known, conducted defence research during World War II, expanding later into other areas including building materials, land resources and woollen textiles. In 1949, the institution was given its present name and today is engaged with solving many of the world's most pressing problems, especially those related to global warming and climate change.

What will they come up with next?

There are different versions of the origins of the Australian kelpie. The best documented story has the iconic working dogs being first bred on George Robertson's 'Warrock' property in Victoria in the mid-nineteenth century.

8

COMMUNITIES

Eliza Batman's £1 Notes

Somewhere in the paupers' section of Geelong cemetery lies Elizabeth Callaghan, one of Australia's forgotten pioneers. Found guilty of passing forged £1 notes, the seventeen-year-old was lucky not be hanged alongside one of her male accomplices. Instead, her death sentence was commuted and in 1821 she was transported for fourteen years. On arrival in Van Diemen's Land, the conduct of the small, dark-haired woman from County Clare, Ireland, was described as 'bad'. From this inauspicious beginning, eighteen- or nineteen-year-old Eliza was destined for an eventful life and a violent death in colonial Australia.

Eliza's record in Van Diemen's Land was one of drunkenness and regular absconding from her assigned duties. Like the many other convict women who refused to bow to the system, she suffered the punishments of the stocks, solitary confinement and the degradation of an iron neck-collar. Her final flight took her to the Tasmanian midlands, where she was sheltered by New South Wales–born settler, John Batman, with whom she soon bore the first of eight children. Although Eliza was still a fugitive, the couple was granted permission to marry in 1828, consolidating Eliza's now-privileged role in her husband's substantial property holdings.

Batman was considered by some a progressive settler in his relations with Traditional Owners, providing assistance to those in need. Yet he played a primary role in the notorious Black War of 1828–1834, which included leading the Ben Lomond massacre of 1829. During this period, Batman also adopted, or otherwise acquired from their families, three First Nations boys. Two-year-old Rolepana was a survivor of the Ben Lomond massacre, insensitively renamed 'Ben Lomond' by the Batmans. The other two boys were Lurnerminner, known as Jack or 'Jacky' Allen, and one simply renamed 'John Batman'.

As mistress of the household, Eliza had responsibility for the boys' education and religious instruction, including their baptism. The boys worked around the Batman's property alongside other workers, convict and First Nations. While this seems like a relatively benign form of servitude, the historians of the Eliza Batman story, Penny Edmonds and Michelle Berry, pointed out that pastoral property 'was a site of colonial domesticity, but it was also an unhomely "contact zone".' Like many other First Nations children, these three boys were 'enfolded in colonial intimacies that recast acts of aggression as acts of kindness and civilisation, and dispersal of Aboriginal families as care.' Their identities as well as their bodies became the property of their captors.

Similar stories unfolded across Australia as colonising Europeans simultaneously attempted to exterminate First Nations people and to incorporate them into their own communities. It was possible for John Batman to abduct Rolepana despite being responsible for the deaths of his people. It was also possible for the Batmans to name their seventh daughter Pelonamena, a reinterpretation of the First Nations 'Pellonymyna' from the Ben Lomond area. Edmonds and Berry sought to understand these entangled complexities of frontier violence and domestic life. Their research 'opens uncomfortable vistas onto the pastoral frontier where colonial women, forced kinship, affection and violence were bound together.'

In 1835, Batman crossed Bass Strait to Port Phillip with his household of convicts and First Nations boys and men. He concluded an agreement referred to as a 'treaty' with the Traditional Owners of the Yarra River regions, now collec- tively referred to as the Kulin Nation. The Kulin were almost certainly unaware of what Batman was proposing. They lost their land while Batman and his family were enriched. He was later honoured as the founding father of Melbourne. But his claim on around a quarter of a million hectares of Kulin country was private rather than official. Batman came under pressure from the colonial authorities to relinquish the property he was occupying. Although John and Eliza had separated, she sailed to England in February 1839 to pursue the family petition to remain in the home they had built together. But the appeal was unsuccessful and when she returned over a year later, John Batman was dead.

The entrepreneurial squatter died rich but with his affairs in disarray. Eliza and other members of the family, as well as some of Batman's employees, contested the will. Eliza ended up losing most of the property while still having responsibility for the children, who were sent to live with family and friends. Rolepana found work but died in 1842. Lurnerminner went whaling and later returned to Tasmania. The fate of the second 'John Batman' is not known.

Eliza married a former Batman employee, William Willoughby, in 1841 but the marriage failed. A second approach to the Crown for compensation of the lost Port Phillip lands was unsuccessful. After the drowning death of her only son in 1845, Eliza fell into difficult circumstances. She was brutally murdered in West Geelong where she was living as 'Sarah Willoughby' in 1852. Described as a woman 'of somewhat abandoned character', Eliza had been brutally attacked and the local press reported that her body 'presents as horrible an appearance as ever human eyes beheld.' She seems to have been involved in a drunken dispute over a bank note of the same forged value that sent her to Van Diemen's Land. As the press described it: 'a disturbance had taken place between the deceased, a woman named Eliza Wilson, and one or two men. This coupled with other information, induced the police to apprehend the woman, Eliza Wilson and a man named John Trigg. On searching the female prisoner at the watchhouse a one-pound note with fresh blood stains on it was found concealed under her arm pit.' Whatever the circumstances that led to this incident, the authorities did not bring charges against the two survivors and they were controversially released a few months later.

Eliza was buried in a still unmarked grave. Although a plaque records her earthly existence, her historical legacy, as both a poor Irish convict woman and a privileged white coloniser, remains uncertain. Her story remains entwined with the controversial life and legend of John Batman, as well as the contradictions and complexities of colonial communities.

An Unlit Beacon

Thomas Raine was still in his teens when he sailed to Australia as a junior officer on the convict ship *Surry* in 1815. An outbreak of typhus left him the only surviving officer. As the acting master, he managed to navigate the ship to China to pick up a cargo and on the way encountered a sandy Barrier Reef island. More than 600 kilometres north-west of Cairns, Queensland, the 32-hectare coral cay was given the young acting captain's name in 1824, but, to the First Nations communities who benefited from it, the island was known by much older names.

The Wuthathi knew it as Thukuruu; the Meriam people as Bub warwar kaur. The island has been used for thousands of years by the Wuthathi, Meriam Le, Erubam Le and Ugarem Le peoples who went there to collect guano and the turtle eggs and hatchlings that also attracted tiger sharks, animals that play an important role in the traditions of the Torres Strait. Wuthathi legend has the island being formed when the body of a tiger shark drifted there after it drowned trying to help carry a crocodile.

The island became of interest to settlers because it was on the sailing route from Australia to Asia. Ships took what was known as the 'outer passage' and then turned west through the Torres Straits. The route was dangerous. In 1842 the 600-odd ton *Martha Ridgeway* was making for Bombay, India, from New Zealand. On the night of 7 July, the ship struck a reef. The crew tried to lighten the ship by cutting down the mizzenmast but they were unable to free the vessel and abandoned it the next day. Three small boats left the wreck, carrying the captain, officers, steward, crew and one passenger. The boats became separated and the captain's cutter was beached on an island. Efforts by one of the other boats to get them off failed and each of the three boats was left to its own fate. Unlike many shipwreck tales, this one ended well, with all being rescued by some of the many ships passing through the busy route.

The *Martha Ridgeway* was not the only vessel wrecked in these dangerous waters and the Admiralty in Britain decided to build a beacon on the island. In 1844 a party of convict stonemasons and labourers were shipped to the island and set to work building a rudimentary lighthouse. Stone was quarried from the island and seashells burned to make lime for mortar. The timbers of the stranded *Martha Ridgeway* were plundered for building materials and after four months' work, a stone tower 12 metres high and topped with wood and canvas stood proudly on the shore ready to warn mariners of dangerous waters.

But the light was never lit. By the time the beacon was ready for operation, a new, safer route to Asia had been opened and there was no further use for a warning light. But there was a big demand for guano, or phosphatic rock, for fertilisers. In 1890 a guano mining company built a jetty, accommodation and tramlines to enable the digging and shipping of the valuable commodity. A hundred Chinese and Malay labourers worked the site for two years under ten European supervisors. The manager, Albert F. Ellis, had his mother living with him on the island. Annie Eliza Ellis died in June 1891, proclaiming her faith in her 'God of Love'. She is buried on the island.

The guano mining operation ceased in 1892 and the island returned to its previous isolation, now bearing the marks and memorials of European endeavour. Traditional Owners were free to return to their customary activities and to begin new practices. The wind- and wave-ravaged stone beacon became an informal message hub. People have left more than 900 legible names or inscriptions in the walls as messages for any who might come there.

By the 1980s, conditions at the beacon's extreme location had seriously degraded the structure. Restoration efforts were carried out then, and again in the early 2020s, this time involving the island's Traditional Owners, some of whom were descended from those who first wrote their names on the beacon. Chairman of the Mer Gedkem Le (Torres Strait Islanders) Corporation, Falen Passi, pointed out that the Traditional Owners of the region 'are part of the seabird at Raine Island, and we are also part of that island.'

Raine Island—Thukuruu, Bub warwar kaur—'is considered one of the most important historical monuments in the Great Barrier Reef World Heritage Area and is listed on the State Heritage Register and the Register of the National Estate.' But there are fears that the island, together with its wildlife, traditional associations and stone tower may not survive severe weather events or the effects of climate change. Even the mytho-logically important tiger sharks are declining. Those involved with the current restoration project hope that the Traditional

Owners, working together with scientists, can preserve the island and, most importantly, its meanings for First Australians and European settlers. As Falen Passi put it: 'You've got to lean on your history, your language, your songs, lean on the history and you will survive'.

How to Build a Village

George Robertson was a man of his era. A believer in the ability of the individual to do whatever was needed in life and to continually improve in every way. A 'man of sterling worth to the community', as his obituary described him in 1890.

George had used his time well, firstly in his native Dundee and from the 1840s, in Victoria. In Scotland the young George not only learned the trades of wood, but excelled in them. He also took the trouble to learn agricultural and architectural skills. When he immigrated, firstly to Tasmania and later to Victoria, he brought his quality tools and his architectural knowledge with him and put them to good use in building one of Australia's most unusual settlements. He started by gaining practical experience in managing the land around Casterton and worked on local farms until he had learned enough and saved enough to purchase the large property, or station, on the Glenelg River known as 'Warrock'. And then he began to build, almost entirely in wood.

He firstly erected a small cottage and a woodshed. Later, he built a larger residence, which he extended in the early 1850s when he married his cousin, Mary Ann Robertson. Eventually, George handcrafted almost sixty buildings—a village. Arranged around a 'green', the self-contained settlement boasted a dairy, grain store, woolshed, blacksmith's shop, stables, a smoke house, accommodation for the station workers, a store for meat, a coach house and, of course, a church. There were also structures for slaughtering animals and drying their skins as well as accommodation for bullocks and pigs, barns and sheds for storing hay. Most of the buildings are of a Gothic style and bear the evidence of a master craftsman's attention to detail and a practical man's understanding of function. George and Mary were keen gardeners and constructed Australia's earliest known greenhouse to further their horticultural interests. There were also dog kennels, closely connected with George's other claim to fame—a part in the origin of the Australian kelpie.

Like most origin stories, there is more than a hint of folklore about the creation of the fabled Australian working dog. It was once widely held that Scottish collies were crossbred with dingoes to produce the original kelpies. This romantically nationalistic myth was scotched, so to speak, a few years ago when scientists showed there is no genetic evidence for this version of events. While kelpies may well have later mated with dingoes, they did not originate from them.

Instead, it is generally accepted that the foundation female that began the line that became the kelpie breed was born at Warrock, offspring of George Robertson's black-and-tan collies. This dog passed to a local, J.D. 'Jack' Gleeson, who called her 'Kelpie' after the Scottish water sprite and later crossed her with a black dog, also bred from a dog imported from Scotland. The resulting litter was 'highly successful and a great line of dogs evolved.' Later mating of Gleeson's dog with another descended from different dogs brought from Scotland produced a female, also named 'Kelpie' after her mother. This dog was considered an outstanding contestant in the first Sheep Dog Trial at Forbes, New South Wales, in 1872. The name 'kelpie' was then given to the entire breed.

Whatever the exact origins and genetics of the kelpie breed, the dogs are considered to be 'worth pretty much a farmhand in terms of the work they help you accomplish on farms and in saleyards', according to Professor Claire Wade, one of the scientists who conducted the research into kelpie genes.

While the subsequent events in the evolution of the kelpie took place elsewhere, George Robertson can rightly claim to have provided the progeny of the iconic animal. He was not a man to seek glory. A generous benefactor of various Christian churches, local mechanics institutes and hospitals, he 'was chary of accepting Honours', preferring a quiet but productive life with Mary. The couple had no children and Mary died in 1886, by which time the family holdings had been significantly enlarged. Warrock was around 6500 hectares and carried more than 18,000 sheep. The station passed to a nephew whose descendants held it for several generations. After being held by other owners, the property was purchased by a local farming family who are currently restoring the National Trust buildings and developing what is probably Victoria's most important pastoral station into a heritage tourism destination.

Goldfields Folk

The Victorian goldfields were bustling, hustling places of aspiration, hard work, violence and grog. Among the thousands seeking their fortunes, usually in vain, were memorable characters of all kinds. Lost to history but for a chance sketch by a passing writer, a few of these people deserve to be remembered for their colour and quirkiness.

The enormous Mrs Bunting, whose bulk was compared to 'a steam-boiler on horseback', was the wife of a McIvor diggings storekeeper in the early 1850s. Well known, and often fined as a sly-grog seller, she cared little for the law, such as it was, or for the dangers of goldfields life. As well as feathering her nest through grog selling, Mrs Bunting had another lucrative business. When other stores were closed for Sunday, she displayed a large sign at the front of her establishment reading 'GOLD BOUGHT THIS DAY'. Turning a profit from this enterprise meant Mrs Bunting had to get the gold to Melbourne, always a dangerous undertaking with bushrangers a very real threat at many points along the way. Undaunted, Mrs Bunting stuck two pistols in her belt and drove a cart down the track towards the city. Cracking her whip and whistling, she drove ahead of the regular gold escort wagon for the entire journey, even promising to protect the escort if they were attacked. 'Everybody knows Mrs Bunting, and has anecdotes to relate of her', wrote her observer.

Another person making a fortune from the diggers rather than the gold itself was an American, Mr Langley. He operated a store tent and an auction tent he called the 'St Louis Stores' and 'St Louis Mart', crying his many wares from a cart or other elevated position. He was described as 'a slight made man, with a rather effeminate style of features, and somewhat sandy whiskers, but especially American, and a regular go-ahead one. He had always a crowd of diggers about him, and sold off their carts, horses, tents, tools, everything, when they were going away. When the diggers' articles were exhausted, he sold his own.'

As well as the necessities of diggings life, Mr Langley also had a thriving trade in books, which he passed off with an impressive spiel:

> You might hear him puffing off old dirty volumes, as 'these splendid volumes;' 'these works that every one ought to know something of; this work which treats of a nation that we all ought to make ourselves acquainted with; this curious work in which the author has said things of illus-trious characters—by the bye, how could this extraordinary volume get here? Why, it is not to be had in London. That is singular, how it escaped the book-hunters in Europe; — this most inquisitive, Paul Pry of a —' all this time turning over the leaves, breaking out in broader and broader smiles, as if quite forgetful of his audience in the piquant pleasantries and secrets of the book; but all the time listening to the five, ten, fifteen shillings of the eager and rapidly advancing biddings; when, knocking off for some nineteen shillings a greasy tome not worth sixpence on a London book-stall, he would say,—'Ah! you've a prize there, my friend; that's the gem of the auction—nay, I should say of the colony; I should have liked to keep that myself.' And then he immediately proceeded to sell some still greater wonder.

These chirpy auction performances involved plenty of feedback from the crowd, with heckling and joking ably parried by the wily American. But one day, he was bested.

Langley was putting on his usual show when a drunken digger stumbled by. He was carrying his 'cradle', a wooden device for separating gold from gravel, on his head. He stopped opposite Langley and proceeded to auction off the cradle, mimicking Langley's flowery turns of phrase and elaborate gestures. The crowd loved it, of course, as the two verballed each other out to uproarious laughter. Eventually, Langley came up with what could have been a master stroke. He simply put up the digger and his cradle for auction as a single lot. But the digger was not to be outdone. He immediately put up the auctioneer's boots for sale. There was so much laughter from the crowd that Langley had to finally concede that he had been bested.

Even if this was a put-up job between Langley and the digger—an early publicity stunt—scenes like this kept the trader high in the public eye. He capitalised even further on that. After finishing work for the day, Langley would place a brightly coloured cap on his head and ride a horse conspicuously around the diggings until someone bought it from him. He was said to be making several hundred pounds a week through these tricks of his trade.

A baker known as Mr Green was yet another American member of the jostling goldfields community. Like Mrs Bunting, he was a very large, 'a sort of baking Hercules'. With an imposing black moustache and whiskers, Green was a friendly character, an attribute probably sustained by the money he was making. He was said to be worth 20,000 shillings and planned to retire to America within a year.

Despite the rough-and-ready nature of goldfields life, plenty of families tried their luck on the diggings. One such was the Ennis family, who hailed from Hobart and included two parents, an older son and daughter and three younger sisters: Jenny aged eleven, Kitty nine and Lizzy six. While the mother and oldest sister looked after the tent, the father and brother worked a claim. The three younger girls were in charge of the horses, which they rode bareback like experienced equestrians and handled as skilfully as any adult as they hauled firewood back to camp. After seeing to the horses, the girls went fossicking through the old tailings, finding an ounce or so each week. The plan was to make enough in two or three years to return to their beloved Hobart, and it would be nice to think they did.

Goldrush communities were rough and very temporary. Nobody planned to stay longer than necessary. When the gold ran out, the diggers left and those who serviced their needs and wants left with them. Some went home with perhaps enough money to improve their lives. Others followed the hopeful crowds trudging to the next rush—somewhere.

God's Line

This colloquial name is sometimes given to an imaginary line proposed by South Australian Surveyor Goyder in the mid-1860s. The line is usually said to run from Ceduna in the west of South Australia to Spencer Gulf, then north to Orroroo and south and east to Pinnaroo on the Victorian border, joining places where average annual rainfall was measured at around 250–300 millimetres (the exact figure varies). Land to the south of the line was considered suitable for growing crops and land to the north suitable only for grazing. While this seems like a useful piece of practical mapping, it was controversial from the time Goyder put it forward and, for some, it still is today.

George Woodroffe Goyder trained in England as a surveyor and emigrated to Australia in 1848. He worked in Sydney as a draftsman and after a few years joined the South Australian public service. By 1861 he had risen to become the colony's surveyor-general. An energetic and committed official, Goyder advised the government on all aspects of land management, town planning, resource development and agriculture. During his time as surveyor-general, there was an unfounded belief that the arid north of the colony, which then included what is now the Northern Territory, could be made to grow crops. It was said that 'rain would follow the plough' and that planting trees would ensure the necessary levels of precipitation. Until the mid-1860s, the apparent absence of drought in the colony gave support to these beliefs. When drought came in 1864–65, crops began to fail and farmers went broke. Goyder was given the job of finding out how far north farmers could expect to success-fully operate. He travelled through the devastated country, marking those locations where crops had not been blasted by the heat. He drew a 'Line of Rainfall' from west to east and recommended agriculturists should not sow seed further north.

Reactions were swift and strong. 'Goyder's folly' was criticised by many in the north. Property owners feared the valuation of their land would drop. There were debates in parliament and the surveyor-general was widely pilloried. Probably as a result of the reaction and the fact that, if he were right, the government would need to financially support northern farmers from the public purse, nothing further was done with the proposal. The return of good rains after the mid-1860s drought seemed to support the Goyder critics and it was not until the return of drought in the 1880s that the wisdom of the line was officially recognised and it was eventually given his name.

As with most things to do with water, that was not the end of controversy. While Goyder's work and proposal were recognised and rewarded at his retirement, arguments about the accuracy of the line continued. In 1927, a front-page article in the *Adelaide Mail* argued that 'Goyder unerringly separated the land where the rainfall is good from that where it is poor is one of the romances of agricultural development in this State.' According to the detailed analysis: 'much of the country outside the line has been brought into productivity owing to modern methods of cultivation, the imaginary boundary delineated by Goyder as long ago as 1865 is still recognised by the Lands and Survey office, and is regarded as an infallible guide by pastoralists.' Despite this, the state's Land and Survey Office still recognised the line, as did the pastoralists. The boundary is still used today, though it is moving further south as climate change threatens northern cropping and the state's famous winegrowing industry.

On the ground, the number of monuments and memorials erected to Goyder's work is a testament to its continuing significance in the history and industry of South Australia. Monuments Australia records twelve markers, statues and plaques expressing community appreciation of the line and its creator. The latest, unveiled in 2015, celebrated the 150th anniversary of the line and takes the form of a corrugated iron statue by Dudley Siviour, unveiled at Orroroo by two of Goyder's great-great-grandchildren. Interviewed at the ceremony, Chair of the Orroroo Carrieton District Council, Kathie Bowman, observed that the line 'seems pretty obvious to us who live here. It does define a lot about the Orroroo district, about the more reliable cropping country south of the line and the more marginal cropping and grazing country north of the line.'

Today, the Regional Council of Goyder describes that part of the line running through its territory—Ngadjuri country— 'from a little north of Pinnaroo in a curve past Eudunda and Burra to Terowie, then between Yongala and Peterborough, then north-west to Mount Remarkable and south to Moonta.' It is considered 'a very accurate guide to the separation point between lands suitable for all sorts of agriculture on a long-term sustainable basis and lands suitable only for grazing.'

Melbourne's Pleasure Dome

In August 1873 a peculiar yarn appeared in the classified advertisements section of the Melbourne *Herald*. A Mr Thomas Jones had discovered human beings with tails living on an island off New Guinea. After a week of nonsense, the story about the 'Elocwe' concluded with the truth. It was a hoax cooked up to advertise the wares of a trader with a market stall called Cole's Cheap Book Store. 'Elocwe' was E.W. Cole spelled backwards and Edward William Cole was one of the most remarkable entrepreneurs and optimists in the history of Australia.

After emigrating from England to South Africa, the twenty-or-so-year-old adventurer turned up in Victoria for a share of the great rush in 1852. He had plenty of competition but made a more or less successful career plying a variety of businesses and schemes that eventually brought him to Melbourne. There, with energy, acumen and some style, he went from selling cheap books in the markets to building the grand institution known as Cole's Book Arcade that eventually stretched between Bourke Street and Little Collins Streets. Imposing though the arcade was, that name does not begin to do it justice. The business was an emporium on steroids, and then some.

Anticipating some modern architectural trends, Cole had the existing structure on the site hollowed out and its roof replaced with a glass dome. Along the side wall, he built balconies with plenty of mirrors and brass fittings, creating a light-flooded space to display his stock. And what a stock it was. As well as 'over a million books', Cole filled his urban pleasure dome with toys, art, stationery, perfumes, lollies and a music department. The place was also a mini zoo, with birds, monkeys and a fernery. Customers could enjoy refreshments at a tea salon, have their printing done, get their photographs taken or enjoy a ceramics display. If you didn't wish to buy a book, you could borrow one or two from the lending library. Or you could just giggle in the 'Wonderland' of optical illusions and be amused at the mechanical toys and slot machines, all presided over by scarlet-clad sales staff. Cole was famous for not pressuring his customers to buy. He preferred the softest of selling techniques, cosseting customers with his extravaganza, sometimes enhanced with live music.

Mostly self-educated, Cole was something of a utopian and cultural activist. He believed in the social benefits of reading and knowledge and his no-pressure-to-buy approach was designed to foster a better world through books. He followed this part of his business with special energy, establishing a publishing operation whose most famous product was known usually as *Cole's Funny Picture Book*, full of 'Choice Riddles, Games and pieces of reading for Adults'.

In keeping with Cole's irrepressible talent for promotion, he claimed, possibly with justification, that 'This is the funniest picture book in the world for children.' Cole also knew his market. He included a shrewd message to those with the money to buy it:

> To Parents, Grandparents, Uncles, Aunts, and Friends.
> Every Good Child should be given one of these Books for being Good.
> Every Bad Child should also be given one to try and make it Good.

A mishmash of rhymes, riddles and stories, mostly purloined from other publications, it was one of the few available books aimed at children, family entertainment and with some educational value added. It was a hit and continued to be for many years, long before there was a children's book industry in Australia.

Cole's unusual approach to sales did not mean he was a poor businessman. He was a master of what would today be called marketing, not only with his advertising fantasy but through a clever gimmick. From 1879, Cole minted medallions finished in gold, bronze, silver and copper, brass and aluminium. These featured inspirational and uplifting quotes such as 'Reading and Thinking Bring Wisdom' and, of course advertised the business. Employees scattered them through the city on their way to and from work, a brilliant way to spend the advertising budget. They also returned income to the business as the medallions could also be purchased for three pence as admission tickets to the arcade when the crowds became too large to handle.

Historians say that Cole's Arcade was at the centre of Melbourne life over the four decades of its existence. It was the place to be and be seen; no visit to the city was complete without a trip to Cole's Arcade to meet and greet, eat, shop and marvel at the glittering array of goods and services. It was a unique physical projection of the man and his vision.

For all his business acumen, Cole was driven more by his social and religious convictions, which he promoted, mostly without much success, in publications he authored. By the time Cole was in his forties, the business was booming and he decided, of course, to advertise for a wife. Just a month later he married Eliza Frances Jordean from Tasmania. The couple would eventually have two sons and four daughters before Eliza died in 1911. Cole then went into semi-retirement, working on his theories about almost everything until his death in 1918.

Although Cole tried to engineer a suitable group of trustees to carry on his ideals and his legacy, his business was such a reflection of the man that it was unlikely to long outlast him. Within ten years of his passing the grand arcade closed down, along with its branches in Sydney and Adelaide.

Copies of the various editions of the picture book, as well as examples of the 300,000 or so medallions, are eagerly sought collector's items today. They are all that remains of one of Australia's greatest little stories of a man who made his expansive dream come to life and, for a while, created a unique community of employees and customers.

MacRobertson's Steam Confectionery Works

A place with a name like this must have a tale to tell. Quite a few, in fact. They begin with a young man named Macpherson Robertson whipping up batches of boiled lollies in his bathroom in Melbourne's then-dodgy Fitzroy in 1880.

'Mac', as he was known, was born in 1859 and brought up in difficult circumstances. Unable to further his education, he became an apprentice in the confectionery industry. Determined to improve his situation, he began making his own lollies and hawking them round the local shops. By the late 1880s, the sugar start-up had expanded beyond the bathroom to engulf several blocks. He adapted his name to the catchier 'MacRobertson' brand and after only a few years MacRobertson's Steam Confectionery Works spread across 1.2 hectares of Fitzroy and employed more than 250 workers. By the late 1920s the entrepreneur's factories reportedly covered 12 hectares and employed 2500 people. Many locals found employment at the works, often through several generations.

Always alert to a good promotional gimmick, Mac had his buildings painted in an eye-catching white to contrast with the grimy industrial suburb in which they stood. To amplify the effect, he dressed in an all-white suit and hat, becoming a well-known local figure. His rags-to-riches story was a press favourite and he embellished it with his autobiography, *A Young Man and a Nail Can: An industrial romance*, published in 1921.

Mac Robertson's continued success owed a good deal to the larger events of the period. Federation ended trade barriers between the former colonies and expanded markets, while World War I ended the former domination of the Australian confectionery market by British manufacturers. The Australian industry, originally staffed mainly by males, became increasingly female as it became more mechanised. Outside Mac Robertson's enterprises, working conditions were generally poor. There were attempts to organise trade unions from the 1880s but these had limited success until the formation of the Female Confectioners' Union (FCU) in 1916, specifically to represent the interests of the many women in the industry, particularly in the quest for wages more in line with those of male workers. Up to this point, the sweated labour of women and girls in the confectionery industry was notorious and it had led to a royal commission in 1917. Unlike most other employers in the industry, Mac was in favour of trade unions. He supported the FCU at his factory and created an internal compensation fund for workers who were ill or injured.

The lollies that rolled out of the steam confectionery included sherbert fizzers, columbines and milk kisses. After a visit to the United States, Mac returned with 'cotton candy', known to us as 'fairy floss', as well as a much better form of gum than Australians had been chewing. He began marketing the improved product with various flavours like celery, kola and tutte frutte. He also invented Old Gold chocolate and the Cherry Ripe bar, with its filling liberally wrapped in that smooth, dark coating.

In the late 1920s, British confectionery interests returned to the Australian market and MacRobertson's responded with a boost in publicity and promotion. This included the introduction of a new chocolate product destined to become a staple of show sample bags: the Freddo Frog. The story goes that MacRobertson's planned a new novelty chocolate to be launched in 1930. It was to be a mouse, but a young employee named as

'Harry Melbourne' suggested that children and women might not react well to chocolate mice and that maybe a frog would be a better choice. Mac agreed and so Freddo Frog was brought into the world. By the 1940s there were at least twelve varieties, each sold for a penny. The shape, size, packaging and depiction of Freddo have changed over the years and for a while, between 1979 and 1994, the confection was taken off the market altogether. But Freddo hopped back into production and can still be purchased.

Throughout his illustrious career, the white-suited entrepreneur promoted his products through publicity stunts and promotions of all kinds, including aviation and the MacRobertson Round Australia motor truck expedition of 1928. He supported Antarctic exploration and donated generously to many causes, including the building of public works in Melbourne during the 1930s depression. He was given imperial honours in the 1930s. A man of modest tastes—other than his fleet of Packard cars—Mac looked after his health with a daily exercise program. Even in his sixties he was able to jump over a 1.4 metre-high bar and he 'cut a dapper, upright and serious figure, with silver hair and clear complexion.'

Macpherson Robertson died in 1945 and family members took over the business until 1967 when MacRobertson's was acquired by its old competitors. They still manufacture Old Gold, Cherry Ripe and, of course, Freddo Frogs.

The Grain Races

For the first five years of her life Elizabeth Jacobsen knew little but the sea. She was the daughter of a Norwegian sailing ship captain. When she grew up, Betty, as she was known, convinced the captain of the *Parma* to take her on as an apprentice. Even in the 1930s, the world of the few remaining commercial sailing ships was completely masculine. Although he allowed Betty to join his ship and learn the ropes, the captain told her that 'No woman will ever be a sailor.' She soon found out what he meant. The all-male crew, following the sailors' superstition that women aboard a ship brought bad luck, resented Betty and made sure she overheard their not-entirely-playful jokes about how they might cause her to fall from the rigging. In her book about her experience afloat, published in 1934, Betty wrote that the sailors 'like to think they can do what I cannot do. They like to fight the sails by themselves, and to feel that, here at least, is something that a woman will never do.'

The vessel Betty sailed aboard was part of a largely Finnish fleet bringing Australian grain to Britain. Each year, between 1921 and 1949, a dozen or so square-rigged ships arrived in South Australian or Victorian harbours to load mostly wheat, but also other grains, bound for British brewers and distillers where much of it ended up as alcohol. These ships were the heirs of the nineteenth-century tea clipper trade, a notoriously dangerous business involving hazardous passages around Cape Horn. Famous clippers like the *Cutty Sark* were driven through mountainous seas by hard-bitten masters bent on being first into port with their precious cargoes. Sailing ships were eventually succeeded by powered vessels, and the clippers, despite some amazingly fast passages, became obsolete. But the 'grain races', as the trade was unofficially known, managed to continue commercial sailing until the middle of the twentieth century. Although the glory days of the big wind ships were over, their small fleet of successors kept the tradition alive through an informal competition for the fastest passage between Australia and the United Kingdom.

By contrast with the ship owners of the clipper-ship era, the Finish and German companies discouraged their captains from racing. There was no commercial advantage in being first and it was hard on the equipment and the sailors, with expensive repairs potentially required. As one historian of the trade put it, 'Unlike the hell-bent racing captains of the celebrated tea-clippers of the 1860s . . . the captain of a grain ship who lost gear more likely would lose his job.' But that didn't stop the racing. By the 1930s, the annual event was so well established that it was widely reported in the Australian press.

The annual grain race between the windjammers from Australia to Falmouth has begun. The ships *Archibald Russell* and *Abraham Rydberg* are already beating down towards the Horn, and the Herzogin Cecilie is a hive of activity at Port Adelaide with all hands preparing for its long trip, which will probably begin late next week. Sails are being repaired, new ropes bent, and all gear overhauled carefully, for when a man's life depends upon a rope 50 feet [15 m] from the deck in a howling gale off the Horn he likes to know that everything is trim and safe.

They say that the only certainties in life are death and taxes but, in Australia at least, there is a third. The grain races, inevitably, supported a robust gambling industry with some feverish speculation on which vessel would make the fastest passage of the year—unofficially, of course, as the captain of the *Herzogin*

Cecilie told a reporter in 1933: 'Questioned about the time he hoped to make, Capt. Erickson smiled and looked up at his trim rigging. "If I told you the time I wish for," he said with a laugh, "you would laugh at me but I will say that I hope to get to Falmouth round the hundred-day mark."'

Erickson's ship would win the race more times than any other contender, but it did not win that year. Instead, it was Betty Jacobsen's ship, *Parma*, with a passage of only eighty-three days from Port Victoria to Falmouth, the fastest time achieved by any of the grain ships. Perhaps women aboard were not unlucky, after all? In fact, women were not infrequently present aboard sailing vessels. Nineteenth-century captains of whalers and other ships might take their wives on the lengthy voyages they usually undertook, a practice that seems to have flourished in later years. In 1949, the last year of the grain races, the captain and first mate of the *Pamir* were both accompanied by their wives, who were signed on as paid stewardesses. After leaving Australia, the *Pamir* battled through two hurricanes, lost sails in a storm off West Africa and was becalmed for fifty-seven days. The ship did not win but gained the honour of being the last windjammer to round the Horn with a commercial cargo.

The last Cape Horners became sail training ships, ghosts of a past era remembered only in Betty Jacobsen's memoir and *The Last Grain Race* (1956) by English traveller and writer, Eric Newby, who sailed in the largest of the grain ships, *Moshulu*, in 1939. The great wooden vessels that came here in the era of sail and those who sailed in them were part of a small but once important community of seafarers connecting Australia to the wider world.

A Community of the Air

If you grew up in the era of radio, before television came to Australia and for a while after, you will remember *The Argonauts Club*. You might even have been one. A little later, on early television, you probably watched the zany puppet with a pencil for a nose, named Mr Squiggle. Between 1990 and 2001, the favourite seems to have been *Round the Twist*. And, of course, almost everyone watched *Playschool*, still entertaining children after more than fifty years on ABC television.

What children hear, watch and read is one of those often overlooked but very important influences on their values and attitudes in later life. Until the dominance of the internet and the omnipresent 'devices', Australian kids were entertained, informed and formed by programs on radio and television.

Beginning in 1933, *The Argonauts Club*, in one form or another, was broadcast nationally until 1972. As well as the stories, music, poems and plays on the program, young listeners could send in their own contributions. They could also join the club if they were between seven and seventeen years of age. Thousands did, especially during the peak of the program's popularity in the 1950s. Members had a badge, a club name, usually based on characters from classical mythology or ancient history, and a number. Many remembered theirs all through life, some going on to become prominent in many fields, from show business to politics, including comedian Barry Humphries who, as 'Ithome 32' was a prominent contributor to the program. Tim Fischer, Ken Done and Dame Joan Sutherland were a few of the members who went on to find fame.

As the television age brought new and exciting visual possibilities to children's entertainment, *Skippy the Bush Kangaroo* was added to the favourites. For children born in the decade between 1981 and 1990, *Round the Twist* and *Play School* were firm favourites. And, along with several other shows from that era, they still are. Research by the Australian Children's TV Foundation (ACTF) published in 2023 found that those kids, now grown up and often with children of their own, frequently revisit their beloved shows. The appeal is both nostalgia and a desire to introduce their children to the favourites of their own childhoods. Streaming television and social media allow those programs no longer in production to live again and to be accessed on demand.

What is it that makes these shows so enduring? According to the researchers it is humour, a healthy dose of the bizarre and the relationship between these perennial kids' favourites and Australian life. Those surveyed for the research said that they identified the shows with 'this kind of gritty, sometimes a little bit crude, really down-to-earth Aussie sense of humour.' The researchers were surprised by the passion with which the now grown-up kids of the 1980–1990 era spoke about these shows. Here are the favourites, together with their production dates:

- *Round the Twist* (1990–2001)
- *Play School* (1966–current)
- *Mr Squiggle* (1959–1999)
- *Skippy the Bush Kangaroo* (1968–1970)
- *Blinky Bill* (1993–2004)
- *The Ferals* (1994–1995)
- *Lift Off!* (1992–1995)

- *Ship to Shore* (1993–1994)
- *Bananas in Pyjamas* (1992–2001)
- *The Genie from Down Under* (1996–1998)

Adults reflecting on the differences between children's television in their childhood and what has been produced since felt that the more recent programs were more 'sanitised' than those of the past and the older shows continued to be 'more upfront with kids'. This is a major point of difference with similar shows produced in the United Kingdom and the United States. The Australian and international smash hit cartoon series, *Bluey*, is sometimes considered to need editing when screened in other countries. The Disney channel recently removed from the popular series references and visuals connected with poo, farting, vasectomies and using the toilet.

These and other edits highlight the Australian tolerance for vulgarity, often an element of our folk humour and colourful folk speech. The Australian idea of a joke does not necessarily translate to other cultures. The reverse can also be the case, of course. While the nuances of cultural identity may be subtle—even when crude—they influence the way people in any national community think of themselves and share a sense of belonging.

Respondents to the survey also felt that children's television was now much more diversified and inclusive in its depiction of people from a range of cultures. There is no doubt a long way to go before the diversity of the Australian community can be adequately reflected in children's television, but the process has started. According to 2023 research by Screen Australia: 'Children's programs have a higher level of cultural diversity than general drama, and this has increased since 2016 in terms of First Nations representation (9.1%) and characters from non-European backgrounds (22%).' On the other hand, representation of disability and LGBTQI+ has a way to go.

These issues were barely known or acknowledged in Australia when the children's session of *The Argonauts* opened with the theme song drawn from English nursery rhymes such as 'Old Mother Hubbard' and 'Jack and Jill'.

Community attitudes and the structure of Australian society have moved on since the 1950s, though kids still want to have fun: that never changes.

Thomas Wood (right) at an unidentified military base in the northwest, 1944. Wood was officially in Australia on a morale-boosting public speaking and fact-finding tour. He was also an agent of the British government, reporting to the Ministry of Information.

9

OURSELVES

People of the Rock

The First Nations people of South Australia's Flinders Ranges are now collectively known as Adnyamathanha—'Adnya' meaning 'rock' and 'matha' a group of people'. Within Adnyamathanha, there are different language groups, including Kuyani, Wailpi, Yadliawarda and Pirlatpa, who identify as the traditional occupiers of country from the northern Flinders Ranges to Port Augusta and east to Broken Hill.

Their story begins with Akurra, a great snake associated with water and the general wellbeing of the land and its people. In one story, Akurra takes the form of two giant serpents named Wartawinha and Ngarnangarrinha, who lived in a waterhole at Arrunha Awi (Aroona). They saw the smoke of the ceremonial leader, the kingfisher, Yurlu, as he cooked a damper near the place now known as Copley while on his way to conduct a big ceremony at Ikara (Wilpena Pound). The two Akurra became greedy and travelled to Copley from where they followed him to the ceremony. There, they surrounded the people and caught them in a large whirlwind. All but one fully initiated man and one partly initiated man were eaten. The hills around the Pound are the two serpents and the pair of hills at Copley where Yurlu left his fire burning are named for the snake couple as they lay waiting for the kingfisher to pass on his way to the ceremony.

In the 1850s the area was taken over by settlers. There was conflict as the Adnyamathanha sought to defend their land and its resources. Warriors killed a stockman named Robert Richardson at Aroona in March 1852. The two men arrested for the killing were never tried due to a lack of evidence. But many years later it came to light that Richardson's boss, Johnson Frederick Hayward, and several others carried out a revenge attack at Brachina Gorge in the Flinders Ranges. They intended to swoop at dawn and capture the warriors, including those they thought had killed the stockman. The ambush killed at least fifteen people, possibly many more. Like other incidents of the frontier wars, this one was never reported or officially documented until publication of Hayward's reminiscences in 1929.

By the start of the twentieth century, the Traditional Owners of the land were completely dispossessed and scattered. They gathered at various traditional sites but by the 1930s most relocated to the United Aborigines Mission at Nepabunna, where some worked in the early workshop of R.M. Williams, crafting the leather goods the firm still sells today. Others worked on stations throughout the region and contributed to the economic development of the state.

Today, the Adnyamathanha continue their rich traditions of story, song and ceremony. They also run a pastoral property and have been successful in their land rights claim to more than 40,000 square kilometres (also recognising the Ngadjuri people's and the Wilyakali people's claims). There are Adnyamathanha enterprises in cultural education and ecotourism and jointly manage the Ikara–Flinders Ranges National Park. Prominent men and women with Adnyamathanha heritage include artists and scholars, and footballer Adam Goodes, famed for his stand against racist AFL crowds.

A memorial in Copley recognises the Traditional Owners of this part of the country. Mounted on a large rock are two plaques, the first of which reads:

In respect and acknowledgement of the traditional owners of the land.
In remembrance of our Aboriginal People who have come from various parts of this country, who were accepted and respected by the Elders of the Adnyamathanha People.
This plaque is erected in remembrance to those who have passed on.
Lest We Forget.
Our loved ones, who are at rest and in our hearts always and forever.
May God bless.
Ngaparla Yura Wangapi Ilkandanapula Inawatana Adnyanga

The spirit of the Adnyamathanha People is remembered in this rock. To the Adnyamathanha People 'Life and Death' is the same.

We are born of our mothers and when we die we return to our mother the Yarta (Land).

Our spirit is then released into the environment which gives us our 'living culture'.

Yesterday, today and forever our loved ones are with us always.

The Hairistocracy

The English writer William Howitt sailed to Australia with two of his sons in 1852. They spent time on the Victorian goldfields and Howitt wrote about what they did, heard and saw there. At this time, British society was based even more on class than today, with the upper and middle classes expecting deferential respect from those deemed beneath them on the social pyramid. Howitt's experiences on the goldfields showed how differently colonial Australia had developed from its beginning a half-century or so before. The well-educated, middle-class Quaker didn't like it much at all: 'There appear to be no gentlemen, or very few, amongst the diggers here. They are the most common, coarsest set of fellows I have seen anywhere. They appear all of the same navvie class, or made up of carters, labourers, ostlers and low fellows, the scum of London cab-drivers, and men about stables.' And there was more: 'One of the things which strikes you everywhere in this colony is the blunt, rude, independent manner of the common people.'

Howitt identified these coarse commoners as the 'rudest and most ignorant of the English population, well sprinkled with felons from Sydney and Van Diemen's Land . . .' As well as their manners and attitudes, Howitt did not like the way they dressed, or their grooming. He labelled them 'truly the *Hairistocracy*' (original emphasis) and predicted that 'It will take a century to work this miscellaneous gathering of rude people out of the scum.' On a more positive note, he thought that, as they prospered, they would, as in America, educate their children and become a 'go-ahead, self-confident, Yankee sort of people.'

Howitt was not completely biased against the Hairistocracy. He wrote of young colonial men who, since childhood, were used to depending on themselves and were 'doing business on their own account before they have a trace of a beard on their chins.' Howitt befriended one of these 'lads', as he called them, a boy of fourteen of fifteen who had already been in business for some years and, with his mate, had accumulated a considerable flock of 200 sheep. The unnamed boy told Howitt the tale of how he and his mate once comprehensively fooled a goldfields commissioner.

The two boys had been selling sly grog from their tent and word of their profitable business venture reached the officials. With the impending threat of a police search, one of the boys managed to get back to their tent in time to send the barrels of alcohol into the bush in the care of the bullock driver they employed, with a bottle of rum for his trouble. The commissioner arrived with a policeman shortly after and ordered the tent searched. Not surprisingly, the policeman was a frequent customer at the sly grog tent. As he went to search the tent, the policeman said to the boy's mate:

> just in a low way like, 'mate,' says he, 'if you have any in the bed, don't pull the clothes off, but only touzle them about pretty well.' The boy's mate responded loudly: 'Off with the clothes, policeman! Out with the bed. Dig up the floor if you liken [sic], and for every drop of grog that you find on my premises, I'll give you an ounce of gold for it.'

The boys kept their gold and the commissioner unhappily departed. But the boys were not going to let things rest there. They cheekily demanded to be compensated for false accusation and 'this scandal on respectable tradesmen'. After some more complaining from the boys, the by then red-faced commissioner asked how much they wanted. 'Twenty pounds' said the boy's mate.

'Twenty pounds! That is preposterous!'

But the boys insisted, eventually agreeing to drop the claim if the commissioner sent men to their tent to make good the damage that evening. He agreed and left. Nobody came that night, so next morning the boys went to the commissioner's office and continued complaining, loudly. Eventually, the embarrassed official relented and offered £10, no more: '"Well", said my mate, still pulling a long face, "that *must* do, if you won't give us any more; but I must say it is a hard case."'

The commissioner handed over the considerable sum of £10 and the boys walked off, laughing to themselves. It took them about an hour to get the tent back in order and they were £10 richer. And there were no more raids on their 'eye-wash' business, as they called the grog trade that had no doubt paid for the sheep.

Howitt thought that 'This is a pretty good specimen of the rising generation of this colony', as did many other observers at the time. The gold rushes rocket-fuelled the population, forcing the rapid development of the less class-bound, independent attitudes and values that were already in evidence among the 'currency', or native-born, generations. Much romanticised in song and story, the independent Australian bush worker, gold prospector and, later, the Anzac digger, would be the basis of the potent myth that modern Australia is a classless society. It is not, and never was. But unlike many other societies, clothes, speech, manners—and grooming—have often not been reliable guides to the wealth and influence of individuals in Australia.

Australian 'Natives'

Dr Benjamin Poulton's obituary was predictably flattering. An outstanding member of the medical profession, teacher and supporter of charities, he was a celebrated public figure in South Australia from the 1880s. He was also one of a growing number of people interested in establishing a uniquely Australian identity.

In June 1890 he gave a lecture to the South Australian branch of the Australian Natives' Association (ANA) on 'The influence of Australian climate and environment on the mental and physical development of Australians'. His basic argument was that the unique environmental conditions in Australia, together with the historical experiences of colonisation, had produced a distinctive national type. He finished his talk with a brief summary of what he believed were the 'prevailing characteristics of the Australian of the present day'. These were:

> his stature; perhaps rather greater than his father's, a general spareness of form, a good muscular development, a pale or even sallow complexion, and his voice with its slight nasal twang and drawl. The fact that he attains maturity at an earlier age than the inhabitant of Great Britain may account for his alleged precocity. He is self-confident, self-reliant, takes generally a hopeful view of things, is not notable for his ambition, as he is certainly for his want of reverence both at home and abroad. He is temperate in his use of spirituous liquors, intemperate in his consumption of meat and tea, hospitable and trustful to strangers, careless of small things even to the fault of thriftlessness, possesses marked powers of self-control, and has a tendency to repress his emotions. He is not demonstrative; he is critical, cautious rather than enthusiastic, candid, fearlessly truthful. He has not, so far as I know developed any remarkable virtues or special vices.

The speaker concluded—to cheers—by saying that the Australian native's 'peculiarities are in the making.'

Dr Poulton's view of the Australian type was restricted to men, and to white men only. Apart from his view that alcohol consumption was 'temperate', most of what he had to say has been echoed by commentators on Australian character ever since, sometimes favourably, sometimes not.

The organisation to which the eminent physician was speaking had its origins in a Victorian friendly society formed in 1871. Before the era of social security, people needed to look after their own medical and other inevitable expenses. Friendly societies, also known as 'fraternal', 'benefit' or 'mutual' societies, were a popular method of providing health insurance and the cost of funerals. 'The Association's objectives were to "raise funds by subscription, donations . . . for the purpose of relieving sick members, and defraying expenses of funeral of members and their wives, relieving distressed widows and orphans and for the necessary expenses of the general management of the Society."'

In the case of this society, its membership was initially limited to 'natives' of Melbourne, meaning those white men who were born there. The society soon changed its name after deciding to admit those born in other colonies. It quickly developed into a significant organisation, most influentially in Victoria, but with 129 branches around the country by the late 1890s. A decade or so later it had almost 30,000 members from a variety of social and economic backgrounds. These members were all born in Australia. The ANA believed, like many at the time, in a 'white Australia', and opposed immigration from non-British countries.

Despite this typical nineteenth-century attitude, the association also had more progressive ideals. It supported the push for federation of the colonies and also the vote for women, though women were only allowed to form a separate ANA organisation and did not become full members until 1964. Free, secular education and a minimum wage were also part of the ANA's more enlightened aims. Despite its restrictive views on race, the association tried to influence government policies related to the wellbeing of First Nations people and promoted the idea of a harmonious—if white—society.

The ANA used its large membership to influence public views, and so politics. Among its adherents were many influential politicians, including prime ministers, premiers, members of parliament and the first Australian-born governor-general, (Sir) Isaac Isaacs. During the 1930s, the influence of the ANA waned. It later focused on its financial, insurance and aged-care activities and, by the 1990s, had merged with another long-established fraternal society to become Australian Unity Ltd.

One initiative of the association remains today. As part of its drive to promote and nurture patriotism, the association established a day for the celebration of the European colonisation of Australia. 'ANA Day', as it was known in Victoria where it began, was on 26 January. In the 1930s, this became 'Australia Day' and it is with us still, if less comfortably, each year.

The story of the ANA is a miniature version of the scope of Australian political and cultural history. It encapsulated a growing national consciousness that involved a distinctive identity that was separate from links to Britain, as the United Kingdom was generally known then. This idea of the Australian people, even in what was for the time its most progressive form, was inevitably tainted with the prevailing views of race and gender. These became embedded in the constitutional formation of the Commonwealth and in legislation passed, or not passed, by early parliaments as struggles for racial, gender and political progress continued into the twentieth century, and beyond. When a nation sending large numbers of its soldiers to war for the first time in 1915 searched for an identity, it drew on many of the ideas expressed by Dr Poulton and espoused by the ANA. The Anzac tradition and its central cultural hero, the digger, was to a significant extent the product of those ideas.

A Broken Soldier

William Thomas Shirley signed up with the Australian Imperial Force (AIF) in January 1916. The Cumbrian stonemason was thirty-nine years old, though his hair was already grey and his weight was low for a man of 1.68 metres. He was probably already suffering from the respiratory problems that his war service only worsened.

Will Shirley seems to have been a reluctant soldier, going absent without leave at least three times before he sailed for the fighting in May 1916. The following year he fought at the battles of Pozières and Bullecourt. He was then shipped back to England after being gassed and also found to be suffering from pleurisy. In and out of hospital, between several more unofficial absences, he was finally invalided home to Australia in October 1917. He was soon discharged but by 1924 was back in hospital at Lady Davidson Home in Sydney's Ku-ring-gai Chase. The home specialised in treating tuberculosis, then an incurable disease.

With time on his hands, Will Shirley began an occupational therapy project using his stonecraft skills. He began to chip and carve the local sandstone near the hospital. After a few hours work each day, sometimes less, a scaled-down replica of the famous Sphinx of Egypt's Giza Plateau slowly began to appear. The connection with Egypt was through the 13th Battalion in which Will had served. The 'Two Blues', as the battalion was known from its colour patches, had originally been based in Egypt. Will and his comrades had strong memories of their time there, especially of the impressive ancient monuments around Cairo.

As well as the roughly one-eighth scale Sphinx, Will also built a couple of small-scale pyramids to flank his unofficial tribute to those who did not return from the war. It took him around eighteen months of continual effort during his long stay at Lady Davidson Home. He was eventually discharged and was living on the central coast of New South Wales when he sickened and later died in Randwick Military Hospital on 27 August 1929.

It would be another two years before Will's spontaneous memorial was dedicated. The work, now with pathways and a wishing well based on a spring discovered during further construction by ex-AIF members, was unveiled by Governor Sir Philip Game:

> [he] hoped the memorial would serve as a triple reminder of the fallen, of the best ideals of the soldiers and sailors who had so valiantly fought, and of the obligation to do all possible to bring about and maintain the ideals for which they suffered. He earnestly desired that in these difficult days it would be an inspiration to everyone who looked upon it to follow in the footsteps of the men of the A.I.F.

Mr W.C. Cridland, president of the T.B. Sailors' and Soldiers' Association, 'described as the most unique and appropriate war memorial in the world, since it was carved by a Digger in his closing days in honour of his old comrades of the A.I.F.'

Will Shirley had created a memorial not only to those killed in action—'my glorious comrades'—but to those many others who survived the war but suffered the peace carrying wounds and afflictions that in many cases blighted the rest of their lives and often ended them prematurely. Families, friends and loved ones also suffered. On the first few anniversaries of Will's death, remembrance notices appeared in the *Sydney Morning Herald*. They took the form of stock memorial poems placed by 'his loving friend', Emma Flanagan. In 1930 she wrote:

Always in my mind dear Will,
Sweet memories of you I keep;
Although one year has passed away
My sorrow is just as deep.

In 1931:
In loving memory of my dear friend . . .
There's someone who misses you sadly,
And thinks of you day by day.
But we'll meet again, dear Will,
At the dawn of a beautiful day.

And the next year:

Years cannot alter my fond love for you,
For your voice and your smile I crave,
Your memory will live my whole life through,
As you lie in your silent grave.

There were no further remembrances in the years that followed.

As well as through these personal tributes, Will Shirley was honoured by large crowds visiting the memorial. The unusual location of the structure and the story of Will Shirley's commitment to it drew thousands to the site during the 1930s when the grief of World War I casualties was still strong in community memory. Re-dedicated in 1995, the plaque marking that event reads in part:

In recognition of the selflessness and sacrifices of the
members of the A.I.F.
Lest We Forget
1914 – 1918

Today, the memorial is part of a recreational walking trail through Ku-ring-gai Chase National Park, another of the thousands around the country commemorating the Great War and its enduring hold on the national consciousness.

The Plot to Save Australia

He was an unusual character. Born in Lancashire, England, in 1892, Thomas Wood went to sea with his father around the age of nine, learned piano, gained a scholarship to Oxford University, and became a composer, traveller and an engaging broadcaster and writer on patriotic themes. He achieved all these things, and more, even though he was almost blind. In the 1930s he worked and travelled throughout Australia and wrote a best-selling book about the place and its people, titled *Cobbers*. Although almost completely forgotten today, Thomas Wood deserves to be remembered for all these things. He should also be outed as an agent of Britain's Ministry of Information and for his major role in a plot to manipulate Australia's cultural identity.

Was Australia to be a predominantly British country? Or was it to become an outpost of the United States? These questions may seem odd today but they were on the minds of many people towards the end of World War II. The United Kingdom's inability to help defend its southern hemisphere interests after the fall of Singapore and the subsequent arrival of large American forces suggested that Australia was in danger of falling away from what was then often called the 'Empire family'. Some influential people were so concerned about these possibilities, as well as the threat of Communism, that they decided to do something about it—in secret.

The plot to save Australia from America, communism and itself originated with the then director of Naval Intelligence, a man referred to by his biographer as 'the intrigue master'. Commander Rupert Long, together with several of his intelligence officers, colluded with Western Australian journalist Malcolm Uren and Thomas Wood to establish a post-war 'British-Australia Council' to ensure that the country remained 'British' in character, rather than American or, even worse in the minds of the conspirators, controlled by a left-wing Labor party and trade union movement.

In 1944, Thomas Wood was in Australia, officially to promote his wartime morale-boosting book, *Cobbers Campaigning,* and to continue the round of radio broadcasts, press articles and public events that he initiated more than a decade earlier when he was working in Australia. But this time, Wood was working for the British Ministry of Information to gather intelligence about Australian attitudes to the United States, the United Kingdom and politics in general. He revealed the true nature of his mission in a letter to Charles Patrick Smith, the managing editor and, since 1931, a director of West Australian Newspapers: 'the matter I am writing about is known to six men only—you will be the seventh. The six are the Acting Governor-General, (my host) four others, and myself. That number must not be increased. May I ask you, then, to be so good as to look upon what I am going to tell you as being in the very strictest confidence?'

The letter continued: 'I am asking your help in a matter of the first importance to Australia and the Empire' and explained why Wood had really returned to Australia: 'I came here to tell Australia about Britain, and in turn to tell Britain about Australia. The first I have tried to do, the second I hope to do; but there is something deeper than this. By invitation from the highest quarter at home I am looking into the whole question of British and Australian relations.'

Wood later wrote via secret diplomatic pouch to Brendan Bracken, a member of Winston Churchill's war cabinet and with responsibility for the Ministry of Information in January 1945. In the letter, he outlined the reasons for his visit to Australia and his activities there: 'I left England in February 1944 to tell Australia, informally and unofficially, of Britain at war, and to learn about Australia.' The letter goes on to point out that he met with the British high commissioner as well as the acting prime minister and spoke to many people around Australia and in New Guinea. The letter then went on to directly state the reasons for his anxiety to present himself back in England.

... from military and civilian leaders, business and professional men, pressmen, majors, privates and ratings

I heard the same disturbing facts. Australians in the main were as loyal as ever, but there were unmistakable signs that other nations were at work while the British story was either not being told or could not be heard. On the other hand there was activity, intelligence and zeal shown by the Americans (Characteristically and openly), Russians, (underground but effective), Dutch (competently), and even the Chinese. Everywhere I could see for myself un-British influences at work, and talk after talk I had with all kinds of people brought fresh instances to my notice. One section of the community is, as you probably know, pro-Australian to the exclusion of everything else and that section is very strong politically and industrially.

Through 1944 and into 1945, the conspirators, calling themselves 'the Group', conducted a clandestine series of meetings with most of the Australian political, military, business and industrial establishment, as well as British diplomats and intelligence figures, including the prime minister, John Curtin, and the acting governor-general, Sir Winston Dugan. The result was the Group's 'Report', a 29-page document detailing exactly how the country would be kept within the culture and politics of the empire. This was to be achieved through 'a British-Australian Council which will operate on a two-way basis telling the British story in Australia and finding out and telling about Australia in Great Britain.' This structure 'would not be a recognisably propaganda organization' but would link up all relevant government departments and would aspire not only to influence the current generation but also those to come. To be a success, it was stated, such an organisation would need to be sensitive to Australian 'peculiarities', such as state jealousies. It would also need to take account 'of those traits in the Australian character which make Australians indolent in thought yet super-sensitive to criticism.' The council would aim to 'reach every section of the community and [to] tie up with all other types of organisations including unions, the armed services, press, radio and cultural societies.'

This was nothing less than a full-scale cultural commissariat that would function through the press, radio and the armed services. Cultural societies would be provided with visiting British personalities—'each will be a subtle British propagandist.' Trade unions would be provided with British Labour leaders. Even children were to be propagandised through films and storybooks, including comics, which 'would be essentially British in character.' Women could be appealed to through their interest in 'dress, beauty aids, social activities and feminist news.' In addition to British-originated information services to government, industry and business 'the publication and distribution of British books in Australia is another thing that badly needs doing.' A 'Union Jack League' would provide for 'the direction of interest in the British way of life' and British entertainers were to be brought to Australia to 'show the flag here.'

And there was more. British advertising agents were to be established to encourage the sale of British goods to the Australian consumer—'In selling British goods these advertising agencies will be selling British.' The two-way interchange of information envisaged in the manifesto would be assisted by telling the people of Britain about Australia—'This is aimed at the one family ideal, the blood link between the members of the British Empire.' There would be visits of Royal Navy units and 'crack British regiments'. Ever the musician, Thomas stipulated that they should, of course, come with their bands.

Wood and some other members of the Group assembled in England shortly after the war, intent on presenting their plan to the highest authorities. But the world had changed. Churchill's wartime government was about to be tipped out of office, replaced by a Labour government with a lot more to worry about than Australian attitudes. Most of the influential sympathisers of the plot were retired, dead or no longer powerful. The Group's plans for the cultural engineering of Australia slid silently into the deep dustbin of clandestine history.

'True Thomas', as Wood called himself in his autobiography, returned to his musical work, his country manor house, his London clubs and related interests. One of his patriotic compositions was commissioned for the 1951 Festival of Britain but he died suddenly in November 1951 without hearing it performed. Despite some impressive funeral services befitting a minor but loyal member of the establishment, Thomas Wood was immediately forgotten. Even in the country where he had once wielded considerable influence and hobnobbed with the powerful, his obituaries were few and short. Australia continued its evolution into a modern multicultural nation with strong British and American connections and without a communist regime.

Crossing the Yellow Line

In 2013 an unusual piece of public art was installed in the cobbles of Hobart's famous market area, Salamanca Place. The work was made up of two lightboxes, each measuring 2 metres by 20 centimetres. In one box the words 'Forgive me for not holding you in my arms' are written and backlit, and in the other the words 'In the wake of your courage I swim.' Known as *The Yellow Line*, this artwork by Justy Phillips commemorates a pivotal event in the history of Tasmania's gay community and, by extension, the broader struggles against official persecution by those identifying as LGBTQI Australians.

Sex and gender are fundamental aspects of the human condition. In all times and in all places they have been the subject of various, usually discriminatory, social and legal sanctions. Until modern times in Australia, homosexuality and other forms of non-heterosexual activity and diversity in gender identity have usually been illegal or otherwise proscribed. Since the 1960s, there have been growing efforts to change the laws and the prejudices behind them. The Sydney 'Pride' parade is the most high-profile of these activities but there have been many other significant events contributing to the current recognition of LGBTQI+ rights, including the same-sex plebiscite in 2017. A less well-known landmark took place in Tasmania in 1988.

Convictism has cast a long shadow across Tasmania's past and present. Attitudes of that dark era were long embedded in colonial and, later, state legislation concerning homosexuality. Sodomy was illegal under England's legal system and so that was automatically the case in colonial Australia and after Federation. The last execution in the British Empire for sodomy was carried out in Tasmania in 1867. Even though capital punishment was later abolished, sodomy in Tasmania could still lead to a sentence of twenty-one years in jail. Social and political attitudes contributed to Tasmania's continued outlawry of non-heterosexual behaviour and resistance to calls for decriminalisation.

In the 1980s, a campaign to decriminalise homosexuality in the island state began under the banner of the Tasmanian Homosexual Law Reform Group. A petition calling for the necessary legislative changes was started with the aim of gaining broad popular support. The campaign set up a stall in the Salamanca Place market to collect signatures for the petition in October 1988. In addition to the state's historical reluctance to decriminalise homosexuality, the world was in the middle of the AIDS epidemic, leading to further vilifying of gay men. When the campaigners refused to close or move their stall, the Hobart City Council of the time placed a ban on the operation and requested police arrest anyone approaching the stall to engage with those staffing it, or to take away informational literature. Each Saturday for the coming months, the same ritual was enacted at Salamanca markets, as reported in the *Canberra Times*:

> The homosexuals insisted that they were being discriminated against, and it was a matter of free speech and human rights, and continued with their stall in defiance. On came the police with their paddy wagon. And for the past almost two months, there has been a regular ritual at Salamanca, as the homosexuals set up their stall each Saturday, and the police arrest them for defying a council order. Within the first six weeks, there had been 130 arrests.
>
> There were screams from some quarters about human rights and free speech, but the council remained resolute.

One council alderman, a medical practitioner, was quoted in the same article declaring that 'he certainly wasn't going to support homosexual-rights demonstrations and stalls at a family market when what they were really talking about was "legitimising sodomy". With AIDS rampant, it was hardly appropriate, he said.'

Although many were arrested over the course of the campaign, the council's actions, which included giving some of its officers powers to 'ban from the market anyone considered to be one of the gay protesters or their fellow travellers', were subsequently shown to be without authority and charges were dropped. But the struggle continued for almost another decade.

By 1997 all Australian jurisdictions had decriminalised private sex between consenting adult men, completing a process that began in South Australia in the 1970s. In Tasmania, a prolonged series of campaigns, an appeal to the United Nations, rallies and protests eventually led to decriminalisation, despite strong resistance from some religious and community organisations. The outcome of these conflicting campaigns was an increase in Tasmanian public support for reform from 33 to nearly 60 per cent. This was the highest such level recorded for any state in the country. In 2008, the Hobart City Council officially apologised for the actions of the 1988 council. Today, Tasmania has not only reversed the intolerant image it once had, but it is now regarded as a leader in progressive sex and gender rights.

There seem to be no contemporaneous reports of an actual yellow line on the ground at Salamanca Place. But the installation symbolises a boundary that people were forbidden to cross without the likelihood of being arrested for supporting, or even inquiring about, alternative sexual orientations.

The Clash of Symbols

What are the most popular and powerful symbols of Australia?

Historians have identified many people, events, practices, objects, flora and fauna, ideas, sounds or places that represent our shared ideas of who and what we are as a nation. They include, among others, Vegemite, the surf lifesaver, pavlova, the Holden automobile, Uluru and the famed 'baggy green' cap of Test cricket. These, and other national symbols, past and present, may not resonate with everyone. The life and legend of bushranger Ned Kelly, usually represented in a stylised image of his iron helmet, has been considered by many to sum up basic Australian ideals, such as defiance of oppressive authority and the 'fair go'. On the other hand, many others have insisted that Ned was a murdering thug. One person's emotionally charged symbol is another's trivia or even red flag.

Symbols are a lot more complicated than they might seem; they can mean a lot, as well as having different meanings to different people or groups of people. The Southern Cross, or 'Eureka flag', has been adapted from its original purpose as a rallying banner for the miners' revolt of 1854 to become a symbol of militant trade unions and the radical left in general. In the second decade of the twenty-first century, the flag was also appropriated by far-right political groups, leading to a rush to have Southern Cross tattoos removed from the bodies of those who had previously been proud to display the image. The symbol became, literally, a brand.

Commercial interests, past and present, have also sought to associate their products and services with images and terms identified with Australia. Terms such as 'Boomerang mouth organs', 'Billy tea', and 'Cockatoo clothing', among many more, have been used in an attempt to increase sales. Are these bush images, espoused in the works of Paterson, Lawson, Tom Roberts and many others in the past, still relevant to many Australians? Certainly, the racism and sexism implicit and explicit in their meanings and the stories behind them are no longer appropriate to a more enlightened era.

Everything changes, or at least appears to change. As historians of this subject, Melissa Harper and Richard White, have observed, 'National symbols never stand still.' Ideas and ideals held dear by previous generations inevitably give way to new, younger and imported concepts, lifestyles and values. As some symbols fade, so new ones take their places.

Whether these symbols represent reality or are simply convenient fictions we hold about ourselves is an open question.

The late nineteenth–early twentieth century ideal of 'Miss Australia', sometimes featured in late nineteenth century newspapers, has long disappeared. Miss Australia was a feminine figure of a young, vibrant nation coming into its rightful destiny. After World War II, this figure transmuted into the beginning of the 'Miss Australia' beauty queen contests. They, too, have been mostly left in the past.

As well as figures from the popular and folk culture of different eras, symbols may also be authorised. Many officially sanctioned national symbols are displayed throughout Parliament House, including coats of arms, flags, wattle (the floral emblem), anthems and the national colours of green and gold, among other not very exciting items. These images are taught to schoolchildren and are backed up by some extensive educational resources for classroom use. The history of some reveals a little political tweaking. A subtle change was made to the Commonwealth Star that appears on the national flag to more closely represent the seven states and territories. Similarly, there have been several alterations to the lyrics of 'Advance Australia Fair', firstly when it was adopted as the national anthem in 1984. In 2021 the line 'For we are young and free' was changed to 'For we are one and free', an affirmation of the political need to use symbols to encourage national unity through recognition of Australia's long Indigenous history.

The simultaneous conflicting meanings of many national symbols suggests that they speak to many about shared ideas and ideals that relate to the predominant sense of who and what we are, whatever that may be at a particular time. While old symbols disappear or morph into new forms, others are undoubtedly in the making. What they will be and what sort of Australia might they represent is another open question.

A Pale Blue Dot

In August 2023 there was a brief burst of public interest in outer space. Specifically, in the spacecraft *Voyager 2*. Some routine commands sent from Earth caused the antennae to point the wrong way, rendering the craft unable to transmit. There was concern that the problem—over 19 billion kilometres away from Earth—might not be remedied and *Voyager 2* would no longer send its valuable data back as it continued its momentous journey.

Outside the space science community, most people had either forgotten all about the legacy *Voyager* mission or had probably never heard of it at all, despite its potential significance for the future of humanity. It began in 1977 when the National Aeronautical Space Agency (NASA) launched two spacecraft, *Voyager 1* and *Voyager 2*, from Cape Canaveral in Florida. Their mission was to fly close to the planets Jupiter and Saturn and relay information and photographs back to scientists on Earth. The voyages were planned to take five years and, in that time, accomplished everything the scientists hoped they would—and much more.

As the spacecraft moved on their separate paths through space and time, new technology made it possible to remotely upgrade the technical capabilities of the craft and extend their journeys. After reaching Jupiter and Saturn, they glided on to the most distant planets in the solar system, Neptune and Uranus. Still operating and transmitting data, the two *Voyager*s then kept going, sailing the solar winds further and further away from Earth. Although some of the experiments and onboard equipment to conduct them have since failed and heating has been turned off to conserve the power generated by their nuclear fuel, the *Voyager*s are still able to relay valuable information. They will probably do so for many more years as the two spacecraft drift into eternity.

Extensive technological support from Earth is required to maintain the Voyager mission. The global deep space network (DSN) is responsible for this. One of its vital components is at the Canberra Deep Space Communication Complex at Tidbinbilla. This facility, in collaboration with its sister sites in the United States and Spain, provides 'continuous communication and navigation support for the world's deep space missions'. When *Voyager 2*'s antenna went out of alignment in 2023, it was a technological 'shout' sent through almost 20 billion kilometres of interstellar space from Tidbinbilla that brought the craft back online. Engineers instructed the *Voyager 2* to turn its antennae back towards Earth. The signal took over eighteen hours to reach the spacecraft and it was another eighteen-and-a-half anxious hours for the return signal to confirm that the command had been accepted and *Voyager 2* could continue sending back data.

As well as providing scientific information, the *Voyager*s have another purpose. The two ungainly looking spacecraft have become humanity's best hope of discovering any extraterrestrial life that might exist. They are both supplied with a '12-inch [30 cm] gold-plated copper disk known as "The Golden Record"', a 'kind of time capsule, intended to communicate a story of our world to extraterrestrials.' Selected by a committee led by the late scientist and visionary Carl Sagan, the recording contains examples of languages spoken from 5000 years ago to the present, natural and human sounds, a great variety of music from many cultures and 115 images selected to portray the nature and diversity of life on Earth. Among the items are field recordings of some Australian First Nations songs and a photograph of a crocodile. This unique encyclopedia is intended to give any extraterrestrial space-farers who might one day encounter the *Voyager*s a good idea of who we are as a species, what we do with ourselves and each other, and what the small rock we live on is like. If either of the *Voyager*s is encountered and the Golden Record decoded by another intelligent life form in the thousands of years they will survive, humanity will have communicated its existence to the cosmos.

In 1990, nearly a decade after the *Voyager* mission was supposed to end, *Voyager 1* sent back an unprecedented image of the Earth taken from a distance of approximately 6 billion kilometres. Our world could barely be seen as a tiny speck of blue in an unimaginable vastness. The photograph puts this lonely planet and its fractious peoples into compelling perspective. Carl Sagan would later write in his book *Pale Blue Dot: A vision of the human future in space*: 'Look again at that dot. That's here. That's home. That's us.'

ACKNOWLEDGEMENTS

As always, my thanks to many people who had a hand in the making of this book, including W Benjamin Lindner, Maureen Seal, Kylie Seal-Pollard, Rob Willis, Olya Willis, and especially to publisher Elizabeth Weiss and the always outstanding folk at Allen & Unwin.

IMAGE CREDITS

Chapter 1 | Seeing the Country
'Full length portrait of late Pitcairn Islanders at Norfolk, circa 1861. These men would be descendants of the Bounty mutineers.' Alamy, ID: 2GYGEBW.

Chapter 2 | The Unsettled Land
'Album of photographs of Jenolan Caves / Frank Hurley.' National Library of Australia, ID nla.obj-140633294.

Chapter 3 | Heroes and Heroines
'Copy of Letter from Governor's Secretary', Queensland State Archives, ID 26118.

Chapter 4 | Ratbags and Rebels
'Cattle rustler and bushman Rodney William Ansell in 1987 photo, inspiration for the 1986 film *Crocodile Dundee*, was fatally shot 3 August 1999 by Constable Jim O'Brien after Ansell opened fire on

partner Sergeant Glen Huitson at Sturt Highway road block, Northern Territory. Photographer Clive Hyde.' Newspix, ID NPX72330

Chapter 5 | Troubled Times
'William Roberts and family evicted from their home into the street, Redfern, 28 September 1934.' Mitchell Library, State Library of New South Wales, ID 52280.

Chapter 6 | Celebrations
'Norland Nursing Home Christmas tree, 16 December 1939.' Sam Hood, Mitchell Library, State Library of New South Wales, ID d3d0EyVrlNLKe.

Chapter 7 | Creations
'Man and amp; boy listening to crystal set radio, backyard, Yarraville, circa 1925.' Museums Victoria, ID 1689328.

Chapter 8 | Communities
'Dad's kelpie pups at "Vivaleigh", Hedley (C.C. Rossiter) circa 1916.' State Library Victoria, ID 2158481.

Chapter 9 | Ourselves
'Hughes, NT. c. July 1944. Two RAAF members at a North West base talking to Dr Thomas Wood, author of the book *Cobbers*. Left to right: Squadron Leader J. Lee of Wagga, NSW and of No. 2 (Mitchell) Squadron RAAF; Squadron Leader Darcy Wentworth of Coolah, NSW and Commanding Officer of No. 31 (Beaufighter) Squadron RAAF; Dr Wood.' Australian War Memorial, ID NWA0574.

NOTES

Chapter 1: Seeing the Country

The Superhighways of Sahul

page 10   'sprinkled with red ochre': Malcolm Allbrook, 'Mungo Man (?–?)', *Australian Dictionary of Biography*, National Centre of Biography, Australian National University, https://ia.anu.edu.au/biography/mungo-man-27704/text35292, accessed 9 December 2023.

page 10   'routes and even modern highways': Dana Morse, 'Researchers demystify the secrets of ancient Aboriginal migration across Australia', *ABC News*, 30 April 2021, www.abc.net.au/news/2021-04-30/research-into-ancient-aboriginal-migration-across-australia/100105902, accessed February 2024. Also Corey Bradshaw et al., 'An incredible journey—the first people to arrive in Australia came in large numbers, and on purpose', University of Adelaide: Faculty of Sciences, Engineering and Technology, https://set.adelaide.edu.au/news/list/2019/06/26/an-incredible-journey-the-first-people-to-arrive-in-australia-came-in-large, accessed February 2024.

page 11   'Arnhem Land from around 1700': Erin Parke, 'New study reveals history of Aboriginal trade with foreign visitors before British settlement',

ABC News, 18 July 2021, www.abc.net.au/news/2021-07-18/new-study-aboriginal-trade-before-british-settlement/100290300#, accessed September 2023.

page 12 'for war rather than trade': Lillian Rangiah, 'Archaeologists say Moluccan boats depicted in Arnhem Land rock art, solving mystery', *ABC News*, 29 May 2023, www.abc.net.au/news/2023-05-28/nt-moluccan-boat-arnhem-land-rock-art/102400042, accessed September 2023.

page 12 'Flinders Ranges in South Australia': Michael C. Westaway et al., 'Hidden in plain sight: The archaeological landscape of Mithaka Country, south-west Queensland', *Antiquity*, vol. 95, no. 382, pp. 1043–60.

page 12 'items and ceremonies and songs': Leman Altuntas, 'Australia's Silk Road': The quarries of Mithaka country dating back 2100 years', *Arkeonews*, 4 April 2022, https://arkeonews.net/australias-silk-road-the-quarries-of-mithaka-country-dating-back-2100-years/, accessed September 2023.

page 12 'for more than 2000 years': Chris Urwin et al., 'Archaeology is unravelling new stories about Indigenous seagoing trade on Australia's doorstep', *The Conversation*, 11 April 2019, https://theconversation.com/archaeology-is-unravelling-new-stories-about-indigenous-seagoing-trade-on-australias-doorstep-111528, accessed September 2023; Sean Ulm et al., 'Early Aboriginal pottery production and offshore island occupation on Jiigurru (Lizard Island group), Great Barrier Reef, Australia', *Quaternary Science Reviews*, vol. 333, 1 June 2024, 108624, https://doi.org/10.1016/j.quascirev.2024.108624.

page 12 'of cockatoos in medieval Sicily': Heather Dalton et al., 'Frederick II of Hohenstaufen's Australasian cockatoo: Symbol of detente between East and West and evidence of the Ayyubids' global reach', *Parergon*, vol. 35, no. 1, pp. 35–60, https://search.informit.org/doi/10.3316/informit.649258641527441, accessed February 2024.

page 13 'even forming family attachments there': Erin Parke, 'Gold teeth and a broken heart: Dirrikaya's adventure unravels Australia's hidden history', *Compass*, *ABC News*, 31 March 2024, www.abc.net.au/news/2024-03-31/odyssey-erin-parke-makassar-connection/103476888.

Nurundere Makes the Sea Flow

page 13 'brought about intriguing new interpretations': Timothy Burberry, *Geomythology: How common stories reflect Earth events*, Routledge, London, 2021, accessed May 2024.

page 14   'the last ice age ended': Jonathan Benjamin et al., 'Aboriginal artefacts on the continental shelf reveal ancient drowned cultural landscapes in northwest Australia', *PLoS ONE*, vol. 15, no. 7, https://doi.org/10.1371/journal.pone.0233912, accessed February 2023 and correction 15 June 2023, https://doi.org/10.1371/journal.pone.0287490, accessed February 2024.

page 15   'man, scarcely able to move': Collected by Meyer and quoted in George Taplin, *The Native Tribes of South Australia*, E.S. Wigg & Son, Adelaide, 1879, pp. 60–1.

page 15   'be around 10,000 years old': Patrick Nunn, *The Edge of Memory: Ancient stories, oral tradition and the post-glacial world*, Bloomsbury, London, 2018; Patrick D. Nunn and Nicholas J. Reid, 'Aboriginal memories of inundation of the Australian coast dating from more than 7000 years ago', *Australian Geographer*, vol. 47, no. 1, pp. 11–47, https://doi.org/10.1080/00049182.2015.1077539, accessed February 2024.

page 15   'be consumed by the fire': Duane Hamacher, 'Finding meteorite impacts in Aboriginal oral tradition', *The Conversation*, 4 March 2015, https://theconversation.com/finding-meteorite-impacts-in-aboriginal-oral-tradition-38052, accessed July 2023.

page 15   'extinct by 40,000 years ago': Patrick D. Nunn & Luiza Corral Martins de Oliviera Ponciano, 'Of bunyips and other beasts: living memories of long-extinct creatures in art and stories', *The Conversation*, 15 April 2019, https://theconversation.com/of-bunyips-and-other-beasts-living-memories-of-long-extinct-creatures-in-art-and-stories-113031, accessed January 2020.

page 15   'oldest oral traditions in existence': Erin L. Matchan et al., 'Early human occupation of southeastern Australia: New insights from $^{40}Ar/^{39}Ar$ dating of young volcanoes', *Geology*, vol. 48, no. 4, https://pubs.geoscienceworld.org/gsa/geology/article/doi/10.1130/G47166.1/581018/Early-human-occupation-of-southeastern-Australia, accessed February 2024.

Star Stories

page 17   'where it has various meanings': For example, the Boorung clan, part of the Wergaia speaking people of the Kulin nation of northwest Victoria. Patricia Christies and Martin Bush, 'Stories in the stars: The night sky of the Boornong people', *Teacher notes*, https://museumsvictoria.com.au/media/1860/stories-in-the-stars.pdf, accessed July 2023.

page 18   'the field of cultural astronomy': Ray P. Norris & Barnaby R.M. Norris, 'Why are there seven sisters?', in Efrosyni Boutsikas, Stephen C. McCluskey and John Steele (eds), *Advancing Cultural Astronomy: Studies in honour of Clive Ruggles*, Springer International Publishing, n.p., 2021. www.dropbox.com/s/np0n4v72bdl37gr/sevensisters.pdf?dl=0, accessed January 2024.

page 18   'endeavour we continue to pursue': Boutsikas, McCluskey and Steele, *Advancing Cultural Astronomy*.

Meeting the Tiwi

page 19   'of First Nations artefacts': Wendy van Duivenvoorde et al., 'Van Delft before Cook: The earliest record of substantial culture contact between Indigenous Australians and the Dutch East India Company prior to 1770', *Australasian Journal of Maritime Archaeology*, vol. 43, pp. 27–49, https://search.informit.org/doi/10.3316/informit.994273997469601, accessed February 2024.

page 22   'four days after reaching Macassar': The surviving primary source details of the van Delft voyage are contained in a report from Batavia to the Seventeen Gentlemen—effectively the corporate board—of the VOC, in R.H. Major (ed.), *Early Voyages to Terra Australis now called Australia . . .*, The Hakluyt Society, London, 1859, pp. 165ff.

A Mystery Island

page 23   'been chipped from volcanic rock': Atholl Anderson & Peter White, 'Prehistoric settlement on Norfolk Island and its Oceanic context', *Records of the Australian Musuem*, supplement, vol. 27, pp. 135–41.

page 25   'Oh, that's just the convicts.': Julie Power, 'Norfolk Island find solves part of Pacific's most enduring mystery', *The Sydney Morning Herald*, 29 October 2022, www.smh.com.au/national/norfolk-island-find-solves-part-of-pacific-s-most-enduring-mystery-20221028-p5btr5.html, accessed May 2023.

page 25   'perhaps as early as 1150AD': Though the Norfolk Island Museum states that they were resident between 750 and 1500, https://norfolkislandmuseum.com.au/collections/kavha/, accessed May 2023.

A Peaceable Possession

page 28   '[sic]—also struck out during editing': The edition of Cook's journal used by the National Museum of Australia is at 'Cook's journal',

National Museum of Australia, www.nma.gov.au/exhibitions/endeavour-voyage/cooks-journal/august-1770, accessed June 2023.

page 28   'foot on the bloody island!': 'Bedanug, Thunadha, Bedhan Lag, Tuidin—Possession Island', National Museum of Australia, www.nma.gov.au/exhibitions/endeavour-voyage/bedanug-thunadha-bedhan-lag-tuidin-possession-island, accessed June 2023.

Castaway

page 29   'not verified until much later': Jean Fornasiero & John West-Sooby (transl. and eds), *French designs on colonial New South Wales: François Péron's memoir on the English settlements in New Holland, Van Diemen's Land and the archipelagos of the great Pacific Ocean*, The Friends of the State Library of South Australia Inc., Adelaide, 2014.

page 32   'are yet to be seen': G.F. Moore, 'To the Editor of the "Perth Gazette"', *Perth Gazette and Western Australian Journal*, 5 May 1838, p. 71.

page 32   'settlers, Georgiana Molloy, in 1841': Alexandra Hasluck, *Georgiana Molloy: Portrait with background*, Oxford University Press, Melbourne, 1955.

page 32   'fathered children with Wardandi women': Augustus Oldfield, 'On the Aborigines of Australia', *Transactions of the Ethnological Society of London*, vol. 3, 1865, pp. 215–98, https://doi.org/10.2307/3014165, accessed July 2023. Oldfield mistakenly thought Vasse was one of Baudin's scientists, but his opinion was based on his own observations of the Geographe Bay area.

page 32   'and articles on the subject': Thomas Brendan Cullity, *Vasse: An account of the disappearance of Thomas Timothee Vasse*, T.B. Cullity, Perth, 1992; Edward Duyker, 'Timothée Vasse: A biographical note', *French Australian Review*, no. 51, pp. 39–41, www.isfar.org.au/wp-content/uploads/2016/10/51_EDWARD-DUYKER-Timoth%C3%A9e-Vasse-A-Biographical-Note.pdf, accessed July 2023.

page 32   'and eventually return to France': Alain Serieyx, *Wonnerup: The sacred dune*, trans. David Maguire, Abrolhos Publishing, Perth, 2001.

Stealing the Bones

page 33   'sent the parts to Edinburgh': *Adelaide AZ*, 'William Smith's part in Adelaide trading of Aboriginal people's bodies exposed by 1903 Tommy Walker scandal', (from ABC Radio National *The History Listen*), https://adelaideaz.com/articles/coroner-william-smith-s-part-in-adelaide-trade-in-aboriginal-people-s-bodies-exposed-by-tommy-walker-scandal-in-1903, accessed June 2023.

page 34   'of rum each for them': Grace Karskens, 'Appin massacre', *Dictionary of Sydney*, 2015, http://dictionaryofsydney.org/entry/appin_massacre, accessed June 2023.

page 35   'one was that of Cannabayagal': Paul Daley, 'Restless Indigenous remains', *Meanjin.* vol. 73, no. 1, https://meanjin.com.au/essays/restless-indigenous-remains/, accessed June 2023.

page 35   'protection of First Nations heritage': Else Kennedy & Tamara Clark, 'Looking back on Mungo Man—human remains millennia older than the pyramids—50 years on', *ABC News*, 10 March 2024, www.abc.net.au/news/2024-03-10/mungo-man-anniversary-willandra-lakes-lake-mungo-national-park/103536402, accessed March 2024.

Chapter 2: The Unsettled Land

A Lost People

page 38   'Wyndham back this way': Ben Ward and ORS on Behalf of the Miriuwung and Gajerrong People and ORS v State of Western Australia and ORS—BC9806200, Unreported Judgements, Federal Court of Australia, WAG 6001 of 1995, p. 31, available as 'Native Title Judgment Federal Court', https://mgcorp.com.au/resources/, accessed May 2024.

page 39   'to Sydney, or even Perth': Julie Lenora Parsons, 'Andrew Hickson: Big sculpture and other obsessions', *Ozarts*, Spring 2020, www.ozarts.net.au/images/oz-arts/2020-spring/andrew-hickson.pdf, accessed October 2022.

Land of Monsters

page 41   'and psychic, in particular places': Christine Judith Nicholls, '"Dreamings" and place—Aboriginal monsters and their meanings', The *Conversation*, 30 April 2014, accessed June 2023.

page 41   'everyday life is the Wulgaru': W. Harney, *Tales from the Aborigines*, Rigby, Adelaide, 1959, pp. 90–7, 98–101, 103–6. R. Berndt & C. Berndt *The Speaking Land: Myth and story in Aboriginal Australia*, Penguin, Melbourne, 1989. See also S. Gill, *Storytracking: Texts, stories and histories in central Australia*, Oxford/New York, Oxford University Press, 1998; J. Mathews (comp.) & I. White (ed.), *The Opal That Turned into Fire and Other Stories from the Wangkumara*, Magabala Books, Broome, WA, 1994; D. Rose,

Dingo Makes Us Human: Life and land in an Aboriginal Australian culture, Cambridge University Press, Melbourne, 1992.

page 42   'looking at the passengers inside': Ron Edwards, *The Australian Yarn*, Rigby Ltd, Adelaide, 1978, p. 211.

page 42   'with a fur coat on': 'Encounter #9: More from Maalan', *Yowie Tracks*, https://yowietracks.com/2020/05/08/encounter-9-more-from-the-malaan/, accessed July 2023.

Flesh-Shrivelling Curses

page 44   'proverbial "bullocky" blush with envy': *Morning Bulletin* (Rockhampton), 6 June 1935, p. 8.

page 44   'a Kurdaitcha or a Jarnpa': Yasmine Musharbash & Geir Henning Presterudstuen (eds), *Monster Anthropology in Australasia and Beyond*, New York, Palgrave Macmillan, 2014.

page 45   'not duly attended to': Baldwin Spencer & F.J. Gillen, *The Native Tribes of Central Australia*, Macmillan, London, 1899, pp. 476ff.

page 46   'the 1930s to the 1950s': *The Argus*, 13 July 1937, p. 8; *The Advertiser*, 20 September 1952, p. 3; *Townsville Daily Bulletin*, 31 August 1953, p. 2.

page 46   'museums and curiosity shops . . .': *The West Australian*, 26 January 1939, p. 7. The letter was written by D.C. Cowan, historian, artist and daughter of Edith Cowan, the first woman to be elected to an Australian parliament. Arunta is now more usually spelt Arrernte.

Lone Graves

page 46   'the gold deposit in 1900': Eastern Goldfields Historical Society Inc., 'Duketon', www.kalgoorliehistory.org.au/towns/Duketon/, accessed April 2023.

page 47   'J Duke/R Schwamn': 'Lonely graves', *Outback Family History*, www.outbackfamilyhistory.com.au/records/record.php?record_id=400, accessed April 2023.

page 47   'died of a heart attack': Cristy-Lee Macqueen, 'Finding lone graves in North Queensland to help trace family histories', *ABC News*, 2 February 2021, www.abc.net.au/news/2021-02-02/search-for-lone-graves-whitsundays-family-tree/13109838, accessed April 2023.

page 47   'was her fourteen-day-old infant son': 'Lone graves of the goldfields', *Goldfields Guide: Exploring the Victorian goldfields*, 25 May 2019, www.goldfieldsguide.com.au/blog/69/lone-graves-of-the-goldfields, accessed April 2023.

page 48 'and was later found dead': 'Child's grave', *Goldfields Guide: Exploring the Victorian goldfields*, n.d., www.goldfieldsguide.com.au/explore-location/352/childs-grave/, accessed April 2023.

page 49 'brought up in that community': *The West Australian* 23 August 1889, p. 3.

page 49 'force of other young men': Leah McLennan and Vanessa Mills, 'Lonely graves of the outback: Retirees install 100 plaques at grave sites across the Kimberley', *ABC News*, 14 September 2016, www.abc.net.au/news/2016-09-14/retirees-plan-mark-outback-graves-kimberley/7838784, accessed April 2023.

Devil of a Place

page 50 'devil's meadow", and so on': Jeremy Harte, *Cloven Country: The devil and the English landscape*, Reaktion Books, London, 2023.

page 50 'Satanic dominions should be . . .': 'Lead ore mining families—from Alston to Australia: Try Again Gold Mine at Devil's Kitchen', *The Australasian*, 8 October 1864, http://www.richardson.org.au/try_again_gold_mining_company_devils_kitchen.html, accessed July 2023.

page 51 'Mount Gambier and Mount Schanck': 'C A H', 'The Devil in Australian Place Names', *The Age* (Melbourne), 3 April 1937, p. 26.

page 52 'early history of the area': Dr Dan Catchpoole, 'James McKeown: from fact to folklore to legend to fable . . . and back again!, Part 1', Australasian Cave and Karst Management Association, https://ackma.org/journal/72/James%20McKeown%20-%20Dr%20Dan%20Catchpole.pdf, accessed July 2023.

page 52 'into this stupendous natural structure': *Empire*, 18 January 1871, p. 4 (using the name 'Binda' as well as 'Fish River' for the location of the caves).

page 52 'carried away specimens" of the formations': *The Maitland Mercury and Hunter River General Advertiser*, 23 October 1856, p. 4.

page 52 'formations were already being aired': *Empire*, 26 February 1857, p. 5.

page 53 'bushrangers, convicts and the devil': Juanita Feros Ruys, 'The Devil's Coach House and Skeleton Cave: Colonial tales, the medieval demonic, and the absence of the Indigenous, *Preternature: Critical and Historical Studies on the Preternatural*, vol. 5, no. 2, 2016, pp. 159–88, https://doi.org/10.5325/preternature.5.2.0159, accessed 18 July 2023.

page 53 'next to the Australian flag': *Blue Mountains Gazette*, 13 February 2023, 'Aboriginal flag now flies over site of titanic dreamtime

struggle at Jenolan Caves', www.bluemountainsgazette.com.au/
story/8079823/aboriginal-flag-now-flies-over-site-of-titanic-dreamtime-
struggle-at-jenolan-caves/, accessed November 2023.

A Ghost of Gold

page 55   'are well-known in Coolgardie society': *Coolgardie Miner*,
1 June 1898, p. 5.

page 55   'depression and laughed it away': *The Evening Star* (Boulder),
1 June 1898, p. 3.

page 55   'hunters to encounter the apparition': Richard Davis, *The Ghost
Guide to Australia*, Bantam Books, Sydney, 1998, p. 415.

page 56   'remains of the original headstone': Moya Sharp, 'Gold
and ghosts', *Outback family History*, 11 September 2021, www.
outbackfamilyhistoryblog.com/the-murder-of-nurse-gold/, accessed
December 2023.

The Obliging Dead

page 56   'at Drayton, for forty-five years': *The Courier-Mail*, 1 August 1952,
p. 4.

page 57   'unfortunate man did not transpire': *The Sydney Morning Herald*,
19 May 1870, p. 3 (from the *Toowoomba Chronicle*).

page 58   '"Book Now If You Dare" proclaims the website': 'Paranormal
investigations', Queensland National Trust, https://nationaltrustqld.org.au/
heritage-sites/Royal-Bull-s-Head-Inn/paranormal-investigations, accessed
June 2023.

page 58   'are unconnected to the inn': Paranormal.com.au, www.
paranormal.com.au/public/index.php?topic=11645.0 , accessed June 2023.

page 58   'her not especially dramatic death': Though I've not been able to
find the source of this oft-repeated date.

The Haunted Asylum

page 60   'spectral rider had no face': Richard Davis, *The Ghost Guide to
Australia*, Bantam Books, Sydney, 1998, pp. 206–7.

page 61   'said the spirit was embedded': *Adelaide Observer*, 29 August 1868,
p. 16 (from the *Ararat Advertiser*).

page 61   'in a lonely spot . . .': *Evening Journal* (Adelaide),
24 September 1881, p. 2.

page 61   'in the Ararat Botanical Gardens': *The Horsham Times*,
2 May 1899, p. 2.

page 61 'him to kill his mother': *Bendigo Advertiser*, 3 May 1906, p. 4.
page 62 'including prisons, hospitals and orphanages': David Waldron,
Nathaniel Buchanan & Sharn Waldron, *Aradale: The making of a haunted
asylum*, Australian Scholarly Publishing, Melbourne, 2020. (Aradale is an
alternative name for the asylum.)

A Million Spooky Acres

page 64 'have no chances of stopping': 'Richo', *Grey Nomads Bulletin
Board*, https://thegreynomads.activeboard.com/t42314385/pilliga-princess/,
accessed July 2023 (edited for clarity). Other details have been sourced
from Jen Tucker (personal communication 16 April 2021; 'Yowies,
bunyips and mysterious tales from the Pilliga Forest', 22 July 2011, https://
oldbroadintheoutback.wordpress.com/2012/07/22/yowies-bunyips-and-
mysterious-tales-from-the-pilliga-forest/; 'Re: port wakefield ghost???',
post by 'Fantome', 21 May 2012, https://fordforums.com.au/showthread.
php?p=4273244 and Claudia Hoops, 'The 6 spookiest roads in Australia',
blog post, 14 December 2015, www.teletracnavman.com.au/resources/
blog/the-6-spookiest-roads-in-australia, all accessed July 2023.
page 65 'TRUCKDRIVERS ON THE HIGHWAY': 'Clare Wibson', 24
June 2018, *Find A Grave*, www.findagrave.com/memorial/190844341/
clare-wibson, accessed July 2023. The Australian Cemeteries Index also
has a photograph of a white wooden cross bearing Clare Wibson's name
and her tentative hold on immortality as the 'Pilliga Princess', https://
austcemindex.com/inscription.php?id=9762192, accessed July 2023.

Dangerous Journeys

page 68 'the story in the 1930s': Bill Scott, *The Long and the Short
and the Tall: A collection of Australian yarns,* Western Plains Publishers,
Sydney, 1985; Paul Smith, *The Book of Nasty Legends*, Routledge & Kegan
Paul, London, 1983; Graham Seal, *Great Australian Urban Myths*, Angus &
Robertson, Sydney, 1995.

Chapter 3: Heroes and Heroines

The Great Rescue

page 72 'eleven o'clock at night . . .': 'The floods at Gundagai', *Freeman's
Journal* (Sydney), 8 July 1852, p. 10.
page 72 'of the buildings had disappeared': 'The floods at Gundagai', *The
Maitland Mercury and Hunter River General Advertiser*, 24 July 1852, p. 4.

page 72   'a population of around 250': 'Gundagai flood', *National Museum of Australia*, www.nma.gov.au/defining-moments/resources/gundagai-flood-1852, accessed July 2023.

page 72   'large and thriving family': 'Great floods at Gundagai—loss of sixty four lives', *South Australian Register*, 22 July 1852, p. 3.

page 73   'to have been completely forgotten': 'An old relic', *The Gundagai Independent and Pastoral, Agricultural and Mining Advocate*, 27 March 1912, p. 4.

page 73   'were caught in the flood': 'Great flood of June 1852', *Monument Australia*, https://monumentaustralia.org.au/themes/disaster/flood/display/93945-great-flood-of-june-1852, accessed July 2023.

The Boundary Rider's Wife

page 76   'Of the boundary rider's wife': 'The boundary rider's wife', *Toowoomba Chronicle and Darling Downs General Advertiser*, 10 December 1898, p. 6.

page 76   'in south-west Victoria, in 1884': 'Shocking suicide', *The Ballarat Courier*, 12 November 1884, p. 4.

page 77   'no accounting for such vagaries': 'A wife's conduct', *The Register* (Adelaide), 16 August 1907, p. 8. Another similar case in the *Macleay Argus* (Kempsey), 5 March 1898, p. 12.

Posties

page 78   'an Australian icon was born': 'First post office', National Museum of Australia, www.nma.gov.au/defining-moments/resources/first-post-office, accessed February 2024.

page 78   'He was paid in tobacco': Emily J.B. Smith, 'Outback mailman who delivered post by walking 700km through the Nullarbor', *ABC News*, 25 August 2022, www.abc.net.au/news/2022-08-25/outback-mailmans-delivery-round-eucla-to-fowlers-bay-nullarbor/101361646, accessed August 2023.

page 80   'within the last few years': 'Perilous journey of a mailman', *The Argus*, 30 August 1879, p. 5.

page 80   'the death of a mailman': 'Australian mailmen and their horses', *Launceston Examiner*, 30 July 1892, p. 3.

page 80   'horse for half a mile': Tim Lee, 'Historical ledger for Halfway Hotel on Victoria's Dargo High Plains reviving stories of travellers past', *ABC News*, 9 November 2023, www.abc.net.au/news/2023-11-09/

historical-halfway-hotel-ledger-dargo-high-plains-preserved/103080134, accessed December 2023.

page 81 'recalled one of his friends': Adriane Reardon, 'Australia's last mounted postie Bruce Dennis farewelled by historic town of Gundagai', *ABC News*, 22 August 2022, www.abc.net.au/news/2022-08-29/mounted-postie-bruce-dennis-dies-gundagai/101380482, accessed August 2023.

page 81 'of Terang from early 1942': 'Terang has two postwomen', *The Argus*, 30 March 1942, p. 5.

page 81 'replace men on active service': 'Postwoman in Brisbane', *Daily Mirror* (Sydney), 3 July 1941, p. 1.

page 81 'trained to replace male telegraphists': 'Girls to drive G.P.O trucks', *Daily Mirror* (Sydney), 15 September 1941, p. 11.

Hell

page 83 'by the officials in charge': 'The transition to peace', *Australian College of Nursing*, www.acn.edu.au/sneak-peek-peace-flu, accessed May 2023.

page 83 'a crematorium, possibly Australia's first': 'Quarantine Station (fmr), Woodman Point', State Heritage Western Australian Government, http://inherit.stateheritage.wa.gov.au/Public/Inventory/PrintSingleRecord/40767f65-2223-41d5-ba74-6ffed70632ae#:~:text=Land%20was%20reserved%20for%20a,station%20finally%20closed%20in%201979, accessed May 2023.

page 83 '"too good to be true," she wrote': Susie Cone's diary is preserved in the State Library of Victoria and can be read online at https://prov.vic.gov.au/archive/VPRS19295, accessed May 2023.

page 83 'had died of the disease': 'History', Friends of Woodman Point Recreation Camp, www.woodmanpointquarantinestation.com/history-of-the-quarantine-station, accessed May 2023.

page 83 'have succumbed to the disease': 'Health—Spanish flu', *Australian Institute for Disaster Resilience*, https://knowledge.aidr.org.au/resources/health-spanish-flu-1919/ and 'Influenza pandemic', *National Museum of Australia*, www.nma.gov.au/defining-moments/resources/influenza-pandemic#:~, both accessed May 2023.

page 83 'with two simple words—"For Valour"': O'Kane Court in the station is also named for Rosa O'Kane. There is a memorial to the 'Boonah Tragedy', as this event has become known, in O'Kane Court.

NOTES

Ambitions of the 'Fair Sex'

page 84 'was strongly supported by women': Geoffrey Blainey, *The Story of Australia's People: The rise and rise of a new Australia*, Viking Australia, Melbourne, 2020 (2015), pp. 99–105.

page 85 'Grand Old Woman of Australia': Susan Magarey, 'Catherine Helen Spence', *SA History Hub*, History Trust of South Australia, https://sahistoryhub.history.sa.gov.au/people/catherine-helen-spence, accessed 18 October 2023.

page 86 'anywhere in the British Empire': Anna Hough, 'The 120th anniversary of women's suffrage in Australia', *Parliament of Australia*, 15 June 2022, www.aph.gov.au/About_Parliament/Parliamentary_Departments/Parliamentary_Library/FlagPost/2022/June/Womens_suffrage, accessed October 2023.

page 87 'the altar of political ambition': 'Edith Cowan', National Museum of Australia, www.nma.gov.au/defining-moments/resources/edith-cowan, accessed October 2021.

page 87 'works, Edith Cowan's "indomitable courage"': Clare Wright, 'Cowan, Edith Dircksey', *The Encyclopedia of Women and Leadership in Twentieth-Century Australia*, www.womenaustralia.info/leaders/biogs/WLE0162b.htm, accessed October 2023.

Almost Sir Lancelot

page 90 'the rest of the war': Accession number RELAWM01900, see 'Model prototype De Mole Tank', Australian War Memorial, www.awm.gov.au/collection/RELAWM01900.

page 90 'below a knighthood—almost Sir Lancelot': Chris Clark, 'de Mole, Lancelot Eldin (1880–1950)', *Australian Dictionary of Biography*, National Centre of Biography, Australian National University, 1981, https://adb.anu.edu.au/biography/de-mole-lancelot-eldin-5950/text10149, accessed October 2023.

Anonymous No Longer

page 92 'book on her Asian travels': Edith Emery, *A Twentieth Century Life: An autobiography*, kindle edition, 2017. Edith also published her *Encounter with Asia*, Ward Lock, London, 1969.

page 93 'the Australian Institute of Architects': Georgia Hitch, 'The remarkable life of Edith Emery—from prisoner of the Nazis to groundbreaking Tasmanian architect', *ABC News*, 4 June 2023, www.

abc.net.au/news/2023-06-04/edith-emery-architect-doctor-prisoner-
legacy/102361834, accessed June 2023.

War Widows

page 94   'help I can give you': Joy Damousi, 'Vasey, Jessie Mary (1897–
1966)', *Australian Dictionary of Biography*, National Centre of Biography,
Australian National University, https://adb.anu.edu.au/biography/vasey-
jessie-mary-11915/text21345, published first in hardcopy 2002, accessed 29
February 2024.

page 95   'they received pensions and allowances': 'Government spied on
war widows', *The Canberra Times*, 19 May 1949, p. 4.

page 96   'Menzies will respect his promises': 'Despair at treatment of war
widows', *Barrier Miner* (Broken Hill), 14 March 1950, p. 8.

page 96   'Widows to the National Government': 'History', Australian
War Widows Inc., https://warwidows.org.au/about-us/history/, accessed
October 2023.

The Gumboot Tortoise

page 97   'fine, shuffled on. And on': Phil Essam, 'From gumboots to glory',
http://www.vrwc.org.au/tim-archive/articles/Cliff%20Young.pdf, 2006,
accessed November 2022.

page 98   'previous record for the run': 'Cliff Young (athlete)', *Wikipedia*,
https://en.wikipedia.org/wiki/Cliff_Young_(athlete), accessed
November 2022 (citing contemporary press articles).

page 99   'the Beech Forest Progress Association': 'Cliff Young', Monument
Australia, https://monumentaustralia.org.au/themes/people/sport/
display/99346-cliff-young, accessed November 2022.

Chapter 4: Ratbags and Rebels

The Only Female Prisoner

page 102   'with a large sledge hammer': Jill Evans, 'Elizabeth Parker, the
Swing riots, and the Tetbury parish clerk', *Gloucestershire Crime History* blog,
14 October 2013 (citing sources from the Gloucestershire Archives, Gaol
Calendars, the Tetbury Poll Book of 1834 and local newspapers), https://
gloscrimehistory.wordpress.com/2013/10/14/elizabeth-parker-the-swing-
riots-and-the-tetbury-parish-clerk/, accessed October 2022.

page 104   'consideration of the Principal Superintendent': *Hobart Town
Gazette*, 3 October 1829, at 'Factory rules and regulations', Female Convicts

Research Centre Inc., www.femaleconvicts.org.au/convict-institutions/ factory-regulations, accessed June 2023.

page 105 'there aged 64 in 1874': 'Elizabeth Studham', *Convict Records*, https://convictrecords.com.au/convicts/studham/elizabeth/115685, accessed February 2024.

Genius Or Fool?

page 105 'great fool, or perhaps both': Bob Reece, 'Robert Lyon Milne', paper delivered to the Royal Western Australian Historical Society, 2016, https://web.archive.org/web/20160707015235if_/http://secure.histwest. org.au/files/ROBERT%20LYON%20MILN1.pdf, accessed October 2023.

page 108 'British colonies in this hemisphere': Lyon, 'To the Editor of the Perth Gazette', *Perth Gazette*, 11 January 1834, p. 215.

page 110 'the attics . . . [original emphases]': J.M.R. Cameron (ed.), *The Millendon Memoirs: George Fletcher Moore's Western Australian diaries and letters, 1830–1841*, Hesperian Press, Perth, 2006, p. 224.

A Convict Transformed

page 111 'escorting him to Castlemain [sic]': 'Victoria', *Colonial Times* (Hobart), 7 November 1856, p. 2.

page 112 'he pleaded guilty to manslaughter': 'Victoria', *Empire* (Sydney), 18 September 1857, p. 5.

page 112 'to be spent in irons': 'Trial of Gypsey Smith and Twigham, for the murder of Serjeant McNally', *Goulburn Herald and County of Argyle Advertiser*, 14 March 1857, p. 3.

page 113 'about getting out of it': 'Illegally at large', *The Argus*, 15 September 1864, p. 6.

page 113 'work in New South Wales': 'Police Department, Sydney, 28th February, 1866, *New South Wales Government Gazette*, 6 March 1866 (issue 51), p. 643.

page 114 'sentiments and healthy feelings': 'Victoria', *The Cornwall Chronicle* (Launceston), 24 February 1866, p. 2.

page 114 'New South Wales to Victoria': 'The death of a bushranger', *The Argus*, 18 July 1879, p. 7.

page 114 'of Great Britain and Ireland': 'Conditional pardon', *New South Wales Government Gazette*, 6 March 1866 (issue 70), p. 803. See also 'William Sydneham Smith', *Convict Records of Australia*, https://convictrecords. com.au/convicts/smith/william-sydenham/56796#references, accessed October 2023.

Red Ribbons and Bright Gold

page 116   'is indebted to the State': Bendigo Goldfields Petition',
Eurekapedia, https://eurekapedia.org/Bendigo_Goldfields_Petition#The_
Wording_of_the_Petition, accessed December 2023.

page 117   'Red Ribbon movement, George Thomson': Dorothy Kiers,
'Thomson, George Edward (1826–1889)', *Australian Dictionary of Biography*,
National Centre of Biography, Australian National University, https://
labouraustralia.anu.edu.au/biography/thomson-george-edward-4716/
text7761, accessed 4 December 2023.

page 117   'the reduction of the license-tax': 'Mount Alexander', *The Argus*,
5 September 1853, p. 7.

You Can't Wipe Out Carr-Boyd

page 118   'William Carr-Boyd wrote of him': Battler, 'Exit Potjostler',
Morning Bulletin (Rockhampton), 9 June 1925, p. 7.

page 119   'and language of the time': 'The North-West Expedition',
The Queenslander, 8 December 1877, p. 13.

page 119   'some distance from the camp': E.S. Wilkinson, 'Out "Where the
pelican builds"', *The Brisbane Courier*, 17 September 1932, p. 19.

page 121   'and hardihood, and dangerous enterprise': 'Interviews with
William Carr-Boyd', *Coolgardie Miner*, 16 November 1898, p. 3.

page 122   'can't wipe out Carr-Boyd': Needle, 'Points', *The Daily News*
(Perth), 22 September 1899, p. 2.

page 122   'in it kept him alive': Mary Durack, 'Carr-Boyd, William Henry
James (1852–1925)', *Australian Dictionary of Biography*, National Centre
of Biography, Australian National University, https://adb.anu.edu.au/
biography/carr-boyd-william-henry-james-3168/text4743, accessed
November 2023.

The Legend Of Galloping Jones

page 123   'the newspapers of the 1920s': Thomas J. Lonsdale, 'More about
buck-jumpers', *The Brisbane Courier*, 23 February 1924, p. 17; Thomas J.
Lonsdale, 'Outlaw horses', *The Brisbane Courier*, 9 August 1924, p. 16.

page 124   'was known as "Galloping Jones"': Greg Barron, *Galloping
Jones: and other true stories from Australia's history*, Stories of Oz Publishing,
Sydney, 2017.

page 124   'of "Alex Brown" was recorded': 'Chillagoe plebiscite', *Townsville
Daily Bulletin,* 8 June 1925, p. 4; 'Severe punishment', *Morning Bulletin*
(Rockhampton), 29 July 1927, p. 13.

page 124   'showed signs of former battles': 'Babinda notes', *Cairns Post*, 22 October 1926, p. 11. Another fight in 'Boxing', *Cairns Post*, 5 October 1926, p. 4.

page 124   'Australia at the present time': Bill Bowyang, 'Horsemen of the past', *Townsville Daily Bulletin*, 30 August 1928, p. 11. Bowyang also published a highly romanticised poem based on Jones: 'On the track', *Townsville Daily Bulletin*, 16 October 1934, p. 9.

page 125   'silly as a wet hen': Bill Bowyang, 'The real horsemen', *The Scone Advocate*, 5 July 1929, p. 8.

page 125   'as a "hardy, bow-legged Australian"': 'Wild horses at showground', *The Labor Daily* (Sydney), 22 December 1933, p. 10.

page 125   'as horsemen of high order': 'Rodeo at show', *The Newcastle Sun*, 15 February 1934, p. 15; 'Rodeo programme', *The Newcastle Sun*, 19 February 1934, p. 8, and 'The rodeo', *Newcastle Morning Herald and Miners' Advocate*, 22 February 1934, p. 5.

page 126   'touch of a human hand': 'Strange but true', *Smith's Weekly* (Sydney), 29 June 1940, p. 10. Another recollection in the *Chronicle* (Adelaide), 11 October 1945, p. 39.

page 126   'on Jones's activities in 1941': Bill Bowyang, 'Buck jumpers at Bowen River', *Townsville Daily Bulletin*, 21 June 1941, p. 10.

page 126   'and admired for his brawling': *Townsville Daily Bulletin*, 4 June 1953, p. 3.

page 126   'in verse during the 1980s': George Crowley (ed.), *The Bronze Swagman Book of Bush Verse*, Winton Tourist Promotion Association, Winton, Qld, 1988.

page 126   'a bank robbery, of sorts': Ron Edwards, *The Australian Yarn*, Rigby Ltd, Adelaide, 1978.

A Poet of the Kerb

page 130   'the United Kingdom and Australia': But for the research of the late Hugh Anderson, Paddy's modest but evocative contributions to popular literature would be entirely unknown, Hugh Anderson, *Paddy Collins: A Sydney street poet*, Red Rooster Press, Melbourne, 2010.

The Death of Crocodile Dundee

page 132   'a deadly shootout with police': Robert Milliken, 'Ansell, Rodney William (Rod) (1954–1999)', *Obituaries Australia*, National Centre of Biography, Australian National University, https://oa.anu.edu.au/obituary/ansell-rodney-william-rod-16153/text28096, accessed June 2023.

page 133   'the gunman stopped moving': Inquest into the deaths of Glen Anthony Huitson and Rodney William Ansell [2000] NTMC 43, pp. 40–1, https://justice.nt.gov.au/__data/assets/pdf_file/0018/206703/glen-huitson-rodney-ansell.pdf, accessed February 2024.

Chapter 5: Troubled Times

Rights and Wrongs

page 137   'known as the "Scottish martyrs"': John Earnshaw, 'Palmer, Thomas Fyshe (1747–1802)', *Australian Dictionary of Biography*, National Centre of Biography, Australian National University, https://adb.anu. edu.au/biography/palmer-thomas-fyshe-2535/text3441, published first in hardcopy 1967, accessed online 7 October 2023.

page 138   'in the cells and punished': 'Thomas Fyshe Parker', quoted in Ingeborg van Teeseling, 'Thomas Fyshe Palmer—"Obnoxious to the Ministry of Britain"', *Australia Explained*, 11 December 2021, www. australia-explained.com.au/mavericks/thomas-fyshe-palmer-obnoxious-to-the-ministry-of-britain#_edn2, accessed October 2023.

page 139   'Dharug were hung "on gibbets"': Frederick Watson et al, *Historical Records of Australia*, Series 1, Library Committee of the Commonwealth Parliament, 1914, p. 499.

page 139   'observed, one of "unparalleled severities"': Thomas Fyshe Palmer, quoted in Michael Martin, *On Darug Land. An Aboriginal perspective: A social history of western Sydney*, Greater Western Educational Centre Collective, Sydney, 1988, p. 42.

page 140   'of men, women and children': Lynley Wallis, Bryce Barker & Heather Burke, 'How unearthing Queensland's "native police" camps gives us a window onto colonial violence', *The Conversation*, 26 September 2018, https://theconversation.com/how-unearthing-queenslands-native-police-camps-gives-us-a-window-onto-colonial-violence-100814, accessed October 2023.

page 140   'made hundreds of such attacks': Georgia Moodie, 'Coming to terms with the brutal history of Queensland's Native Mounted Police', *The History Listen*, ABC News, 24 July 2019, www.abc.net.au/news/2019-07-24/native-mounted-police-indigenous-history-aboriginal-troopers/11296384, accessed October 2023; *Archaeology on the Frontier* blog, https://archaeologyonthefrontier.com, accessed October 2023.

page 140   'murdering possibly 60,000 people': Raymond Evans & Robert Ørsted–Jensen, 'I cannot say the numbers that were killed': Assessing violent mortality on the Queensland frontier', *SSRN* 2014, https://papers. ssrn.com/sol3/papers.cfm?abstract_id=2467836, accessed October 2023.

page 140   'the approach of different researchers': The most detailed research is at *Colonial Frontier Massacres in Australia, 1788–1930*, The Centre for 21st Century Humanities, University of Newcastle. Researchers identify more than 11,000 Aboriginal and Torres Strait islander victims of massacres by colonists across the country.

page 141   '*A family story*': David Marr, *Killing for Country: A family story*, Black Inc., Melbourne, 2023.

page 141   '"a devastating impact" upon them': 'Introduction', *Colonial Frontier Massacres in Australia, 1788–1930*, The Centre for 21st Century Humanities, University of Newcastle, https://c21ch.newcastle.edu.au/ colonialmassacres/introduction.php#definition, accessed October 2023.

The Devil Himself

page 146   'the honor [sic] to belong': Jesse Dowsett, 'The capture of Ned Kelly', *The Latrobe Journal*, 11 April 1973, p. 60, at https:// latrobejournal.slv.vic.gov.au/latrobejournal/issue/latrobe-11/t1-g-t2. html, accessed January 2024 (there are some discrepancies in the times given in this document).; see also Police Commission, 'Minutes of evidence taken before Royal Commission on the Police Force of Victoria, together with appendices', National Library of Australia, https://nla.gov.au/nla.obj-34169454/view?partId=nla.obj-34169465, accessed February 2024.

Cutting Cane

page 148   'was a hard job': Francesco Ricatti, 'Migration and place: Italian memories of north Queensland', *Queensland Review*, vol. 21, no. 2 (special issue on migration) 2014, pp. 177–90, https://doi.org/10.1017/qre.2014.24, accessed February 2024.

page 149   'valued part of community life': Catherine Dewhirst, 'Italians in north Queensland', *Queensland Historical Atlas*, 2010, www.qhatlas. com.au/content/italians-queensland, accessed November 2022; Barbara Bortolanza, 'The canecutter monument: A monument to the sugar pioneers of the Johnstone Shire', in *A Pictorial History of the Early Italian Settlement in the Innisfail District*, at *Making Multicultural Australia*, http:// www.multiculturalaustralia.edu.au/doc/innisfail_pioneers.pdf, accessed November 2022.

We Gave Them Hell

page 150 'away to their cars': Eddie Stephenson 'We met them at the door:
Resisting evictions in the Depression', *Red Flag*, 24 July 2023, https://
redflag.org.au/article/we-met-them-door-resisting-evictions-depression,
accessed November 2023.

page 151 'hooted and shouted insulting remarks': 'Desperate fighting', *The
Sydney Morning Herald*, 20 June 1931, p. 13.

page 152 'met them at the door': Graham Seal, prod., *On the Steps of the
Dole-Office Door*, Larrikin Records LP, 1977.

page 152 'than Victoria's unemployed were given': Blainey, *The Story of
Australia's People*, Viking Australia, Melbourne, 2020 (2015), p. 277.

page 152 'of around 70 per cent': Australian Bureau of Statistics. 'Housing
Occupancy and Costs', ABS, 2019–20, www.abs.gov.au/statistics/people/
housing/housing-occupancy-and-costs/latest-release, accessed July 2024.

page 153 'those aged 25 to 29': The Treasury, *2023 Intergenerational
Report*, Australian Government, https://treasury.gov.au/publication/2023-
intergenerational-report, accessed November 2023.

The Battle of Brisbane

page 154 'forms of Australian sexual relations': Danielle Miller, 'Battle of
Brisbane—Australian masculinity under threat', *Queensland Historical Atlas*,
15 November 2010, www.qhatlas.com.au/battle-brisbane-%E2%80%93-
australian-masculinity-under-threat, accessed November 2023.

page 156 'gaoled for six months': 'The Battle of Brisbane—26 & 27
November 1942', *Australia at War*, www.ozatwar.com/ozatwar/bob.htm,
accessed November 2023. The information on this site is derived primarily
from Barry Ralph, *They Passed this Way: The United States of America, the
states of Australia and World War II*, Kangaroo Press, Sydney, 2000.

The Peace Ship

page 159 'allowed to leave the country': Amanda Harris, Tiriki Onus &
Linda Barwick, 'Performing Aboriginal rights in 1951: From Australia's
Top End to southeast', *Australian Journal of Politics and History*, vol. 69, no. 2,
June 2023, pp. 227–47.

page 159 'hours later! Yeh, that's true': *Ray Peckham interviewed by Rob
Willis in the Activists for Indigenous rights in the mid 20th century oral history
project*, 21 March and 30 April 2012 in Dubbo, NSW, ORAL TRC 6430,

National Library of Australia, available at Trove, https://nla.gov.au/nla.
obj-213880846/listen, accessed February 2024.

page 160   'leaders in Melbourne were conspicuous': 'Farewell to
Delegates', *The Age* (Melbourne), 9 June 1951, p. 2.

The First Boat People

page 161   'a week of their arrival': 'Lam Tac Tam', National Archives
of Australia, www.naa.gov.au/explore-collection/immigration-and-
citizenship/migrant-stories/vietnam/lam-tac-tam, accessed December 2023.

page 161   'renamed Ho Chi Min City': 'Vietnamese just ahead of the
police', *The Canberra Times*, 17 May 1977, p. 9.

page 162   'arrive from the late 1980s': Janet Phillips & Harriet Spinks, 'Boat
arrivals in Australia since 1976', *Parliament of Australia*, www.aph.gov.au/
about_parliament/parliamentary_departments/parliamentary_library/pubs/
rp/rp1314/boatarrivals, accessed December 2023.

page 162   'were eventually resettled in Australia': Vietnamese Museum
Australia, https://vietnamesemuseum.com.au/, accessed December 2023.

Playing With Covid

page 166   'one has a knife': The quoted examples are sourced from
Childhood, Tradition and Change, https://ctac.esrc.unimelb.edu.au/index.
html; the *Pandemic Play Project*, https://pandemicplayproject.com/; and the
author's own collection.

page 167   'spread of the coronavirus': Judy McKinty & Ruth Hazleton, 'The
Pandemic Play Project—documenting kids' culture during COVID-19',
International Journal of Play, vol. 11, no. 1, 2022, pp. 1–22.

page 167   'forget that play is serious': David Hockney, 'The day my
father died', *The Independent*, 15 October 1993, www.independent.co.uk/
life-style/the-day-my-father-died-david-hockney-is-par-excellence-an-
artist-who-speaks-to-us-direct-in-words-as-well-as-art-here-he-tells-
with-his-usual-beguiling-directness-about-pleasure-and-sorrow-life-and-
work-1511161.html, accessed March 2024.

Chapter 6: Celebrations

A Horse of Light

page 171   'messages between sergeant and officers': 'Yeerakine Rock—
Kondinin water tank art—Western Australia', *Australian Silo Art Trail*,
www.australiansiloarttrail.com/yeerakine-rock, accessed April 2023; and

Lois Tilbrook, *Nyungar Tradition: Glimpses of Aborigines of south-western Australia 1829–1914*, University of Western Australia Press, Perth, 1983, p. 139, https://aiatsis.gov.au/sites/default/files/catalogue_resources/m0022954.pdf, accessed February 2024.

page 171 'Kambarang—season of birth: October–November': 'Indigenous weather knowledge', Bureau of Meteorology, http://www.bom.gov.au/iwk/calendars/nyoongar.shtml, accessed April 2023.

page 171 'including some from other states': *ABC News*, 'A unique ANZAC Day ceremony in WA's wheatbelt paid tribute to the 10th Light Horse regiment', www.youtube.com/watch?v=gqvQmdfamtE, accessed April 2023; 'Kondinin Anzac horse', *Artforms*, https://artforms.com.au/klondinin-anzac-horse/, accessed April 2023. The designers and makers of the Light Horse memorial, Artforms, have also supplied a smaller version to Melbourne's Remembrance Parks.

One Long Party

page 173 'Australia, and by many others': Australian Government, Department of Home Affairs, 'Permanent migration from India', www.homeaffairs.gov.au/research-and-statistics/statistics/country-profiles/profiles/india, accessed December 2023.

page 173 'special foods and outdoor events': Widia Jalal, 'Celebrating in style', *ABC News*, 19 November 2023, www.abc.net.au/news/2023-11-19/types-of-indian-outfits-over-diwali-and-festive-occasions/103103664, accessed December 2023; Widai Jalal, 'When is Diwali 2023? How is the Festival of Lights celebrated and where can I join in the fun?', *ABC News*, 12 November 2023, www.abc.net.au/news/2023-11-12/when-is-diwali-2023-and-where-to-celebrate-in-australia/103072966, accessed December 2023.

page 174 'ritual to more public events': A. Barlow, 'Festivals' in Gwenda Beed Davey & Graham Seal (eds), *The Oxford Companion to Australian Folklore*, Oxford University Press, Melbourne, 1993, pp. 116–17.

page 174 'may also identify six seasons': Helen Halling (ed.), *From Ochres to Eel Traps: Aboriginal science and technology resource guide for teachers*, Science Educators Association of the ACT, Indigenous Consultative Body, 1999; Bureau of Meteorology, 'Indigenous Weather Knowledge', http://www.bom.gov.au/iwk/, accessed July 2024.

page 174 'episodes of fire and flood': Alan Reid, 'Seasons', *Encyclopedia of Melbourne* online edition, Cambridge University Press, 2005, School of

Historical & Philosophical Studies, The University of Melbourne, 2008, www.emelbourne.net.au/biogs/EM01345b.htm, accessed May 2024.

Keeping Christmas

page 175   'they scramble for the treats': Emily Bissland, 'The simple joy of the Dixie Santa night, an 86-year Christmas tradition', *ABC News*, 23 December 2021, www.abc.net.au/news/2021-12-23/dixie-santa-night/100715240, accessed January 2024.

page 176   'and disappear until next Christmas': Erin Parke & Vanessa Mills, 'In the Kimberley community of Warmun, this black bird delivers the Christmas presents', *ABC News*, 23 December 2021, www.abc.net.au/news/2021-12-23/aboriginal-christmas-tradition-wangkarnal-crow-western-australia/100715128, accessed January 2024.

page 176   'between them or four each': James Scott, *Remarks on a Passage to Botany Bay, 1787–1792. A First Fleet journal*, entry for December 25 1787, State Library of New South Wales, SAFE/DLMSQ 43.

page 176   'topic in the nineteenth century': *The South Australian Advertiser*, 23 December 1865; *South Australian Register,* 20 May 1889, p 6; *Sydney Morning Herald*, 18 August 1864, p. 3; *The Cornwall Chronicle* (Launceston), 6 May 1868; *The Queenslander*, 25 December 1875, p. 4. Also, the *Hobart Town Courier*, 11 June 1838, p. 4, for a rundown of the many calendar traditions observed in Britain at the time.

page 176   'drinking a glass or two': Frank Cusack, *The Australian Christmas*, Heinemann, Melbourne, 1966, p. 13.

page 177   'with salt pork and rum': Cusack, p. 45.

page 177   'picture worth travelling to see': 'Christmas Eve', *The Daily Telegraph*, quoted in Madeline Shanahan, 'A festive feast of fish and fruit: the creation of the Australian Christmas dinner', *The Conversation*, 25 December 2020, https://theconversation.com/a-festive-feast-of-fish-and-fruit-the-creation-of-the-australian-christmas-dinner-151201, accessed December 2023.

page 178   'season, known as "Gravy Day"': Sarah Motherwell, 'Paul Kelly's How to Make Gravy gets new lyrics and new meaning for Christmas in 2021', *ABC News*, 21 December 2021, www.abc.net.au/news/2021-12-21/paul-kelly-what-is-gravy-day/100715890, accessed January 2024.

Light Up the Night

page 179   'remember the fifth of November': R. Gifford, 'Guy Fawkes: Who celebrated what? A closer look at 5th November in the light of Captain

Swing', in T. Buckland & J. Wood (eds), *Aspects of British Calendar Customs*, Sheffield Academic Press, Sheffield, UK, 1993.

page 179   **'a mob of juvenile patriots'**: In which year it was recorded in 'Weekly Occurrences', *Sydney Gazette and New South Wales Advertiser*, 10 November 1805, p. 1, though was probably already well established by that date: see A. Barlow, 'Festivals', in Gwenda Beed Davey & Graham Seal (eds), *The Oxford Companion to Australian Folklore*, Melbourne, 1993, p. 117.

page 179   **'be taken to the police'**: *The Sydney Monitor*, 31 October 1829, p. 3, also *The Australian* (Sydney) 8 November 1833, p. 2.

page 179   **'what it had been—"Gun-powder Treason"'**: 'Government Notice', *The Perth Gazette and Western Australian Journal*, 27 April 1833, p. 66.

page 180   **'various parts of his body'**: 'Accidents, Offences &c.', *Sydney Herald*, 11 November 1833, p. 2.

page 181   **'hat and uniform on . . .'**: *The Queanbeyan Age*, 16 November 1867, p. 3.

page 181   **'Latrobe Valley during the 1990s'**: Gwenda Beed Davey, 'The Moe Folklife Project: A final report', prepared for the Department of Communications and the Arts and the National Library of Australia, Melbourne, National Centre for Australian Studies, April 1996.

page 182   **'the audience than the participants'**: M. Day, 'A cracker of a night', *West Australian*, 4 November 2000. See R. Birch, *Wyndham Yella Fella*, Magabala Books, Broome, WA, 2003, p. 76 for Guy Fawkes night in Wyndham in the 1940s. Empire Day became Commonwealth Day from 1958 and has since disappeared from the calendar.

page 182   **'already in bushfire season'**: Nicole Curby, 'Why the Northern Territory is Australia's last bastion of Cracker Night', *ABC News*, 1 July 2023, www.abc.net.au/news/2023-07-01/territory-day-australias-last-cracker-night/102541428, accessed July 2023.

page 183   **'the time has obviously backfired'**: Myles Morgan, 'Buttocks burnt as cracker stunt backfires', *ABC News*, 30 July 2012, www.abc.net.au/news/2012-07-30/man27s-bottom-explodes-as-party-trick-backfires/4163238, accessed January 2024.

Hunting for Halloween

page 184   **'Scots formed around the 1820s'**: James Jupp (ed.), *The Australian People: An encyclopedia of the nation, its people and their origins*, Cambridge

University Press, Melbourne, 2001 (rev. edn, first published 1988), pp. 646ff.

page 184 'at Forrest Creek in 1858': 'Forest Creek', *Mount Alexander Mail*, 22 October, 1858, p. 4.

page 184 'Perth kept it in 1911': 'Halloween', *The Daily News* (Perth), 31 October 1911, p. 5.

page 184 'other amusements for the children': 'Halloween', *The Bundaberg Mail and Burnett Advertiser*, 28 October 1912, p. 3.

page 184 'will be out that night': 'Halloween', *Macleay Argus* (Kempsey), 16 October 1942, p. 2.

page 184 'in action, New York style': Leona Deane, 'Australian at World's Fair', *Lachlander and Condobolin and Western Districts Recorder*, 25 January 1940, p. 2; *The Henty Observer and Culcairn Shire Register*, 2 February 1940, p. 7. Originally published in the Adelaide *Observer*.

page 185 'Halloween in Melbourne in 1952': 'Perth Girl stayed at millionaire's mansion in America', *Sunday Times* (Perth), 12 October 1952, p. 7. 'Young Americans get ready for lively evening', *The Herald* (Melbourne), 28 October 1952, p. 10. Lex Lammoy of the NSW Scouting Association claims to have seen trick-or-treating in Cairns during the 1950s, *Wilson's Almanac*, www.wilson's almanac.f2s.com/index.html, accessed February 2002 (link no longer live).

page 185 'of a visiting American academic': 'Trick or treat', *The Canberra Times*, 31 October 1970, p. 8.

page 185 'town of Dampier in 1972': 'Youth activities', *Hamersley News* (Perth), 23 November 1972, p. 10.

page 185 'to have influenced Australian kids': Annika Dean, 'The origins of Halloween', *University of Sydney*, 27 October 2017, www.sydney.edu.au/news-opinion/news/2016/10/27/the-origins-of-halloween.html, accessed October 2023.

page 186 'pagan rites for the dead': J. Simpson & S. Roud, *A Dictionary of English Folklore*, Oxford University Press, Oxford, 2000, p, 163; see also Ronald Hutton, *The Stations of the Sun: A history of the ritual year in Britain*, Oxford University Press, Oxford, 1996, pp. 369–70.

page 186 'to rival those of Christmas': In 2023, it was estimated that over five million Australians would observe Halloween, spending almost five hundred million dollars on the event. ARA-Roy Morgan Snap SMS survey, Finding No: 9331, www.roymorgan.com/findings/ara-roy-morgan-media-release-halloween-2023, accessed May 2024.

One Day in September

page 187   'a "grand final" took place': 'Football', *The Herald* (Melbourne), 29 September 1893, p. 3.

page 187   'ground should be well filled': 'Sport and play', *Melbourne Punch*, 1 October 1896, p. 20.

page 189   'of the community over decades."': Nicola Heath, 'Miles Franklin–winning author Amanda Lohrey takes on Australia's renovation obsession in her new novel, *The Conversion*', *ABC News*, January 2024, www.abc.net.au/news/2024-01-19/miles-franklin-winner-amanda-lohrey-new-book-the-conversion/103308426, accessed January 2024.

More Than a Meal

page 190   'Kelly's donkey . . .': 'The Country', *The Advertiser* (Adelaide), 13 September 1917, p. 11.

page 192   'Our project exists for them': 'The Barossa Cookery Book', *Those Barossa Girls*, www.thosebarossagirls.com.au/barossa-cookery-book-project/, accessed December 2023.

page 192   'the Tanunda Soldiers' Memorial Hall': Sarah Jane Shepherd Black, '"Tried and tested": Community cookbooks in Australia, 1890–1980', PhD Thesis, University of Adelaide, 2010.

page 193   'indeed, "more than a meal"': Emma Siossian, 'More than a meal', *ABC News*, 16 December 2023, www.abc.net.au/news/2023-12-16/treasured-old-cookbooks-and-recipes-and-why-they-matter/102608174, accessed December 2023.

Chapter 7: Creations

Creative Convicts

page 196   'than by playing the violin': The petition was dated 11 November 1848: see Peter MacFie, 'A petition from fourteen fiddlers', https://petermacfiehistorian.net.au/publications/fourteen-fiddlers/, accessed July 2023.

page 197   'used to astonish me . . .': Peter MacFie, 'A Fiddler, a Piper and Two Guitarists', at https://petermacfiehistorian.net.au/publications/fiddler/, accessed July 2023.

page 198   'at their own houses': From the *Sydney Gazette*, 28 October 1820, p. 2, quoted in Heather Blasdale-Clarke, 'François Girard, dancing master, convict', *Australian Historical Dance*, 28 October 2013, www.historicaldance.au/francois-girard-dancing-master-convict/, accessed July 2023.

page 198   'aged around sixty-seven in 1859': Kenneth R. Dutton,
'A colonial entrepreneur: François Girard (1792?–1859)', Institute for the
Study of French Australian Relations, www.isfar.org.au/wp-content/
uploads/2016/10/39_KENNETH-R.-DUTTON-A-Colonial-Entrepreneur-
Francois-Girard-1792-1859.pdf, accessed February 2024.

page 199   'important enough': 'Convict artists in the time of Governor
Macquarie', State Library of New South Wales, www.sl.nsw.gov.au/
stories/convict-artists-time-governor-macquarie, accessed July 2023.

page 199   'poverty in Hobart in 1853': 'Gould's Sketchbook of Fishes',
Libraries Tasmania, https://libraries.tas.gov.au/allport-library-and-museum-
of-fine-arts/goulds-sketchbook-of-fishes-tasmanian-curriculum-resource/,
accessed July 2023.

The Dreaded Tomhooka!

page 200   'the bellowing of a calf': 'The Track', *Townsville Daily Bulletin*,
4 October 1939, p. 12.

page 202   'to sack him right away': Bill Bowyang, 'On the track', *Townsville
Daily Bulletin*, 1 March 1922, p. 5.

page 203   'money, credit cards and passport': Graham Seal, *Great Australian
Urban Myths* (rev. edn), Angus & Robertson, Sydney, 2001, pp. 120ff.

page 203   'we a nation of bastards': Manning Clark, 'Are we a nation of
bastards?', *Meanjin*, Winter 1976, https://meanjin.com.au/essays/are-we-a-
nation-of-bastards/, accessed September 2023.

Where's Christina?

page 204   'correspondent to a Queensland newspaper': The *North
Queensland Herald*, in the *Evening Journal* (Adelaide), 23 November 1901,
p. 5.

page 207   'of the poet, Paterson': W. Benjamin Lindner, *Waltzing Matilda—
Australia's Accidental Anthem*, Boolarong Press, Brisbane, 2019.

page 207   'Waltzing Matilda Centre at Winton': W Benjamin Lindner,
Winton's Waltzing Matilda Centre: From a song a home is born, Waltzing
Matilda Centre, Winton, Qld, 2024.

The Anzac News

page 208   'appeared, including the *Anzac Argus*': 'Newspapers in the
trenches', *Tweed Daily* (Murwillumbah), 31 August 1915, p. 2.

page 209   'nearly smothered him with kisses': 'Australians rush to
surrender', *The Herald* (Melbourne), 23 August 1915, p. 1.

page 210   'Moving On': A.B. Paterson, 'Moving On', *The Kia Ora Coo-ee*, 15 May 1918, p. 13.

page 211   'Printed "Somewhere in France"': Graham Seal, *The Soldiers' Press: Trench Journals in the First World War*, Palgrave Macmillan, Basingstoke UK, 2013.

A Special Kind of Magic

page 214   'poles as she went': Patricia Milne, 'The School Magazine of Literature for Our Boys and Girls', *Readers' Memories Celebrate its Centenary*, National Centre for Australian Children's Literature, 2016 (posted June 2021), www.ncacl.org.au/articles-about-the-national-centres-collection/, accessed August 2023.

page 215   'magazines for years to come': *The School Magazine*, https://theschoolmagazine.com.au/, accessed August 2023.

Louie The Fly

page 216   'So did Louie': 'Louie the Fly', www.mortein.com.au/about/about-louie/, accessed October 2023.

page 216   'Louie was an instant hit': Amanda Diaz, 'The making of an iconic jingle', National Film and Sound Archive of Australia, www.nfsa.gov.au/latest/louie-fly, accessed October 2023. White was also the composer of another classic jingle for the polishing wax marketed as 'Mr Sheen'.

page 217   'has continued to the present': Colin Ward, 'Dung beetle program', *CSIROpedia*, 21 February 2011, https://csiropedia.csiro.au/dung-beetle-program/, accessed October 2023.

page 218   'more dangerous insect pest': 'Louie is back: Mortein brings back brand mascot in new avatar', *ET Brand Equity*, https://brandequity.economictimes.indiatimes.com/news/advertising/louie-is-back-mortein-brings-back-brand-mascot-in-new-avatar/89971365, accessed October 2023.

A Crystal Mystery

page 219   'to make the reception enjoyable': Proton, 'Our Wireless Circle', *Sunday Mail* (Brisbane), 3 July 1932, p. 23.

page 220   'to build the following year': Proton, 'Our Wireless Circle', *Sunday Mail* (Brisbane), 16 April 1933, p. 19.

page 222   'from his location in Florida': Robert Weaver, 'The "mystery"
    crystal set', 2012 (revised March 2023) *Electron Bunker*, https://
    electronbunker.ca/eb/CrystalSet01.html, accessed November 2023.

page 222   'rather than the modern equivalent': Ken Harthun, 'Improvement
    of the "mystery" crystal set', *Electron Bunker*, March 2001, www.qsl.net/
    kc4iwt/xtal/mysteryimproved.htm, accessed November 2023.

page 222   'some perhaps about crystal sets': 'Tune into Radio 100', National
    Film and Sound Archive (NFSA), nfsa.gov.au/collection/curated/radio-100

Wi-Fi

page 223   'the "Silver City Writing Tablet"': Carla Howarth, 'End of an
    era as 173yo Birchalls book store to close', *ABC News*, 6 January 2017,
    www.abc.net.au/news/2017-01-06/end-of-an-era-as-173yo-bookstore-
    birchall27s-to-close/8165770, accessed February 2024.

page 225   'wireless connectivity we enjoy today': 'Wi Fi', National
    Australia Museum, www.nma.gov.au/defining-moments/resources/wi-fi,
    accessed February 2024.

page 226   'global warming and climate change': Colin Ward, 'Brief history',
    CSIROpedia, 10 December 2015, https://csiropedia.csiro.au/our-history/,
    accessed December 2023; *Encyclopedia of Australian Science and Innovation*,
    Swinburne University of Technology, November 2023, www.eoas.info/,
    accessed December 2023.

Chapter 8: Communities

Eliza Batman's £1 Notes

page 231   'and violence were bound together': Penny Edmonds & Michelle
    Berry, 'Eliza Batman, the Irish convict reinvented as "Melbourne's
    founding mother", was both colonised and coloniser on two violent
    frontiers', *The Conversation*, 8 June 2023, https://theconversation.com/
    eliza-batman-the-irish-convict-reinvented-as-melbournes-founding-mother-
    was-both-colonised-and-coloniser-on-two-violent-frontiers-206189,
    accessed June 2023. The authors treat the story in more detail in their
    'Eliza Batman's house: unhomely frontiers and intimate overstraiters
    in Van Diemen's Land and Port Phillip', in Penny Edmonds & Amanda
    Nettelbeck (eds), *Intimacies of Violence in the Settler Colony*, Cambridge
    Imperial and Post-Colonial Studies Series, Palgrave Macmillan, Cham,
    Switzerland, 2018, https://doi.org/10.1007/978-3-319-76231-9_6.

page 232   'woman "of somewhat abandoned character"': P.L. Brown, 'Batman, John (1801–1839)', *Australian Dictionary of Biography*, National Centre of Biography, Australian National University, https://adb. anu.edu.au/biography/batman-john-1752/text1947, published first in hardcopy 1966, accessed June 2023.

page 232   'under her arm pit': 'Geelong', *The Argus*, 1 April 1852, p. 2.

page 232   'released a few months later': 'Geelong', *The Argus*, 1 July, 1852, p. 4.

An Unlit Beacon

page 235   'who might come there': Queensland Heritage Register, 'Raine Island Beacon', *Queensland Government*, https://apps.des.qld.gov.au/ heritage-register/detail/?id=600432, accessed June 2023.

page 235   'Register of the National Estate': Department of Environment, Science and Innovation, 'Raine Island National Park (Scientific)', *Queensland Government*, https://parks.des.qld.gov.au/parks/raine-island/ about/culture#cutlure_and_history, accessed June 2023.

page 236   'history and you will survive': Holly Richardson, 'Convict-built stone tower on Great Barrier Reef's Raine Island restored by rangers, traditional owners', *ABC News*, 18 June 2023, www.abc.net.au/ news/2023-06-18/convict-built-beacon-raine-island-great-barrier-reef-restored/102332494, accessed June 2023.

How To Build a Village

page 236   'obituary described him in 1890': 'Death of Mr George Robertson', *The Hamilton Spectator*, 18 June 1890, p. 3. There are some discrepancies in the available sources: see Merron Riddiford, 'Passing of the pioneers', *Western District Families*, 28 January 2019, https:// westerndistrictfamilies.com/2019/01/28/passing-of-the-pioneers-67/, accessed November 2023.

page 237   'did not originate from them': Tracy Chew et al., 'Genomic characterization of external morphology traits in kelpies does not support common ancestry with the Australian dingo', *Genes*, vol. 10, no. 5, 2019, p. 337, https://doi.org/10.3390/genes10050337.

page 238   'given to the entire breed': 'Origin of the kelpie', *The Working Kelpie Council of Australia*, www.wkc.org.au/About-Kelpies/Origin-of-the-Kelpie.php, accessed November 2023.

page 238   'the research into kelpie genes': Courtney Fowler, 'Kelpie DNA study unravels mysterious origins of Australian working dog, but finds no dingo', *ABC News*, 28 June 2018, www.abc.net.au/news/rural/2019-06-28/kelpie-study-finds-no-detectable-dingo-dna/11250106, accessed November 2023.

page 238 'into a heritage tourism destination': Warrock Homestead, https://warrockhomestead.com.au/, accessed November 2023.

Goldfields Folk

page 242 'return to their beloved Hobart': William Howitt, *Land, Labour and Gold, or, Two Years in Victoria: With visits to Sydney and Van Diemen's Land*, Longman, Brown, Green & Longmans, London, vol. 1, 1858, p. 259.

God's Line

page 243 'of their land would drop': *The South Australian Advertiser*, 4 February 1865, p. 2.

page 243 'There were debates in parliament': 'Appeal to the country', *South Australian Register*, 22 February 1865, p. 2.

page 244 'was eventually given his name': The line was included in the *Waste Lands Alienation Act* of 1872, but this was repealed after several wet years.

page 244 'line, as did the pastoralists': 'Goyder's line of rainfall', *The Mail* (Adelaide), 2 April 1927, p. 1.

page 244 'the line and its creator': 'Drought', https://monumentaustralia. org.au/themes/disaster/drought, accessed September 2023.

page 245 'country north of the line': Michael Dulaney, James Jooste & Daniel Keane, 'Goyder's Line moving south with climate change, SA scientists say, forcing farming changes', *ABC News*, 2 December 2015, www.abc.net.au/news/2015-12-02/goyders-line-climate-change-wheat-wine-grapes/6919276, accessed September 2023.

page 245 'lands suitable only for grazing': Regional Council of Goyder, 'Goyder Master Plan 2022–2037 V1', www.goyder.sa.gov.au/__data/assets/pdf_file/0039/1197678/FINAL-GMP-2022-2037.pdf, accessed September 2023.

Melbourne's Pleasure Dome

page 247 'children's book industry in Australia': Jodi Kok, 'Marvellous Melbourne's own Willy Wonka—E.W. Cole and his famous Book Arcade', State Library Victoria blog, 6 September 2022, https://blogs.slv.vic.gov.au/our-stories/ask-a-librarian/e-w-cole-and-his-famous-book-arcade/, accessed October 2023.

page 248   'to spend the advertising budget': 'Cole's Book Arcade Collection', Museums Victoria, https://collections.museumsvictoria.com. au/articles/1900, accessed October 2023.

page 248   'until his death in 1918': E. Cole Turnley, 'Cole, Edward William (1832–1918)', *Australian Dictionary of Biography*, National Centre of Biography, Australian National University, https://adb.anu.edu. au/biography/cole-edward-william-3243/text4897, published first in hardcopy 1969, accessed online 30 October 2023.

MacRobertson's Steam Confectionery Works

page 249   'hectares and employed 2500 people': 'MacRobertson', *Table Talk* (Melbourne), 23 May 1929, p. 13.

page 251   'and can still be purchased': 'MacRobertson's Confectionery Factory', Victorian Collections, https://victoriancollections.net.au/stories/ macrobertsons-confectionery-factory, accessed September 2023, from 'Nail Can to Knighthood: The Life of Sir Macpherson Robertson KBE' exhibition which took place at the Royal Historical Society of Victoria in 2015.

page 251   'hair and clear complexion': John Lack, 'Robertson, Sir Macpherson (1859–1945)', *Australian Dictionary of Biography*, National Centre of Biography, Australian National University, https://adb.anu.edu. au/biography/robertson-sir-macpherson-8237/text14421, published first in hardcopy 1988, accessed online 22 September 2023.

The Grain Races

page 252   'a woman will never do': Betty Jacobsen, *A Girl before the Mast*, Charles Scribners, New York, 1934.

page 253   'likely would lose his job': Spencer Apollonio, (Ed), *The Last of the Cape Horners, Firsthand Accounts from the Final Days of the Commercial Tall Ships*, Brassey's, Washington, DC, 2001, p. xxv.

page 254   'round the hundred-day mark.'': 'Windjammers grain race to Britain is on', *The Mail* (Adelaide), 14 January 1933, p. 12; *Daily Commercial News and Shipping List* (Perth), 16 March 1934, p. 4.

page 254   'Horner's became sail training ships': 'Calms, gales in last grain race', *The Daily Telegraph* (Sydney), 4 October 1949, p. 3.

A Community of the Air

page 255   'went on to find fame': 'Argonauts Registration form', Friends of the National Film and Sound Archive, https://web.archive.org/

web/20110217113137/http://www.archivefriends.org.au/index.php/
argonauts-registration-form, accessed October 2023.

page 256   'Foundation (ACTF) published in 2023': Joanna McIntyre et
al., *Kids' TV Memories: Audience perspectives on the roles and long-term value
of Australian children's television*, Report 2, Australian Children's Television
Foundation, Melbourne, 2023.

page 258   'has a way to go': Screen Australia, 'Seeing ourselves 2: diversity, equity and inclusion in Australian TV drama', April 2023, www.
screenaustralia.gov.au/fact-finders/reports-and-key-issues/reports-and-
discussion-papers/seeing-ourselves-2, accessed October 2023.

Chapter 9: Ourselves

People of the Rock

page 262   'his way to the ceremony': 'Akurra Trail', *Mobile Language
Team*, https://mobilelanguageteam.com.au/learning-resources/leigh-
creek-akurra-trail/, accessed November 2022; Jacinta Koolmatrie, 'Friday
essay: histories written in the land—a journey through Adnyamathanha
Yarta', *The Conversation*, 11 October 2019, https://theconversation.
com/friday-essay-histories-written-in-the-land-a-journey-through-
adnyamathanha-yarta-124001, accessed November 2022.

page 262   'of Hayward's reminiscences in 1929': 'Brachina Gorge Flinders
Ranges', *Colonial Frontier Massacres*, https://c21ch.newcastle.edu.au/
colonialmassacres/detail.php?r=695, accessed November 2022.

page 264   'ones are with us always': 'Traditional Owners of the land',
Monument Australia, https://monumentaustralia.org.au/display/116631-
traditional-owners-of-the-land, accessed November 2022.

The Hairistocracy

page 264   'cab-drivers, and men about stables': Howitt, *Land, Labour and
Gold*, pp. 338–50.

Australian 'Natives'

page 267   'Poulton's obituary was predictably flattering': 'Obituaries',
Observer (Adelaide), 30 July 1921, p. 31.

page 268   '"peculiarities are in the making."': 'Australian Natives'
Association', *South Australian Register*, 10 June 1890, p. 6.

page 269   'general management of the Society."': John E. Menadue,
A Centenary History of the Australian Natives' Association 1871–1971,
Melbourne Horticultural Press, 1971, p. 9.

page 269   'of social and economic backgrounds': 'Australian Natives'
Association', National Museum of Australia, www.nma.gov.au/defining-
moments/resources/australian-natives-association, accessed October 2023.

A Broken Soldier

page 272   'comrades of the A.I.F': 'The Sphinx', *The Sydney Morning Herald*,
4 May 1931, p. 7; Jim Low, 'Remembering Private Shirley', *Simply Australia*,
22 November 2022, www.simplyaustralia.net/remembering-private-
shirley/, accessed December 2022. The page also refers to Jim Low's song
about Will Shirley, titled 'The Broken Soldier'.

page 273   'killed in action—"my glorious comrades"': 'Sphinx Memorial',
New South Wales War Memorial Register, www.warmemorialsregister.
nsw.gov.au/memorials/sphinx-memorial, accessed December 2022.

page 273   'sorrow is just as deep': Emma Flanagan, 'In Memoriam', *The
Sydney Morning Herald*, 27 August 1930, p. 12.

page 273   'dawn of a beautiful day': Emma Flanagan, 'In Memoriam', *The
Sydney Morning Herald*, 27 August 1931, p. 8.

page 273   'lie in your silent grave': Emma Flanagan, 'In Memoriam', *The
Sydney Morning Herald*, 27 August 1932, p. 11.

The Plot to Save Australia

page 275   'biographer as "the intrigue master"': Barbara Winter, *The Intrigue
Master: Commander Long and Naval Intelligence in Australia, 1913–1945*,
Boolarong Press, Brisbane, 1995.

page 276   'British and Australian relations': Letter from Thomas Wood to
Charles Patrick Smith, 21 September 1944. Copy in author's possession.

page 279   'obituaries were few and short': This story is based on research
by the author in the United Kingdom and Australian archives and libraries,
including the National Library of Australia; the British Library; Exeter
College, Oxford; the National Archives, Kew; the BBC Archives, Reading;
the Cumbria Archives Service, as well as the usual secondary sources.
There is a biography of Wood by Australian historian Russel Ward in the
Australian Dictionary of Biography, in which entries on most others associated
with the Group also appear, though without mentioning the conspiracy.

Crossing the Yellow Line

page 280 'place in Tasmania in 1867': Rodney Croome, 'Gay Law Reform', *The Companion to Tasmanian History*, Centre for Tasmanian Historical Studies, University of Tasmania, www.utas.edu.au/library/companion_to_tasmanian_history/G/Gay%20Law%20Reform.htm, accessed September 2023. While the term 'gay' was in use in the 1980s to describe homosexuals and lesbians, the growing diversity of sex and gender identities is now usually recognised through the acronym LGBTQI (lesbian, gay, bisexual, transexual, queer and intersexual) to which 'A' may sometimes be added for 'asexual'. Exact usage varies considerably.

page 282 'protesters or their fellow travellers': 'Hobart getting used to bizarre protests', *The Canberra Times*, 14 December 1988, p. 9. Reports also in *Tribune* (Sydney), 23 November 1988, p. 2, and 30 November 1988, p. 12. The exact number of people arrested varies in other sources.

The Clash of Symbols

page 283 'proud to display the image': Richard White, 'The slippery symbols of Australia', *Openbook*, Summer 2021, State Library of New South Wales, www.sl.nsw.gov.au/stories/slippery-symbols-australia, accessed January 2024.

page 284 'symbols never stand still': Melissa Harper & Richard White (eds), *Symbols of Australia: Imagining a Nation*, NewSouth, Sydney, 2021 (first edition 2010), p. vii.

page 284 'mostly left in the past': Marilyn Lake and Penny Russell, 'Miss Australia' in Melissa Harper & Richard White (eds), *Symbols of Australia: Imagining a nation*, Newsouth, Sydney, 2021 (2010), pp. 156ff.

page 285 'educational resources for classroom use': Department of the Prime Minister and Cabinet, *Australian Symbols*, https://peo.gov.au/understand-our-parliament/parliament-house/national-symbols-in-parliament-house, accessed May 2024; 'National symbols in Parliament House', Parliamentary Education Office, https://peo.gov.au/understand-our-parliament/parliament-house/national-symbols, accessed March 2024.

A Pale Blue Dot

page 286 'the world's deep space missions': 'Deep space network', *NASA*, www.nasa.gov/communicating-with-missions/dsn/, accessed March 2024.

page 287 'could continue sending back data': NASA Jet Propulsion Laboratory, California Institute of Technology, 'NASA mission update:

Voyager 2 communications pause', *Voyager*, 28 July 2023, www.jpl. nasa.gov/news/nasa-mission-update-voyager-2-communications-pause, accessed November 2023.

page 287   'of our world to extraterrestrials': NASA Jet Propulsion Laboratory, California Institute of Technology, 'The golden record', *Voyager*, https://voyager.jpl.nasa.gov/golden-record/, accessed November 2023.